THE
SPECIAL
STUDENT

Practical help for the classroom teacher

THE SPECIAL STUDENT

Practical help for the classroom teacher

C. M. CHARLES, Ph.D.

Elementary Education, San Diego State University,
San Diego, California

IDA M. MALIAN, Ph.D.

Special Education, San Diego State University,
San Diego, California

with 24 illustrations

The C. V. Mosby Company

ST. LOUIS • TORONTO • LONDON   1980

The C. V. Mosby Company
11830 Westline Industrial Drive, St. Louis, Missouri 63141

Library of Congress Cataloging in Publication Data

Charles, C   M
   The special student.

   Bibliography: p.
   Includes index.
   1.   Mentally handicapped children—Education—
United States.   2.   Mainstreaming in education—
United States.   3.   Handicapped children—Education—
Law and legislation—United States.   I.   Malian,
Ida M   1950-   joint author.   II.   Title.
LC4601.C44   471.9   80-13053
ISBN   0-8016-1132-6

AC/M/M   9 8 7 6 5 4 3 2 1   01/A/026

Preface

Throughout history, the handicapped have been education's forgotten children. Until this century, little provision was made for educating the blind, deaf, or crippled. Virtually none was made for educating the mentally retarded or severely emotionally disturbed. The situation boiled down to this: If you couldn't behave like nonhandicapped students, use the same facilities they used, and learn right along with them, you were out of luck. School was no place for you.

That unfortunate situation began to change in the early 1900s, especially in the United States, where we idealistically believed that every person had intrinsic worth and deserved a fair chance in life. That idea implied, more than anything else, a fair chance in education. Education was supposed to provide a command of fundamental skills—the 3 R's—plus training in economic self-sufficiency, effective participation in democratic processes, and the pursuit of personal aptitudes. To get a fair chance at attaining those marvelous fruits, every person, regardless of race, color, creed, or personal make-up, had to have access to appropriate learning, teaching, materials, and facilities.

The press toward providing quality education for the handicapped began slowly, but like the proverbial snowball it gained increasing momentum. We have seen this movement progress from earlier confinement to a few special institutions to the 1970s' attention to every aspect of handicap—physical, emotional, learning, and communication. Key litigation opened the federal tills, so that the finest facilities, materials, and teachers became available for educating the handicapped. Every school district, agency, and institution of higher education became involved. The civil and educational rights of all handicapped persons were at last being recognized.

Or were they? Special education (the name by which education for handicapped students became known) was conducted largely apart from the regular classroom. That meant isolation from nonhandicapped students. True, the finest educational materials and facilities were available. True, special education teachers were highly trained to meet the needs of handicapped students. Still, something seemed to be missing. The missing ingredient, so worrisome to parents and professionals alike, seemed to be interaction with nonhandicapped students. In short, the handicapped were segregated from the mainstream of education.

Concern about this segregation mounted during the 1960s and 1970s. Its rationale lay in two observations. First, it was believed fundamentally wrong, morally speaking, to keep handicapped and nonhandicapped people apart. We are all people, equal under the skin, with equal stakes in the great human concerns of our times. It is wrong to consider some people all right and other people less than human. Interaction between handicapped and nonhandicapped should be very instructive to both groups, facilitate positive relations, and allow the display of individual abilities that reduce derision, prejudice, and fear.

Second, it was believed educationally wrong to segregate handicapped students from nonhandicapped students. The handicapped profit greatly from the intellectual and social stimulation that nonhandicapped students provide. Similarly, nonhandicapped students profit socially and emotionally, and sometimes intellectually, from close association with the handicapped.

Both these views were basic to the great push of the later 1970s toward maximum integration of the handicapped into regular education. This push was formalized in Public Law 94-142, The Education of All Handicapped Children Act of 1975. This national law mandated that handicapped students be identified and educated, up to age 21, in the most appropriate way in the "least restrictive environment." The least restrictive environment was defined as the learning environment that would foster maximum personal and social growth. Further, the law specified that the least restrictive environment was to be considered the "regular classroom," unless the considered opinions of professionals and the student's parents suggested otherwise.

PL 94-142 became fully operative in 1978. School agencies rushed to comply with its many requirements. The movement assumed the label "mainstreaming," to refer to handicapped students being thrust into the mainstream of education.

Naturally the movement has hit a few snags. But those snags have only slowed it slightly. They have never threatened to stop it. The main snag has been the regular classroom teacher, beset with fears of working with the handicapped and not adequately prepared for the task.

You have to understand this about teachers: They are fine people, well intentioned, extremely dedicated, eager to do the best they can do for every student under their direction. But they have not worked with handicapped students very much. Those students, if unable to function adequately in regular classrooms, were placed in special facilities with special teachers. Some were put there because they were behaviorally or emotionally handicapped. They were, in common parlance, "terrors" in the classroom. You can see why teachers are troubled at the prospect of reorganizing instruction and procedures to accommodate handicapped students.

This book is for teachers, experienced and brand new. Its purpose is twofold: (1) to allay teachers' fears by describing the law, its requirements, and the students who are involved, thus removing the fear of the unknown; and (2) to present basic knowledge and practical skills for working effectively with the handicapped. The overall result should be teacher awareness, skill, confidence, and readiness for providing the best education possible to all students, whatever their abilities and needs might be.

C. M. Charles
Ida M. Malian

Contents

PART THREE

Teaching the special students

7 Teaching students with behavior disorders, 115

PART FOUR

A look into the future

14 Future special education, 229

PART ONE

Preparing for mainstreaming

CHAPTER 1

Educating all handicapped students

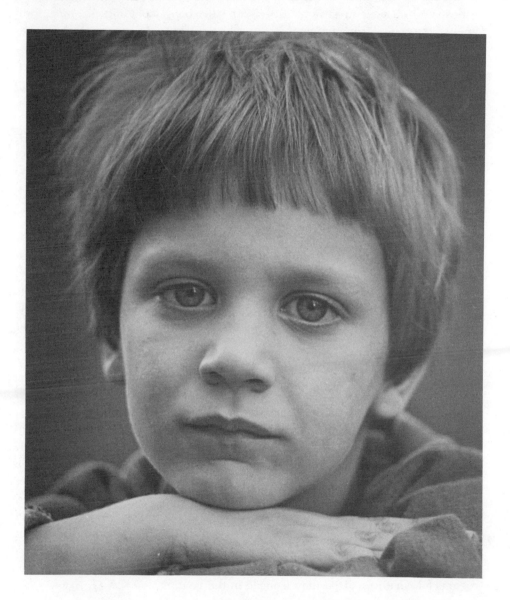

On November 29, 1975, the United States Congress enacted Public Law 94-142, The Education For All Handicapped Children Act of 1975. This law, which became fully effective in fiscal year 1978, made many specific directives regarding the education of handicapped children; those directives are producing widespread changes in several aspects of education, including planning, programs, curricula, teaching methods, evaluation, parental input, and teacher training.

PL 94-142 is aimed specifically at the education of handicapped students. However, its implementation is beginning to bring about significant changes in the education of nonhandicapped students as well—in learning environments, class sizes, and the availability of specialized services.

Presented at the end of this chapter are significant excerpts from the text of PL 94-142. There you can read the exact wording of the legal requirements. Preceding that are the following sections, which outline the requirements and implications of PL 94-142.

REQUIREMENTS OF PL 94-142
Who

PL 94-142 requires that school districts take steps to identify *all* handicapped youth among the populations they serve. The law names nine specific categories of handicap: (1) deafness, (2) hard-of-hearing, (3) mental retardation, (4) orthopedic impairment, (5) other health impairment, (6) serious emotional disturbance, (7) specific learning disability, (8) speech impairment, and (9) visual impairment (including blindness).

The search that school districts conduct must be carried out in such a manner that all individuals from ages 3 to 21 who fit within the nine categories are identified, whether they are presently known to the schools or not. The search identifies about 12% of that population, for a total of some 8 million individuals.

Parents of individuals identified in the search have the right to an impartial hearing and to discuss or contest matters of identification, educational placement, educational program, evaluation, and similar matters. They may request such a hearing at any time. Upon making the request, they must be advised of time, place, and their rights guaranteed by the law. They are entitled to be represented by legal counsel. They can be assisted by persons with expertise in the area of handicap. They can present evidence. They can question individuals presenting testimony. They can require the attendance of witnesses. They are entitled to a written transcript of the hearing and a copy of the decision, including specific reasons for whatever disposition is made in the hearing.

Where

PL 94-142 stipulates that the individuals identified through systematic search must be educated in the "least restrictive environment," which is specifically named in the law as "the regular classroom." Thus, all handicapped students are to be taught in the regular classroom *unless* some other setting is required for their optimum development. If a setting other than the regular classroom is required, parents and school personnel must confer on the matter. Documentation must then be prepared that justifies the use of a setting other than the regular classroom.

The strong emphasis on the regular classroom as the least restrictive environment is based on the detrimental effects of segregating handicapped students from normal students. Those detriments include harmful labeling of students, the lack of interaction between handicapped and nonhandicapped students, and the possible violation of basic human rights guaranteed by the United States Constitution.

What and how

The inclusion of handicapped students in regular classrooms does not mean that the curriculum must be the same for all students. On the contrary, PL 94-142 stipulates that the schooling of handicapped students must be differentiated in accordance with their special needs and with the services that are available to them. This differentiation must be shown in educational plans that are specially made for each individual student. The law thus calls for a degree of individualized education not commonly seen in the regular classroom.

Frequently mentioned in PL 94-142 are individualized instruction, individualized plans, and individualized programs. As concerns this stress on individualization, the law calls for *Individualized Education Programs* (IEPs). An IEP must be prepared every year for each student identified as handicapped. It must be a written statement, and it must include the following:
1. Notation of present levels of educational performance
2. Goals for the year, together with short-range objectives that lead to the goals
3. The specific educational services to be supplied by the school, with beginning and ending dates
4. The extent to which the student can participate in the regular classroom
5. Evaluation procedures and schedules, based on stated criteria, to determine whether objectives and goals are being reached; this must be done at least once per year

The IEP must be coupled with a continuous recording and reporting system. This system must include diagnostic results and descriptive profiles that clearly show the degree of exceptionality and the rate and amount of educational growth. Chapter 4 describes in detail how IEPs are formulated and presents a model IEP form (Fig. 1).

Consultative process

PL 94-142 calls for continual parental involvement in the education of their handicapped children. It requires that parent, guardian, or surrogate (individual legally entitled to act in lieu of parent) consult in the indentification, evaluation, and placement of each handicapped student. Parents must document this consultation by signing-off at appropriate points on the individualized education program.

EDUCATIONAL IMPLICATIONS OF PL 94-142

Effective implementation of PL 94-142 has far-reaching implications for schools and teachers. Especially impacted are student clientele, classroom environments, curriculum, teaching methods, documentation, evaluation, and consultation with parents. Other ramifications reach to class size and the possible extension of certain PL 94-142 provisions to nonhandicapped students.

Student clientele

Significant changes must occur in the student clientele of the regular classroom. Rarely during the past few decades have regular classrooms enrolled students who were deaf, blind, mentally retarded, or severely orthopedically handicapped. Students whose emotional or behavioral problems made them disruptive were shuttled between regular and special classes.

PL 94-142 establishes a "zero reject principle." All students, by virtue of existence, are entitled to equal access education, regardless of cost. None can be rejected; none can be excluded because of problems they might cause with facilities, instruction, or disruptive behavior. The law requires that these students be placed in regular classrooms, unless it can be substantiated that their own well-being—not just that of teacher or other students—will be enhanced by placement in special classes. Teachers will therefore be working with students who require unusual accommodations, individualized instruction, special teaching methods, and special materials and services not provided for nonhandicapped students.

Not only does the presence of handicapped students present new challenges for regular classroom teachers—the nonhandicapped students must adjust as well. Regular students rarely come into contact with severely handicapped individuals, much less live and work closely with them. They have to learn to behave with acceptance and understanding. In return, they can profit from personal closeness with people who are contending with life situations different from their own.

Curriculum

PL 94-142 requires that handicapped students be given the most effective education possible. This education must be formulated especially for each student and stated in the Individualized Education Program.

These IEPs call for variations in subject matter, content, instructional materials, and learning activities. Blindness prevents learning from printed material. Deafness renders auditory activities useless. Crippled limbs cannot perform many ordinary physical movements. Mental retardation places greater reliance on concrete rather than abstract learning.

Thus, the curriculum that has become familiar for fourth-grade social studies, tenth-grade English, and so on will not be totally appropriate for many handicapped students. Hence, virtually all regular classrooms enrolling handicapped students employ content, materials, and activities that are, in one way or another, expanded, reduced, or altered from their present form.

Physical environments

Regular classrooms have to undergo some modifications. They must accommodate wheelchairs and allow sufficient space for easy movement. Special equipment and materials are needed for the visually impaired, things such as magnifying devices, relief globes, and braille atlases and rulers.

Special instructional materials must be available for students with specific learning disabilities such as dyslexia, aphasia, and perceptual difficulties.

In addition, the classroom must be arranged and equipped for individualized instruction. Special areas are established for different kinds of activities. Each must be furnished with appropriate instructional materials, readily accessible to the students. Suitable materials and activities for nondiscriminatory evaluation must be included.

Social environments

Until handicapped and nonhandicapped students become fully accustomed to each other, specific attention must be given to their social interaction. Repeated instruction concerning human value and dignity, acceptance, courtesy, and helpfulness will be helpful. Care must be taken to see that all students have a secure feeling of "belongingness" and importance in the classroom. Each must have responsibilities, each must be seen as a contributing member of the group, and each must have the opportunity to display special talents and share interesting experiences.

Teaching methods

PL 94-142 requires the use of teaching practices long advocated, but not frequently used, for regular classrooms. Chief among them is truly individualized instruction, complete with educational diagnosis, long- and short-range objectives, and instructional prescriptions for each handicapped student. These individualized plans are linked to appropriate methods of documentation, evaluation, and reporting. All these elements are included in a written statement—the IEP. Parents collaborate in the planning and are entitled to monitor instruction and student progress.

The approach of necessity reduces the amount of time the teacher spends in teaching the entire class. Increasingly, teaching functions will move away from presenting information and toward diagnosing, prescribing, and tutoring in the individual programs.

Different class management techniques are required as well. Behavior modification techniques and well-defined contingency management programs are necessary, especially for students whose normal behavior disrupts learning for others. Flexible scheduling allows for different activities and different work rates. Nonhandicapped students will spend more time working on their own. New means for attending to their needs must be devised.

Finally, teachers are learning new skills and techniques for working with specific disabilities. They must be conversant with speech disabilities and means of reducing them; they must learn about special optical devices and braille materials for the visually impaired, and about auditory diagnoses and devices and even rudimentary signing for the hearing impaired. They must learn about a variety of devices used by the orthopedically handicapped. They must know about diabetes, allergies, and other health impairments. The list goes on, and it presents a significant instructional challenge. Still, the challenge is being met, and it has a silver lining—the joy of helping students whose needs go well beyond the ordinary.

Evaluation

PL 94-142 requires that individualized educational programs specify appropriate procedures of evaluation. This evaluation must be referenced directly to stated goals and objectives. It must show degrees and rates of progress, and it must show the extent to which the stated objectives are being reached.

The term "appropriate procedures" requires the use of diagnostic and assessment techniques that are new to most regular classroom teachers. Standardized tests, for example, have limited use in this type of evaluation. Such tests are "norm-referenced." They reveal how an individual compares to others across the nation. That information does not help in the kind of evaluation called for in PL 94-142.

Instead of norm-referenced information, teachers must obtain "criterion-referenced" information, which does not compare one student against another. Rather, it reveals progress toward objectives set specifically for a given individual.

Therefore, teachers must use procedures for checking, recording, and reporting the progress of each individual within the individualized program. Paper and pencil tests will be appropriate only for students whose sight, motor coordination, and reading and writing abilities are adequate. Much greater reliance will be put on teacher observations, reports of specialists who observe students in school, samples of student work, and input from parents.

Consultation with parents

Teachers have long recognized the value of close communication with parents. Parents can be powerful allies in teaching. They are usually quite concerned about their children's education. They like to be informed about what teachers are trying to accomplish, how they are going about it, what they themselves can do to help their child at home, and of course how their child is faring in the program.

Unfortunately, keeping close touch with parents is time consuming. It is hard enough for elementary teachers, with their thirty to thirty-five students; secondary teachers may see 150 or more students each day. The best they can ordinarily do is to send home written communiques. They usually make personal contact with parents only when a student is failing or causing trouble.

PL 94-142 changes this picture. Parents are to be included in all phases of placement, planning, and evaluation. They are to check student progress periodically in the ongoing process of educational diagnosis and instruction. They are to be in continual contact with teachers and program specialists. For the first time, parents will be brought closely into their children's educational process.

This closeness requires that teachers devise efficient systems of communicating with parents. They must use written, telephone, and personal messages. Times, places, and schedules must be arranged. This responsibility requires large amounts of time and taxes the ingenuity and stamina of teachers.

Class size

It is evident that implementation of PL 94-142 requires much additional work and time for teachers. It also requires much more individualized instruction and evaluation. This work load and time involvement make it impossible for teachers to attend to the number of students they have traditionally served.

Therefore, class size must diminish if teachers are to properly implement PL 94-142 as required by law. But even small reductions in class size greatly increase the cost of education. Since individual states are reluctant to increase their support of education, and since PL 94-142 is a federal law that supersedes state laws, the federal government will likely pour huge amounts of money into public education. Whether this infusion of money will be sufficient to reduce class size remains to be seen. One thing is clear—if PL 94-142 is to be implemented as it is written, class size must be reduced in cases where handicapped students are placed in regular classrooms; otherwise the task becomes impossible for teachers.

Teacher education

PL 94-142 requires that all teachers be prepared to implement its requirements. New teachers must show such preparation before they can obtain teaching credentials. Teachers already credentialled must undergo inservice training so that they meet the requirements.

This requirement is causing much activity in school districts and schools of teacher education. Every teacher's outlook will be reoriented toward working with all students, regardless of their special abilities, disabilities, and requirements. They must learn to individualize instruction, use criterion-referenced evaluation for each student, and communicate effectively with parents. They must learn what to expect in specific disabilities, how to work with such students, and how to reorganize their classrooms.

These may seem monumental tasks. They are formidable, to be sure, but not impossible. All the expectancies, procedures, and techniques can be learned. Helping teachers learn them is what this book is about.

Extension to all students

PL 94-142 is directed *only* to the education of the handicapped. Implementing the law, however, also affects nonhandicapped students. Possibly some of the requirements will be extended to all students, handicapped or not.

As teachers individualize instruction for handicapped students, their contact time with other students will be reduced. They may find it easier to individualize instruction for everyone. As they prepare communication devices and procedures for parents of the handicapped, they can extend the written communiques to all parents without much extra effort. Activities for developing social acceptance, belongingness, and responsibility apply equally to all students in the classroom.

New record-keeping devices can be utilized for all students. Thus, PL 94-142 has heavy impact on nonhandicapped students, too.

An additional reality may strike down the remaining barriers between education for the handicapped and the nonhandicapped. Early on, some parents of nonhandicapped students began calling for equal treatment for their children. They, too, wanted the quality that comes with individually planned education programs and close consultation with parents. Thus it may happen someday that the requirements of PL 94-142 will become the requirements for all students.

SUMMARY OF PL 94-142: KEY ELEMENTS AND IMPLICATIONS

This section presents selected elements of PL 94-142, showing their original wording. Where appropriate, they are followed by a listing of implications for classroom teachers.

1. *The purpose of PL 94-142 is to provide the best possible free education to handicapped youth, ages 3 to 21.*

   P.L. 94-142
   Sec. 3
   "(c) It is the purpose of this Act to assure that all handicapped children have available to them, within the time periods specified in section 612(2)(B), a free appropriate public education which emphasizes special education and related services designed to meet their unique needs, to assure that the rights of handicapped children and their parents or guardians are protected, to assist States and localities to provide for the education of all handicapped children, and to assess and assure the effectiveness of efforts to educate handicapped children."

2. *The law names nine categories of handicap.*

   P.L. 94-142
   Sec. 602
   Handicapped children are defined as "mentally retarded, hard of hearing, deaf, speech impaired, visually handicapped, seriously emotionally disturbed, orthopedically impaired, or other health impaired, or children with specific learning disabilities, who by reason thereof require special education and related services."

   Children with specific learning disabilities are defined as "those children who have a disorder in one or more of the basic psychological processes involved in understanding or in using language, spoken or written, which disorder may manifest itself in imperfect ability to listen, think, speak, read, write, spell, or do mathematical calculations. Such disorders include such conditions as perceptual handicaps, brain injury, minimal brain dysfunction, dyslexia, and developmental aphasia. Such term does not include children who have learning problems which are primarily the result of visual, hearing, or motor handicaps, of mental retardation, of emotional disturbance, or of environmental, cultural, or economic disadvantage."

3. *A diligent search must be conducted by every school district to identify handicapped youth.*

   P.L. 94-142
   Sec. 612(2)
   The State shall assure that . . .
   "(C) all children residing in the State who are handicapped, regardless of the severity of their handicap, and who are in need of special education and related services are identified, located, and evaluated, and that a practical method is developed and implemented to determine which children are currently receiving needed special education and related services and which children are not currently receiving needed special education and related services . . ."

4. *Handicapped students must be educated in the "least restrictive environment." This means the regular classroom, unless written justifications for other settings are made.*
   Implications for teachers:
   a. Teachers can expect to have in their classes students with various kinds of handicap.
   b. Significant changes will be required in teaching methodology, learning environments, and methods of classroom management.
   c. Teachers will need special preparation for working most effectively with handicapped students.
   d. Teachers must learn to work collaboratively with specialist itinerant teachers.

5. *An individualized education program (IEP) must be prepared each year for each handicapped student.*

   P.L. 94-142
   Sec. 4(a)
   "(19) The term 'individualized education program' means a written statement for each handicapped child developed in any meeting by a representative of the local educational agency or an intermediate educational unit who shall be qualified to provide, or supervise the provision of, specially designed instruction to meet the unique needs of handicapped children, the teacher, the parents or guardian of such child, and, whenever appropriate, such child, which statement shall include (A) a statement of the present levels of educational performance of such child, (B) a statement of annual goals, including short-term instructional objectives, (C) a statement of the specific educational services to be provided to such child, and the extent to which such child will be able to participate in regular educational programs, (D) the projected date for initiation and anticipated duration of such services, and appropriate objective criteria and evaluation procedures and schedules for determining, on at least an annual basis, whether instructional objectives are being achieved."

Sec. 612

"(4) Each local educational agency in the State will maintain records of the individualized education program for each handicapped child, and such program shall be established, reviewed, and revised as provided in section 614(a)(5)."

Implications for teachers:

a. Teachers must learn to prepare IEPs in accord with legal requirements.

b. Appropriate skills must be acquired for assessing and diagnosing academic performance, stating short- and long-range goals, and conducting nondiscriminatory evaluation for determining progress toward those goals.

c. Time must be set aside for participation with the group that establishes the IEP.

d. Teachers must acquire skills for individualizing instruction. These skills include (1) varying content, objectives, activities, or time in accord with learner needs; (2) setting up a management system that facilitates individual study; (3) providing appropriate materials and activities; and (4) establishing individualized procedures for diagnosis, evaluation, recording, and reporting.

6. *All materials and procedures for testing, assessment, and evaluation must be nondiscriminatory, as regards race, culture, or nature of handicap.*

P.L. 94-142

Sec. 612(5)

"(C) procedures to assure that testing and evaluation materials and procedures utilized for the purposes of evaluation and placement of handicapped children will be selected and administered so as not to be racially or culturally discriminatory. Such materials or procedures shall be provided and administered in the child's native language or mode of communication, unless it clearly is not feasible to do so, and no single procedure shall be the sole criterion for determining an appropriate educational program for a child."

Implications for teachers:

a. Care must be taken to see that language, cultural backgrounds, physical skills and abilities, and specific learning disabilities do not render evaluation procedures invalid.

b. Evaluation of learning must be carried out on an individual basis, judging student progress in terms of goals specifically stated in the IEP.

7. *Parents who object to any aspect of their handicapped child's education are guaranteed the right of due process.*

P.L. 94-142

SEC. 615(b)(1)

Agencies receiving funds under this Act shall provide . . .

"(E) an opportunity to present complaints with respect to any matter relating to the identification, evaluation, or educational placement of the child, or the provision of a free appropriate public education to such child.

"(2) Whenever a complaint has been received under paragraph (1) of this sub-section, the parents or guardian shall have an opportunity for an impartial due process hearing which shall be conducted by the State educational agency or by the local educational agency or intermediate educational unit, as determined by State law or by the State educational agency. No hearing conducted pursuant to the requirements of this paragraph shall be conducted by an employee of such agency or unit involved in the education or care of the child."

SEC. 615

"(d) Any party to any hearing conducted pursuant to subsections (b) and (c) shall be accorded (1) the right to be accompanied and advised by counsel and by individuals with special knowledge or training with respect to the problems of handicapped children, (2) the right to present evidence and confront, cross-examine, and compel the attendance of witnesses, (3) the right to a written or electronic verbatim record of such hearing, and (4) the right to written findings of fact and decisions (which findings and decisions shall also be transmitted to the advisory panel established pursuant to section 613(a)(12))."

8. *States must furnish personnel development to permit implementation of the law.*

P.L. 94-142

SEC. 613(a)

The State plan shall . . .

"(3) set forth, consistent with the purposes of this Act, a description of programs and procedures for (A) the development and implementation of a comprehensive system of personnel development which shall include the inservice training of general and special educational instructional and support personnel, detailed procedures to assure that all personnel necessary to carry out the purposes of this Act are appropriately and adequately prepared and trained, and effective procedures for acquiring and disseminating to teachers and administrators of programs for handicapped children significant information derived from educational research, demonstration, and similar projects, and (B) adopting, where appropriate, promising educational practices and materials development through such projects. . . ."

Implications for teachers:

a. Teachers can expect to receive information and training necessary for carrying out the requirements of the law.

b. School administrators must be trained as well.

Note: Laws have been enacted in the various states to comply with the personnel development act. As an example, California makes the following requirements for new teachers and administrators:

80032.2 (a) *Special Education Training for Teachers and Administrators.* The Special Education training requirement specified in Section 67.5 of Chapter 1247 of the statutes of 1977 shall be required of each applicant for a clear Multiple or Single Subject teaching credential or an Administrative Services credential issued in accordance with the provisions of Section 44259 of the Education Code. This requirement may be satisfied by a course of study, which may be offered or accepted by an approved college or university. The college or university recommending the applicant for a clear Multiple or Single Subject teaching credential or Administrative Services credential shall submit a plan for Commission approval indicating how this requirement will be met. Each plan submitted to the Commission shall include but not be limited to the following:

1. A description of the program elements which lead to the demonstration of the competencies as provided herein;
2. A description of how such program elements relate to each specified competency for each credential;
3. A description of the specific program options available to each candidate for completing the competencies;
4. Provisions for giving credit or establishing equivalency toward completion of this requirement in the form of in-service training, work taken for credit at other institutions, including out-of-state institutions, or a combination of these or other options.

(b) After July 1, 1979 no institutional recommendation shall be issued for the clear Multiple or Single Subject teaching credential unless the recommending institution has presented evidence, consistent with its approved plan, of the completion by the candidate of all the following competencies consisting of the demonstrated ability to:

1. Diagnose children's academic strengths and weaknesses, perceptual characteristics, and preferred learning modalities (i.e., auditory, visual, kinesthetic) through formal and informal assessment procedures;
2. Demonstrate the ability to assess the characteristics and behavior of exceptional pupils in terms of program and developmental needs;
3. Recognize the differences and similarities of exceptional and non-exceptional pupils;
4. Analyze non-discriminatory assessment including a sensitivity to cultural and linguistic factors;
5. Produce and evaluate short- and long-term educational objectives based on Individualized Education Program goals;
6. Utilize various diagnostic/prescriptive materials and procedures in reading, language arts, math, and perceptual-motor development;
7. Apply diagnostic information toward the modification of traditional school curriculum and materials for selected children;
8. Identify and teach non-academic areas, i.e., socialization skills, career and vocational education;

9. Discuss inter- and intra-personal relationships with students and be able to communicate appropriate information in a non-threatening manner to teachers and parents;
10. Explain current enabling legislation dealing with Special Education.

(c) After July 1, 1979 no institutional recommendation shall be issued for the Administrative Services credential unless the recommending institution has presented evidence, consistent with its approved plan, of the completion by the candidate of all of the following competencies consisting of the demonstrated ability to:

1. Demonstrate the ability to assess the characteristics and behavior of exceptional pupils in terms of program and developmental needs;
2. Recognize the differences and similarities of exceptional and nonexceptional pupils;
3. Analyze non-discriminatory assessment including a sensitivity to cultural and linguistic factors;
4. Discuss interpersonal relationships and human relations problems and issues with students and parents;
5. Communicate information in a non-threatening manner to teachers and parents;
6. Evaluate the concept of least restrictive environments and its implications for the instructional process;
7. Define and explain the admission, review, and dismissal processes;
8. Formulate and illustrate an individualized educational program for individuals with exceptional needs;
9. Identify and select alternative instructional programs;
10. Contrast and explain individual protections as it pertains to parents, teachers and students.

Clearly, PL 94-142 adds significant new requirements for regular classroom teachers and administrators. Already heavily burdened, they must develop new skills, establish new teaching and management procedures, and find the extra time that will be needed.

The task may be cumbersome, at least at first, but it is far from impossible. The actual number of handicapped children per regular classroom will be small, no more than two or three on the average. The majority will receive significant help from specialists. Many will spend part of the day in regular classes and the remainder of the day in special classes. Teachers can count on much support from appropriate specialists. Moreover, suitable training must be provided to teachers. They cannot and will not be left to fend for themselves without preparation.

The purpose of this book is help provide the information and training needed by teachers and support personnel. Its chapters deal in practical and explicit terms with basic knowledge and skills. Reading the material, discussing it with others, and performing the suggested activities will calm anxieties and build confidence.

You will come to see that working with handicapped students, while a challenge, can also be pleasant and highly rewarding.

SUGGESTED ACTIVITIES

1. Invite a special education teacher or administrator to discuss his or her district's steps in implementing PL 94-142.
2. In class discussion, identify regular teachers' greatest fears or concerns about working with handicapped students. List possible steps for allaying those fears.
3. Find out what your state requires in teacher education for complying with PL 94-142. Discuss training program components that will assure that the competencies are developed.

SUGGESTED READINGS

Charles, C.: Individualizing instruction, ed. 2; St. Louis, 1980, The C. V. Mosby Co.

Corrigan, C.: Political and moral contexts that produced PL 94-142, J. Teacher Educ. **29:** 3-7, 1978.

Introducing Public Law 94-142—The Education of All Handicapped Children Act of 1975, Council For Exceptional Children, Reston, Virginia, 1976.

The Education of All Handicapped Act—PL 94-142, Council for Exceptional Children, Reston, Virginia, 1977.

CHAPTER 2

Handicapped students: who are they?

A handicap is any permanent condition that severely inhibits normal functioning. The great majority of us have physical, mental, or emotional traits that do not permit us to function completely normally at all times. However, most of the little aches, pains, depressions, vision losses, and so on do not interfere in any significant way with our daily life functions. When an impairment reaches a level that is not overcome even by special attention, it is considered a handicap.

Public Law 94-142 is concerned with education of students who suffer from one or more of the following nine categories of handicap: (1) deafness, (2) hard-of-hearing, (3) mental retardation, (4) orthopedic impairment, (5) other health impairment, (6) serious emotional disturbance, (7) specific learning disability, (8) speech impairment, and (9) visual impairment.

Some 12 to 15% of school-age youth in the United States are considered handicapped; the total runs past 12,000,000. If every one of these people were able to attend regular school classes, teachers could expect, on the average, to have about four handicapped students in each class. Of course, some students, especially those with profound mental retardation and very severe health and orthopedic impairments, cannot attend or cannot profit from regular classrooms. Thus the number of handicapped students to appear in regular classes is somewhat lower. Still, regular teachers can expect to work with two or more handicapped students per class, at least part of the time.

Some handicapped students require special services, while others do not. Special services include instruction, materials, equipment, transportation, care, and other things not required by nonhandicapped individuals.

Gearheart and Weishahn (1976) conservatively estimated that over six million students between the ages of 5 and 18 were sufficiently handicapped as to require special services, with less than half actually receiving those services. By categories, their estimates were:

Visually impaired	55,000
Hearing impaired	330,000
Speech impaired	1,925,000
Health and orthopedically impaired	275,000
Emotionally disturbed	1,100,000
Mentally retarded	1,375,000
Learning disabled	1,100,000

Public Law 94-142 requires that all teachers be prepared to work with handicapped students who can profit from regular classroom attendance. The following chapters of this book will deal explicitly with how teachers can meet this legal requirement. The remainder of this chapter will describe briefly the traits and disabilities typical of individuals in the nine categories of handicap.

THE HEARING IMPAIRED: DEAF AND HARD-OF-HEARING

PL 94-142 names deaf and hard-of-hearing as separate categories of handicap. They are grouped together here for two reasons. First, they represent degrees along the same continuum of hearing acuity. Second, regular classroom teachers rarely work with profoundly deaf students, but they almost always have in class students who have some degree of hearing loss.

Hearing impairments, usually referred to as "hearing loss," are of two types. The more common type has to do with *volume and pitch*, loudness of sound at low, medium, and high frequencies. The other type of hearing loss has to do with *intelligibility*. The volume may be adequate but the sound, as in the case of speech, may appear garbled. Impairments of both types can be helped through speechreading (lipreading, expressions, gestures) and the use of hearing aids.

Hearing losses, especially in volume and pitch, are assessed through use of the pure tone audiometer. The audiometer can produce pure sounds at different pitches (frequencies) and volumes (measured in decibels). By charting one's perception of volumes at different frequencies, an audiogram is prepared that shows levels of hearing acuity and loss.

Students with mild hearing losses seldom have auditory problems in school. They have difficulty hearing very soft voices, but they compensate on their own by speechreading, listening carefully, and asking for repetitions. Most are never identified except through routine tests.

Those with moderate hearing losses require special attention, but they can remain in the regular classroom full time. Moderate loss falls in the 40- to 50-decibel range. Normal conversation cannot be heard clearly unless the speaker is quite close, and even then background noise may render the speech unintelligible. Students with moderate hearing loss must be seated near the teacher. They will speechread a great deal, and they may require hearing aids.

With greater degrees of hearing loss, speech is affected. A moderately severe loss—in the 60- to 70-decibel range—makes normal conversation difficult. Speechreading and hearing aids are required. The loss will probably be accompanied by some speech defects. Pronunciation may be inaccurate and rhythm and intonation abnormal. Vocabulary may be limited. The individual will be hesitant about speaking in class and participating in class discussions. Special speech instruction will be required.

Severe and profound hearing losses, 70 decibels and beyond, prevent most learning through auditory means. With much help, these students can learn to speechread fairly well. They can also learn to speak, but not in a way that sounds normal. Most of their academic learning will come from printed material. They can participate well in regular classrooms in subjects that do not require speaking and listening, but they also require special instruction outside the classroom.

While *deafness* is detected in early childhood, mild hearing losses frequently go unnoticed. Often it is the regular teacher who notices hearing difficulties in students. Tell-tale signs include: (1) odd position of head while listening, perhaps favoring one ear over the other, (2) inattention during discussions, (3) repeatedly saying "Huh?" and asking for repetitions, and (4) asking classmates for directions. Teachers who suspect hearing loss should notify the school nurse or audiologist to check the student. Meanwhile the following provisions are suggested:

1. Seat the student near the front
2. Look at the student while speaking
3. Speak loudly and distinctly
4. Assign a "buddy" to the student to assist with directions and verbal information

THE MENTALLY RETARDED

Individuals vary greatly in their intellectual capabilities. The great mass of us who fall between the high and low extremes are considered "normal." Those at the upper extreme are called "gifted" and those at the lower extreme are called "retarded." In making these judgments, individuals are compared against all other individuals of their same age.

Ranges and cut-off points for establishing levels of mental retardation are set by experts. Intelligence quotient (IQ) tests assess individuals in areas of logical reasoning, abstract thought, spatial and verbal relationships, and areas of knowledge (such as vocabulary) thought commonly available to all. Average IQ is set at 100. The range from 90 to 110 takes in 50% of the population; it is considered the "normal" range. Just below the normal range is a category called "dull normal"; its boundaries are often set at 75 to 90.

Students who repeatedly score below 75, and whose scores are not believed to be caused by specific language or emotional problems, are categorized as mentally retarded. That category's upper range, 50-75, marks mild levels of mental retardation. Individuals included therein are usually referred to as "educable mentally retarded" (EMR). Two or three students out of a hundred fall into this category. They profit from work in the normal elementary school curriculum, modified to a slower pace with little or no abstract thought required. Their secondary school programs concentrate on basic literacy, functional math, and job-related training.

Generally speaking, mentally retarded students have shorter attention spans, a slower work pace, poorer language skills, and limited ability to deal with abstractions. Their concepts of self are apt to be low, and they often prefer to play with younger children. For many years EMR students have been taught only in special classes. PL 94-142 returns them to regular classrooms for much of their instruction.

Care must be used in labeling students as mentally retarded. PL 94-142 makes very clear that materials and procedures used for testing, evaluation, and placement must be nondiscriminatory, which means they must not falsely categorize students whose language, reading, culture, or specific learning disabilities may depress their test performance.

The law also says that no single criterion can be used for placement. Teachers and specialists need to look for several indicators that point toward the same conclusion. Evidence can be found in class work, language ability (if native speaker of standard English), performance on Piagetian-type tasks, ability to see the point, ability to generalize, and so forth.

Students judged to be mentally retarded require high levels of motivation and constant success. Their learning activities should be sequenced into small steps. They should be reinforced continually. Repetition and careful feedback help them acquire correct knowledge and skills.

Basic literacy, math, and human relations skills are especially important for mentally retarded individuals, who often become skilled and highly valued workers. They tend to be punctual, steady, dependable, and loyal. Many business people prefer hiring them for positions such as maids, waitresses, stock clerks, carpenters, mechanics, and manufacturing jobs, in which boredom is more likely to afflict people of normal intelligence.

THE ORTHOPEDICALLY IMPAIRED

The word "orthopedics" refers to diseases and deformities of the muscles, joints, and skeletal system. The most common orthopedic impairments among school-age students are those associated with cerebral palsy, amputations, birth defects, and diseases such as arthritis and muscular dystrophy. Not included here are injuries such as fractures and torn cartilage, ligaments, and tendons; these are correctable and are not considered handicaps.

Cerebral palsy. Cerebral palsy is a severe impairment of the ability to make voluntary movements. It results from brain injuries, usually sustained at birth. Deformities of the skeletal system result as well.

Cerebral palsied individuals show spastic (jerky) or athetoid (uncontrolled) movements. Some are able to walk; others are confined to wheelchairs and are virtually helpless. The brain injury often produces hearing and speech problems as well.

Most cerebral palsied individuals have normal intelligence. That enables them to learn adequately in regular classrooms. However, their special orthopedic and language needs often require work in special facilities with therapists part of the time.

Amputation. Amputation refers to absence of limbs and parts of limbs that have been removed surgically. The amputations, some done during infancy, are done because of injury or disease.

Previously, amputees accepted their missing arms, legs, hands, or feet and made the best of it, using crutches and wheelchairs. Now, artificial limbs, hands, and feet are fitted whenever possible. Many amputees learn to use artificial legs and feet so well that they go unnoticed in crowds. Artificial arms and hands can be used well, too, but they cannot be concealed as easily.

School students with amputations can spend all or most of their time in the regular classroom. Only slight accommodations must be made for them. They will be highly noticeable, however. Care must be taken to provide tolerance and acceptance from members of the group.

Birth defects. Birth defects leave many children with malformed limbs, hands, and feet. Most foot defects can be corrected surgically. They usually go unnoticed, except that the individual may not be able to run as well as others. Defects of the legs, arms, and hands are more noticeable and make certain movements difficult or impossible. Students with these defects may receive some physical therapy in school. For the most part they will be in regular classrooms full-time.

Diseases of joints, bones, and muscles. Diseases of the joints, bones, and muscles include arthritis, osteomyelitis, muscular dystrophy, and other rare diseases. *Arthritis* is usually considered a disease of age, but it afflicts children, too. The most common form is *rheumatoid arthritis*. It affects mainly the joints in the fingers, hands, toes, and feet; it occurs also in the elbow, knee, shoulder, and hip. It makes joints sore, swollen, and stiff. It may deform the joints as it progresses, drastically changing the appearance of hands. Sometimes rheumatoid arthritis affects organs such as the liver, spleen, and heart.

Arthritic students function perfectly well in the regular classroom. Some movements are difficult for them, and they may not be able to play running, jumping, and throwing games. Otherwise, they do not require extensive special attention.

Osteomyelitis is an infection of the bones and bone marrow. Proper treatment with antibiotics usually halts the disease before it has crippling effects. Occasionally, the limbs, even the jaw, may be seriously affected, leaving permanent damage. Students with these effects are disabled in movements of major limbs. They often require crutches for mobility.

Muscular dystrophy is the most serious of the diseases that now affect the muscles. It has various forms. The most serious affects children, usually striking before the age of 10. The cause is unknown, and the condition is irreversible, ending in death.

In muscular dystrophy, the muscles simply begin to waste away. The individual, thus weakened, becomes unable to walk. These individuals then spend much of their remaining lives in wheelchairs. In later stages they are bedridden.

The disease produces some limb deformity as well, because opposing muscles do not weaken at the same rate. The stronger set dominates the weaker, thus pulling body parts out of shape.

The present philosophy is to allow muscular dystrophied children to lead lives as normal as possible. That means they should participate in regular classrooms as much as their condition allows. In earlier stages of the disease they are active, productive, and contributing members of the class. Progressively they are able to spend less time in the classroom, and sooner or later they must withdraw altogether.

Teachers encounter a few difficulties in working with orthopedically impaired students. They make a few accommodations for wheelchairs and crutches. They familiarize themselves quickly with the requirements of braces and false limbs. Mainly, they need to help normal and orthopedically handicapped students accept each other and work together respectfully and harmoniously.

THE HEALTH IMPAIRED

"Health impairments" is a loosely defined group of handicapping conditions that includes physical malfunctions of vital organs and certain body tissues. These malfunctions are relatively permanent, not transient as in colds, injuries, or infections. The most common of these debilitating conditions are allergies, diabetes, asthma, and epilepsy.

Allergies. Allergies are body reactions to various substances common in the physical environment. They most commonly afflict the skin and mucous membranes. Symptoms include watery discharge, sneezing, coughing, blisters, rashes, and itches. Their effect often goes beyond the obvious affliction to produce overall lethargy, discomfort, chronic indigestion, or hyperactivity.

Diabetes. Diabetes is a very serious condition in which the pancreas does not produce sufficient insulin to burn the blood sugar. Various symptoms accompany diabetes, including thirst, hunger, frequent urination, irritability, and general weakness and listlessness. In advanced stages the eyes are affected; blindness sometimes results. Diabetes sometimes leads to death.

Diabetes is usually treated by daily injections of insulin. The proper level of insulin is very difficult to maintain. If there is too much insulin, it burns up the available blood sugar, resulting in hypoglycemia (very low level of blood sugar, accompanied by trembling, perspiration, and faintness); it can be quickly corrected by taking orange juice, candy, or raisins. If too little insulin is present, the body cannot use the sugar present in the blood. Severe instances can result in diabetic coma and require hospitalization. Labored breathing, nausea, and vomiting may occur. The condition is corrected by an injection of insulin.

Asthma. Asthma is a special allergic condition that involves spasms of the muscles of the bronchial tubes. Its causes are not fully known, and treatment is only partially effective. Asthma attacks produce coughing, wheezing, and labored breathing. They often occur during heavy exercise. They may last from several seconds to several hours. Special inhalants are used to reduce the symptoms and allow freer breathing.

Epilepsy. Epilepsy is a common condition among school-age students, affecting about 2% of the population. The cause of epilepsy is not known. The process occurs as an excessive electrical discharge in the brain. Its main symptom is the seizure, or muscular convulsion, occurring when the brain, during the discharge, loses control over muscles, senses, and consciousness. Most seizures can be controlled fairly well with anticonvulsant drugs. The seizure may be very light, short, and unnoticed. Such is the *petit mal* seizure that may occur several times a day in some children. Stronger seizures may result in unusual, though not grossly bizarre, behavior. The student may rub the arms, smack the lips, walk around, or even take off articles of clothing. This often happens during a *temporal* seizure, which may last from several minutes to a few hours. The individual will not remember what happened during the seizure and will want to sleep afterward. Frightening behavior may occur during a *grand mal* seizure. The individual will fall down and have jerking convulsive movements, perhaps shouting or gurgling and emitting quantities of saliva. Afterward, the person will remember nothing of the event and will want to sleep. Even though a grand mal seizure may appear terrible to onlookers, there is little danger except through injury by falling into objects. Everyone should remain calm. Nothing will stop the seizure once it has begun. A doctor need not be called, though the parents should be informed. After a short rest, the student can resume normal activities in the classroom.

●   ●   ●

Health impairments are never treated by teachers. They do need to know about the existence of such conditions in students so as to know what to expect.

That allows them to make necessary adjustments in instruction, make allowances for unusual behavior, prepare and inform other students for occurrences such as epileptic seizures, and know what to do if signs of diabetic difficulties appear.

No medication is ever given by the teacher. The school nurse or family doctor is summoned when medication is indicated. With careful instructions the teacher can be allowed to give orange juice or sugar during a hypoglycemic attack. It is still best to call for help, however, since the symptoms of hypoglycemia and those of diabetic coma can be confused.

THE EDUCATIONALLY HANDICAPPED: THE EMOTIONALLY DISTURBED AND THE LEARNING DISABLED

PL 94-142 calls for specific attention to students with serious emotional handicap, and to students with specific learning disabilities. Schools usually subsume these disabilities under the single heading "educationally handicapped" (EH), a large category that encompasses several disabilities; it includes not only emotional problems and specific learning disabilities, but behavior problems as well.

Behavioral problems. From the teacher's point of view, disruptive behavioral problems present the greatest concern. They are usually symptoms of other problems. Still, the teacher must deal with them. Hyperactivity is common: the student cannot keep quiet or still. Hostility and aggression toward other students and the teacher are also common, along with downright refusal to comply with adult authority. These behaviors vex teachers sorely. Chapter 6 deals with the management of behavior.

Emotional problems. Several emotional problems are related to some of the disruptive behaviors. Often, however, the emotional problem does not result in "bad" behavior. Individuals may be very withdrawn and incapable of interacting with students or doing group work. They may be chronic daydreamers; they may be very fearful; they may cry miserably; they may show streaks of cold cruelty. These behaviors, too, are symptoms of deeper problems.

Specific learning disabilities. Specific learning disabilities refer to dysfunctions—sometimes physical, sometimes intellectual—that interfere with learning. Chief among them are *dyslexia* (a severe reading disability involving perception of printed words); *perceptual disorders* such as reversals, mirror images, and inability to differentiate among various shapes and sounds; *memory disorders*, in which a student may have poor short-term memory or poor memory for some things but not others; and *specific subject disabilities*, in which they have great difficulty learning isolated parts of the curriculum, such as reading, spelling, or mathematics, while being adequate to excellent in others.

Teachers can only work gently with the manifestations of severe emotional problems; they can work directly, however, with specific learning disabilities. Some disabilities, such as perceptual reversals, improve and even disappear after careful attention. Others such as dyslexia usually remain, but teachers can work around them and students learn to cope.

Special materials and effective methods have been devised for diagnosing and correcting learning disabilities; many of these approaches are described in Chapter 8.

THE SPEECH IMPAIRED

The speech impaired comprise the largest category of handicapped students. Over two million school-age students in the United States have one or more kinds of speech problems.

With time many speech defects correct themselves. Some, such as lisping, may be considered cute and encouraged in the young. Despite their frequency, speech impairments do not significantly affect educational progress unless they (1) interfere with communication, (2) produce feelings of inadequacy, or (3) result in alienation from the group.

Poor articulation and nonfluency. Two types of speech impairment are prevalent and require attention. They are poor articulation (producing inaccurate speech sounds) and nonfluency (stuttering and halting speech). Both these types interfere somewhat, though not greatly, with communication. Their greatest danger is in attracting unfavorable attention, with resultant poor self-image.

Much more likely to interfere with school communication are nonstandard English and English inability. Examples of nonstandard English are ghetto language and pidgin English. English inability is often seen in students whose parents speek Spanish, Arabic, and other languages in the home.

These difficulties are not considered speech impairments, however; neither are ethnic or regional accents. Impairments come from physical or emotional conditions. The language inabilities mentioned here are matters of learning that are attended to through standard instructional procedures.

Articulation errors are most commonly shown in distorted pronunciation. These distortions may result from inappropriate models or habituated "baby talk." If so, they are easily corrected. If they result from physical impairments, they require prolonged special attention. Such physical impairments include hearing loss, cleft lip or palate, deformities of tongue, gums, teeth, or nose, and cerebral palsy. Some deformities can be corrected surgically; of those that cannot, resultant speech impairments are difficult to correct.

Nonfluency problems, such as stuttering, are very hard to correct. They appear to be tied into emotionality. Fluent speech is usually easier for stutterers in calm, relaxed situations. Often, the trait disappears as individuals reach adulthood. But students who stutter in school invariably attract attention, which only worsens the problem.

Speech-impaired students usually receive regular help from specialists. Meanwhile, they attend regular classes most of the time.

Teachers have two special duties to carry out with their speech-impaired students. The first is to provide direct help with articulation difficulties. The speech specialist will advise on what to do and how to do it.

The second duty is to provide a climate of tolerance and acceptance for speech-impaired students. Their classmates tend to laugh, mimic, and make fun of speech disorders. A healthy climate is established and maintained by: (1) discussing the matter with the entire class; (2) showing no reaction at all when students stutter or misarticulate; (3) not finishing sentences for students who are having difficulty; and (4) showing acceptance for students as they are, and being sure other class members do so, too.

THE VISUALLY HANDICAPPED

Two levels of visual impairment require attention under PL 94-142. People who fall into these two levels are referred to as *educationally blind* or *partially sighted*.

Educational blindness is not the same as legal blindness. To understand this point, first consider *legal blindness*, which is a technical definition put forth by the National Society for the Prevention of Blindness. A legally blind person has visual acuity of no more than 20/200 *after correction* in the better eye, *or* has a defect that reduces the angle of vision to no more than 20 degrees. In the first case, an individual can see at 20 feet only what a normally sighted person can see at 200 feet. In the second case, an individual can see only a small "spot" within the large visual field that the normal eye can see.

Bear in mind that some legally blind people can see well enough to read and move about without special assistance. Others must read braille and use devices or assistance in walking from one place to another.

People classified as *partially sighted* can read printed materials. This is an educational rather than a technical definition. The print must sometimes be held very close to the eye. It must be larger than the standard for a given age. If not, it must be enlarged with a magnifying device before students can read it.

Because there is a large overlap between legally blind and partially sighted, most schools use an educational definition to differentiate between the blind and partially sighted. The educational definition for *partially sighted* is that individuals can read printed material, but that material must be larger than standard or else enlarged with magnifying devices. The educational definition for *blindness* holds that printed materials cannot be read at all. The individual must learn from voice, audio tapes, and braille reading.

Students with severe visual impairment will have been identified very early. They will have been using magnifying devices or learning to read braille before entering the regular classroom. Students with less severe loss of vision often escape detection for several years. Still, their ability to function normally in and out of the classroom is hampered.

Regular teachers may be the first to notice sight defects. The students themselves do not know. They have nothing against which to compare, and parents often do not recognize signs of vision loss.

Behaviors that hint at vision loss include: (1) squinting at the chalkboard, (2) holding a book very near or very far from the eyes, (3) blinking, distorting the eyes, and holding the head at odd angles, and (4) showing unusual sensitivity to light. Teachers who observe these behaviors should alert the school nurse. Properly fitted glasses usually alleviate the problem.

Students who are partially sighted even after correction require some special materials and help. Great quantities of magnifying devices, braille materials, and audio materials are available. The itinerant specialist provides help in their proper use.

● ● ●

This concludes a brief overview of the areas of handicap named in PL 94-142, along with traits of students included in the areas.

Subsequent chapters present detailed suggestions for methods, materials, and management strategies useful in working with students in the different categories of handicap.

SUGGESTED ACTIVITIES

1. Invite a blind or orthopedically handicapped college student to speak to your class. Request commentary on difficulties and successes encountered in school learning and in relations with nonhandicapped students.
2. Arrange to examine the variety of materials used by the partially sighted and the blind, such as magnifying devices, large print materials, braille typewriters, and audio discs and tapes.
3. Visit a class or adult workshop for the mentally retarded. Note the curricula, materials, and learning activities. Talk with the students, if allowed.
4. Learn and practice a rudimentary signing vocabulary, as used by the deaf.
5. Arrange for a demonstration by a speech therapist, to review common articulation problems and how they are treated.

SUGGESTED READING

Gearheart, B., and Weishahn, M.: The handicapped child in the regular classroom, St. Louis, 1976, The C. V. Mosby Co.

CHAPTER 3

New roles for classroom teachers

THE MANDATE FOR CHANGE

Teachers have new roles to fill under PL 94-142, there is no getting around it. A few of these roles are brand new, and several are modifications of traditional roles; they add up, though, to a rather different way of teaching. The changes do not please most teachers—changes rarely do. Teaching is a tough job, and when you find things that work you want to stay with them. When you find a comfortable groove, you like to stay in it.

Teachers *are* making the required changes, however. They have little choice. The law's the law. But they are also finding a silver lining in the cloud. The new roles called for in PL 94-142 make for better teaching. They may be aimed at handicapped students, but they benefit everyone—handicapped students, non-handicapped students, parents, and perhaps most of all the reluctant teacher.

The benefits lie in greater teaching precision, greater control of students, and improved communication with parents. Why and how these benefits accrue are explained in this chapter.

TRADITIONAL TEACHER ROLES

Let us take a moment to review traditional roles filled by the teacher—they are numerous, indeed. We will note only the major roles that have to do with instructing. They provide a background against which to consider the new and modified roles. Traditionally teachers have been expected to:
1. Plan instruction
2. Arrange physical learning environments
3. Establish productive social climates
4. Organize students into working groups—large, small, and individual
5. Present instruction, using methods suited to topics and students
6. Manage students, materials, and activities
7. Communicate effectively with students
8. Maintain class control
9. Evaluate student progress
10. Report student progress to parents and administrators

Of course teachers fill many noninstructional roles, too: they supervise playgrounds, study halls, and lunchrooms; they communicate with parents; they attend parent-teacher association meetings; they have committee assignments (the list is very long). Let's return to basic instructional roles and see what PL 94-142 demands.

NEW ROLES REQUIRED FOR MAINSTREAMING

Three new roles are expected of teachers: (1) planning individualized education programs (IEPs); (2) using special materials and apparatus; and (3) working closely with specialized personnel. A few teachers will also be named to state advisory panels. Here are some of the requirements of the new roles.

Individualized Education Programs (IEPs)

The most demanding new role is planning and carrying out the Individualized Education Programs. Such programs must be planned for each handicapped student, at least once each year. The IEP plan must be a written statement that includes the following information:

1. Notation of the student's present levels of functioning
2. Statement of goals for the year
3. Statements of specific instructional objectives that lead to those goals
4. Specification of the inputs to come from special education and related services
5. Plans for continual evaluation of student progress

Educators and parents must cooperate in planning the IEP. Whenever possible, the student should also participate.

Carrying out the IEP is the real chore. Planning only scratches the surface. Teachers must play major roles in assessing present levels of functioning, diagnosing special needs, delivering instruction matched to the stated objectives, meshing efforts with the special education teacher, monitoring the individualized work, and conducting ongoing evaluation of the total effort.

These essential elements are discussed briefly in later sections of this chapter. Some of them, such as IEP planning, diagnosis and prescription, evaluation, and behavior management also receive detailed attention in subsequent chapters.

Special materials and apparatus

Some handicaps necessitate the use of special apparatus and instructional materials. Most teachers are not familiar with them. Orthopedically handicapped students use crutches, wheelchairs, braces, and other devices. Visually impaired students require magnifying devices, instruction by audio tape, materials such as atlases, maps, globes, charts, and rulers that have raised surfaces, printed materials with large type, and a variety of materials printed in braille. Hearing-impaired students often use hearing aids.

Teachers must know how the special devices work. They must be able to attach, adjust, or place them. They must store, care for, and manage the instructional materials. These tasks at first appear worrisome. Actually, they are quite interesting. Amazing things are being done to assist physically handicapped people. It is enlightening and enjoyable to know about these devices and materials, how they work and how they benefit students.

Working with specialized personnel

Whenever people work together they find benefits and they find difficulties. Benefits include sharing the load, complementing individual expertise, esprit de corps, a little fun and laughter, someone to share disappointments with, and a greater number of good ideas. Difficulties include extra time required for planning, getting in each other's way, personality conflicts, unequal sharing of the load, petty annoyances, and not being totally your own boss.

Regular teachers must work closely with special education and support personnel. They are required by law to plan together, to work together in delivering the educational program, and to collaborate in ongoing evaluation of the IEP; working together is therefore a requirement, a given, a fait accompli.

Despite growth in team teaching and the use of aides and volunteers, most classroom teachers work alone with their students. When others such as aides are in the class, they have clearly subservient roles. The teacher is completely in charge. But now other professionals besides the teacher are making appearances in the classroom. They work with students, either inside or outside the room. They have equal status with the regular teacher. Neither is in charge of the other.

This collaboration with equality of status has its benefits, as noted previously, which can be significant. Joint efforts can have their drawbacks, too. It thus behooves teachers, specialists, and support personnel to take special pains to maximize the benefits while minimizing the drawbacks. They can do this by (1) remembering their prime purpose, which is to do the best possible for the students; (2) recognizing that they have equal status—neither is in charge of the other; (3) focusing positively on the specific contributions that each can make, (4) clearly outlining in the IEP or elsewhere the specific functions of each; (5) setting up regularly scheduled short conferences to discuss progress, difficulties, and specific needs of students; and (6) never forgetting that each and every person is a mixture of concern, desire to do right and well, insecurity, defensiveness, and easily hurt feelings. Smiles, kind words, and pats on the back do wonders.

MODIFIED EXISTING ROLES

The three roles previously discussed constitute relatively new functions for most teachers. Along with those three come eight roles that already exist for all teachers, but that must be modified somewhat when working with handicapped students. Those eight modified roles are:

1. Working with handicapped students
2. Providing a class climate of acceptance for handicapped students
3. Using behavior management techniques best suited to handicapped students

    4. Using classroom management (organization and deployment of students, materials, and activities) that suit handicapped students
    5. Individualizing instruction
    6. Assessing performance, diagnosing needs, and prescribing solutions
    7. Evaluating continually in nondiscriminatory ways
    8. Communicating closely with parents

Let us consider each of these modified roles briefly.

Working with handicapped students

This may at first glance appear to be a new role, rather than a modified one; it is not, however, and here's why. All student groups show an enormously wide range of variability, in physical, mental, emotional, and behavioral traits. When a trait is so unusual that it prevents the individual from functioning normally, even when given all the help possible, we say the individual is handicapped.

That definition is far from precise. The cut-off marks are arbitrary. Teachers regularly have in their classes students who do not function "normally." Thus in a real sense they have been working with "handicapped" students all along.

True, if a person is officially designated as handicapped, the factors that inhibit normal functioning may be rather more pronounced—it is only a matter of degree, however. The point is, handicapped students are not a separate breed, apart from all others. They are, instead, *like* all others in most ways. The ways in which they are different simply require some special attention.

Thus, teachers find that working with handicapped students is not impossible, terrifying, or utterly disagreeable. It is often fun and very rewarding. Basically, it is just not that different from working with the regular, "nonhandicapped" students.

Providing a climate of acceptance

School-age students show the best and the worst of human traits. They are like adults in that way. When they are good, they can be *very* good, the best; when they are bad, they can be very bad.

Students in classrooms must be helped to relate to handicapped students in positive ways. Positive relations will not occur automatically. Without attention, you can expect some nonhandicapped students to treat their handicapped classmates poorly: they will be prone to make fun of the disabilities, exclude the handicapped from circles of friendship, and discount the contributions they can make to the class. Rarely will they recognize the opportunity for their own positive personal growth that comes from association with the handicapped. Rarely will they be aware of the ways they can contribute to the positive growth of handicapped students.

These realities charge the teacher with a continuing duty to enhance personal relations, show how we learn from each other, and stress how we need support from each other. The emotional climate of the classroom makes such interpersonal relations possible. This climate is delicate in the extreme. Teachers establish and maintain it. Students have their responsibilities, too. Concern, good manners, respect for others' rights and abilities—these are the hallmarks of a climate of acceptance. Students can learn to function in and help perpetuate such climates. But this does not happen automatically; everyone has to work at it.

Behavior management

All teachers have their own methods of classroom control, methods which vary greatly. Some teachers tolerate noise and accept a degree of horseplay; others run a tight ship. Some rule by authority; others use counseling and behavior modification. Most of them, however, would be hard put to explain in detail their method of control.

Teachers who work with emotionally and behaviorally disabled students cannot get by that way. To make schooling profitable for students and life tolerable for themselves, they use carefully devised plans of behavior management.

Behavior management, as used in special education, is based on principles of reinforcement. It is oriented solely toward behavior, toward what students do. Rewards are given for desired behavior. Undesired behavior receives one of three responses: (1) it is ignored, but at the same time a student behaving correctly is reinforced; (2) it is verbally suppressed, through request or authority of the teacher; or (3) it is punished, but not harshly, and only when ignoring or verbal suppression fails.

One of the biggest favors you can do for people is to help them behave in socially acceptable ways. Such behavior is necessary, too, for maintaining adequate learning environments for other students. The carefully planned behavior management programs effectively promote both of these effects.

Most teachers must make some modifications in their customary ways of controlling the class. Those modifications are not difficult to make, however, and their benefits far outweigh the time and effort needed to implement them.

Behavior management is crucially important to all teachers. Chapter 6 explains different management systems that have records of notable effectiveness.

Classroom management

A clear distinction is made here between behavior management and classroom management. Behavior management refers to controlling students' behavior in ways that keep them on task, while reducing or eliminating boisterousness, disruption, aggression, and so forth. Classroom management, on the other hand, refers to the grouping of students, establishment of routines, deployment of materials, presentation of instruction, keeping of records, and similar matters.

Teaching handicapped students calls for large-scale changes in the types of classroom management most teachers use. PL 94-142 stipulates individualized education programs and individualized instruction. Most teachers use relatively little individualized instruction, finding more efficiency and satisfaction in grouped instruction. The individualized instruction mandate is discussed further in the next section.

Organizing the class for receiving special services requires changes, too. Resource specialists now come into the room. Sometimes they call students out for instruction elsewhere. Sometimes they give special instruction in the classroom, while the regular teacher is also teaching. Schedules have to be planned, arrangements made, and records of student activities coordinated.

Special materials and equipment must be kept accessible, yet out of the way when not in use. Space must be allowed for wheelchairs to operate. Listening posts, with tape players and earphones, have to be available.

Time schedules are needed that remind teachers and students who does what, and when and where they do it. Ways must be devised for monitoring student work and for providing help when needed. All these things require thoughtful planning. They force a departure from normal management routines. But once established, once everyone knows when and what to do, the new routines are effective—they may be different, but they work.

Individualizing instruction

The requirements of individualized instruction call for management plans quite different from those used in group instruction. Individual diagnosis, prescription, and record-keeping are routine matters. Students often work at their own pace, instead of together in lock-step fashion. Materials for individual work must be kept readily available; they must also be easy to return to their places and stored. Individual conferences must be fitted into the schedule. Students must be able to work on their own, since the teacher cannot be directly in control of all they do. Other students, "buddies" in the class or from higher grades, may be needed to work with individuals who cannot work alone.

Orchestrating instructional activities for different people, on different topics, at different rates of speed, requires special skills. Those skills can be acquired easily enough. So can a variety of preplanned materials and management systems. Teachers lacking these skills and materials can count on help from the special education services provided in their school district.

Assessment, diagnosis, and prescription

As part of the IEP, teachers are required to help assess levels of performance, diagnose specific needs, and prescribe learning activities related to specific objectives. Those specific objectives provide the backdrop against which assessment, diagnosis, and prescription can be understood.

Assessment comes ahead of objectives. Teachers are to help assess handicapped students' functional abilities, that is, determine what they are presently capable of doing. When referring to academic achievement, assessment means finding out their working level in language, mathematics, reading, and so forth. This assessment is done in several different ways. Among them are:

1. Using standardized tests, where the student is judged against others of his or her age or grade level
2. Using criterion tests, where the student is judged on his or her abilities to perform specific tasks
3. Examining work done by the student
4. Observing the student at work
5. Conferring with former teachers
6. Examining records of past performance
7. Talking with the student
8. Talking with the student's parents

Once this initial assessment is done, teachers are to formulate goals for the year and specific behavioral objectives that lead to those goals. These statements, especially the specific objectives, must be done in behavioral terms. They must stipulate what the student will become able to *do*, that you can see or hear. Most teachers know about behavioral objectives. They can use them, when required. But few in truth actually use them when planning instruction. The IEP requires such statements.

These objectives cannot be validly stated until diagnostic procedures are completed for areas of weakness. Suppose assessment has shown that Sara, in sixth grade, is very weak in math. Diagnosis will reveal two kinds of helpful information: (1) what specific areas of math are weaknesses for Sara—number facts, computational procedures, word problems, fractions, etc., and (2) what specific errors Sara is making in her areas of weakness—errors in carrying, borrowing, interpretation, conversion, etc.

Many devices and procedures are used in diagnosis. As with assessment, tests are plentiful, especially in reading and mathematics. Teachers can observe students at work and detect errors they consistently make. They can examine student work. They can listen carefully to speech patterns, to identify articulation errors. In areas more difficult to diagnose, such as dyslexia, trained specialists are needed. Recommended diagnostic tests and procedures are discussed in later chapters.

Diagnosis, then, shows specific areas of weakness and specific errors that occur within those areas. With this information, teachers can formulate meaningful goals and behavioral objectives for each student.

Prescriptions, which come next, are instructional activities especially selected to correct error patterns and to strengthen weak areas. These prescriptions are named in the IEP. Teachers compose many of the prescriptions. Others are included in preorganized instructional packages. Specialists compose prescriptions for behaviors outside the teacher's expertise.

The prescriptions are delivered in different ways. Teachers may teach lessons directly, either in small groups or tutorial arrangements. Specialists, aides, tutors, and parent volunteers can deliver them one-to-one. The prescriptions may be given as assignments, which students complete and then have checked by the teacher. They may occur automatically as sequential activities in preorganized instructional packages.

Evaluation

Teachers who work with handicapped students have to use individual methods of evaluation. Traditional testing, marking, and reporting systems do not work. Those systems treat all students as if they were equal in ability, with the hardest workers getting the highest marks. They are based on the total class, rather than individualized instruction. No attempt is made to guard against the suppressing effects of inadequate language ability, perceptual difficulties, slower intellectual development, cultural differences, or problems of physical movement and coordination.

The law requires that handicapped students be evaluated in a different way. Evaluation must be consistent with the following key ideas: *criterion-referenced, nondiscriminatory, ongoing.*

Criterion-referenced evaluation. Criterion-referenced evaluation is not mentioned in PL 94-142, but it is implicit in all references made to evaluation. Criterion-referenced evaluation judges individual student progress against goals established for that individual. It matters not in the slightest whether a given student is fastest, slowest, or just average within the class. Standing against others is immaterial. What is crucially important is the progress that individual is making toward his or her own personal goals and objectives.

Those goals and objectives are spelled out in the IEP. Teachers and specialists together decide on realistic goals for Jonathan to reach over a semester's or year's time. Together they compose or select the specific behavioral objectives that mark

Jonathan's steps toward those goals. Those behavioral objectives state, in terms that can be seen or heard, exactly what Jonathan will become able to do:

Count by ones to 100, without error, within 1 minute.

Write the multiplication facts from 1 through 5, in 10 minutes or less, with no more than two errors.

Follow a list of three verbal directions given together, in the proper order, without error.

Jonathan's instruction is directed specifically at helping him reach those behavioral objectives. The emphasis is totally on success. Evaluation focuses on how well and how quickly Jonathan is reaching the objectives. If his progress seems too slow, reasons are sought out. Corrections are made and procedures improved.

Criterion-references evaluation, then, starts with specific behavioral objectives. It focuses on how well the student is reaching *his own* set of objectives. Its purpose is to improve teaching and learning, in order to foster the most rapid student growth. It is never used to crack the whip on the student, motivate through fear of failure, or compare one student against another.

Nondiscriminatory evaluation. *Nondiscriminatory* is a second key idea in evaluating handicapped students. The law stipulates that procedures and materials used for placement and evaluation must not discriminate against individuals because of race or culture.

Cultural background determines language development, value system, and background of experiences that relate to learning. The law is specific in requiring that these factors be avoided in the placement and evaluation of handicapped students. Students who speak little or nonstandard English fare poorly on tests of verbal intelligence. That is not by itself a sign that they are intellectually handicapped. Students from certain cultural groups lack many of the concepts, experiences, and familiarity with objects that figure into standardized tests.

This is not to suggest that there is no place for standardized tests. They are very useful for assessment and diagnosis. But findings must be interpreted correctly. More importantly, their results constitute only one of several sources of information that should be considered.

While the law specifies race and culture as sources of discrimination, specific handicaps are equally important. Students who have specific reading disabilities cannot perform well on tests that require reading. Students who have specific math disabilities may not do well on tests that include logical reasoning and spatial relationships. Students with orthopedic handicaps, perceptual difficulties, emotional problems, and specific allergies may not be able to show their true abilities in test situations. These facts must be considered and not allowed to discriminate against handicapped students.

Ongoing evaluation. *Ongoing* is a third key idea in evaluation. This means that evaluation is a continual process, not one that occurs only at 6- or 9-week intervals.

Ongoing evaluation monitors the daily, even hourly progress of students. Comprehensive records are kept, always with an eye toward improvement of learning and teaching.

Communicating with parents

A few experienced teachers have discovered that they have powerful allies in parents. This is especially true of primary teachers. Instead of shying away from contact with parents, they go out of their way to establish it. Parents sometimes make life difficult for teachers, but those parents are a tiny minority. For the most part they are quite concerned about their children's education. They want them to do well, and they sincerely appreciate teachers showing attention to them.

Most teachers do not cultivate parents. They just want to do their jobs with students. They duly report to parents as required. They send home an occasional note. They conduct personal conferences if required to do so. And they call parents when tough problems arise. That is enough, they feel; they would just as soon avoid further complications in their professional lives.

Parents do not exactly seek out teachers, either. They do somewhat in kindergarten and first grade, but after a while they leave matters in teachers' hands.

That is not the way it goes with handicapped students, however. Parents show continued interest in their child's schooling. Special education teachers expect to know and talk with parents regularly.

Thus, regular teachers working with handicapped students can expect close contact with parents. The law specifies several rights and functions of parents. For example, they are to be involved in the assessment, evaluation, and placement of their child. They are to participate in planning the IEP. They are to check off, at designated times, steps in their child's progress. They are to be consulted on any plans to change placements, IEP, teachers, or objectives. They are to sit on advisory panels.

Anytime parents feel that their child is not getting the instructional program best suited to his or her needs, they are entitled to impartial hearings. They can be advised by experts and represented by legal counsel. If dissatisfied with the results of the hearing, they can appeal to a panel at the state level. If dissatisfied there, the law says they may file for redress through the courts.

It does take extra time and effort to communicate with parents. Most teachers who do a good job of it think it pays off handsomely. They get home support for their instructional programs, and they get help with tutoring.

A system of written messages and telephone calls can be organized easily. The messages tell parents about school instruction and special programs. They ask for support and assistance with homework, study times, and motivation. They stress the benefits intended for the students. This rallies parents to the teacher's side, reduces misunderstanding, and often produces unexpected sources of help.

Devices and procedures for effective communication with parents are discussed in detail later in this book.

TEACHER PREPARATION

Teachers, being after all only human, react with dismay at having to modify traditional teaching roles, while also acquiring new ones. It does not console them to say that things will work out, they always do, and before you know it you'll have everything under control; you may even like the new ways better.

It doesn't provide much consolation, either, to remind them that teachers and administrators must be provided the necessary training. Nobody gets thrown to the wolves. Nobody drowns. It is the states' responsibility to see that teachers are prepared to properly implement the mandates of PL 94-142. Chapter 1 made mention of the teacher competencies required, how they are specified in new state law, and how those competencies are to be verified.

Preservice teachers can receive necessary training through college classes and related field work. People working toward administrative credentials can expect the same. The course work will be nothing greatly different for them. Their training will occur without trauma.

Inservice teachers are not so lucky. They, too, must be trained. But they are already busy; many are overworked and teetering on the brink of psychological overload. Their school districts have the responsibility for providing training. Whatever arrangements they make, whether evening classes, summer classes, or other options, teachers are sure to resent them. The teachers have good reason to do so. They are constantly beleaguered by new requirements and new duties.

Still, states and school districts must comply with the law. The law says training must be provided. Inservice teachers at least have some say in how their training is supplied.

Meanwhile, teachers and administrators on all fronts have been moving toward newer roles. These role changes have been hastened by laws pertaining to educating the handicapped. The laws may have been intended for the handicapped, but the results are inevitably spreading to all students. Nothing is what it used to be, including teaching.

SUGGESTED ACTIVITIES

1. Find a teacher known to be excellent in communicating with parents. Ask that teacher to share techniques, devices, and procedures with the class.

2. Invite a school administrator in special education to describe plans and programs in his or her district used to help regular and special education teachers work together effectively.
3. Interview the inservice education director of a school district to find out how that district provides the inservice training required under PL 94-142 and the appropriate state law.
4. Discuss the pros and cons of setting up college classes on a system of specific behavioral objectives. Should the course be individualized? Should tests be used? If everyone reaches all the objectives, how should grades be assigned? In principle, should college classes differ from the IEP of handicapped students?
5. Students work alone a great deal in highly individualized programs. Discuss ways in which teachers in such programs can ensure desirable amounts of group work, together with adequate amounts of student contact and attention from the teacher.

PART TWO

Working with individuals and groups

CHAPTER 4

Individualized education programs (IEPs)

REQUIREMENTS FOR IEPs

Public Law 94-142 requires that a special "Individualized Education Program" (IEP) be prepared for each handicapped student at least once a year, the purpose of which is to meet the unique educational needs of the student. (The abbreviation, IEP, will be used henceforth in this chapter.) Federal law also stipulates what IEPs must contain and how they are to be prepared. The IEP must:

1. Be a written statement
2. Be prepared at least once a year for each student identified as handicapped
3. Be prepared jointly by a group comprised of:
   a. A special educator or administrator named by the educational agency
   b. The classroom teacher
   c. The parents or guardian of the child
   d. The child, when appropriate
4. Contain the following information:
   a. Statement of present levels of the child's educational performance
   b. Statements of annual goals for the child
   c. Statements of short-range objectives that lead to those goals
   d. Statement of the specific educational services to be provided
   e. Indication of the extent to which the child will be able to participate in the regular classroom programs
   f. The beginning dates for the services to be provided, and the projected date on which the services will end
   g. Evaluation procedures for determining whether the stated objectives are being met; included must be appropriate nondiscriminatory evaluation procedures, and schedules to be followed; this evaluation must be done at least once a year
5. Be coupled with a continuous recording and reporting system, which includes:
   a. Diagnostic results
   b. Descriptive profiles that show
      (1) degree of exceptionality
      (2) rate and amount of educational growth
6. Provide for continual parental involvement at all stages; this involvement is to be documented by parent sign-offs at various points on the IEP

IEP FORMS

Clearly, the IEP is intended to be specific, objective, appropriate to needs, and easily monitored. It is clear, too, that preparing the IEP requires considerable time. In efforts to cut down the time required for preparation, and to ensure

Student's legal name _____

Last _____ First _____ Middle _____

Student number _____

Birthdate _____

M   F

Circle

School _____ Grade _____

To _____

Date of program _____

Certification _____ (Exceptionality) _____

Level of service _____

Formal evaluation _____ Date _____

Parental permission:

I hereby certify that I, the parent or legal guardian of the aforementioned child, have been fully informed of the results and recommendations of this assessment and hereby grant permission to proceed with this recommended Individualized Educational Program and placement. I have had an opportunity to participate in the development of my child's program and agree with its contents.

Signature of parent/legal guardian _____ Date _____

Child study team members _____ (Signatures) _____

Statement of educational services and special instructional materials: Special education self-contained classroom, resource room, occupational therapy, physical therapy, special remedial reading, braille, hearing aid, large print, special transportation, etc.

Special ed/related services	Delivery mode/comments	Hrs/wk
	Special education total hours per week	
Regular education		
	Regular education total hours per week	

Special education busing: Special conveyance required ☐   Special program location ☐

Program location _____ Bus pickup location _____ Parent contact phone _____

Fig. 1. Pupil personnel services Anchorage School District Individual Education Program (IEP).

Continued.

Student's legal name _____ Birthdate _____

CURRENT LEVEL OF FUNCTIONING

Test data (include test name, scores, date given, specialist):

Observation:

Medical findings:

Environmental, cultural, or economic factors:

Ability/achievement discrepancy:

Conclusions/comments:

Educational strengths:

Signature title:

Certification:

Weaknesses:

Fig. 1—cont'd. Pupil personnel services Anchorage School District Individual Education Program (IEP).

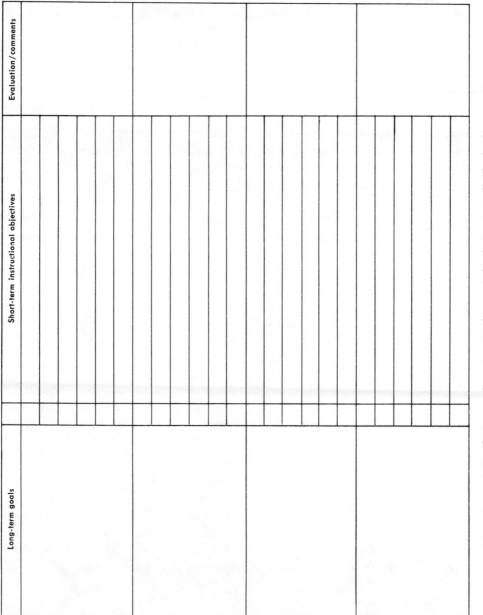

Fig. 1.—cont'd. Pupil personnel services Anchorage School District Individual Education Program (IEP).

completeness and accuracy, school districts across the country have developed their own IEP forms. These forms contain space for filling in all necessary information for each child. They have places for parents and other participants to sign. Some contain reminders of parents' rights. These IEP forms vary considerably in format. Fig. 1 shows an IEP form used in Anchorage, Alaska. (It is reproduced by permission.)

ELEMENTS OF THE IEP

We noted that IEP contents are stipulated by law; among the required contents are statements of present levels of educational performance, annual goals, short-range objectives, specific educational services to be provided, and appropriate nondiscriminatory evaluation procedures.

Levels of performance

Levels of educational performance describe what the student is capable of doing in curricular areas at the time of assessment. Those levels mark the base line upon which educational plans are made.

In addition, good assessment points to areas of strength, weakness, and special need. This is called diagnosis, and we will consider it briefly at this point. Specifically, we will give attention to the diagnosis of difficulties and needs of handicapped students. This diagnosis is called for in the IEP, and it forms the basis for the other IEP contents—short- and long-range objectives, specific plans for instruction, and the evaluation procedures deemed suitable for the student.

Handicapped students are diagnosed in somewhat different ways from regular students. In the first place, to have been identified as handicapped, one must have a disability that does not permit normal functioning even after the best corrections have been made. The severity of that difficulty calls for a much more precise diagnosis of its underlying cause. Very poor reading, for example, might be due to a condition called dyslexia. The student's perception might be faulty. Words and letters might be indistinguishable, or reversed, or seen as mirror images.

The severity and importance of such learning disabilities call for special tests, to be administered and interpreted by trained personnel. Classroom teachers are seldom involved in these diagnostic procedures. Still, they find it helpful to acquaint themselves somewhat with tests that are most often used. Among such tests are the following:

Intelligence tests
Stanford Binet Intelligence Scale
Wechsler Intelligence Scale for Children (WISC)

Diagnostic tests

Bender Visual Motor Gestalt Test—A test of perception and spatial relationships.

Detroit Tests of Learning Aptitude—Tests that show innate but unrealized learning potential. Widely used with older students.

Durrell Analysis of Reading Difficulty—Diagnostic test for students with problems in reading.

Hiskey-Nebraska Test of Learning Aptitude—Test of visual perception and spatial reasoning, originally designed for the deaf but now used for the hearing as well.

KeyMath Diagnostic Arithmetic Test—Test that identifies specific disabilities in mathematical reasoning and computational patterns.

Peabody Individual Achievement Test—A school achievement test designed for individual rather than group administration and interpretation.

Picture Story Language Test—For assessing language capabilities of younger students.

Oseretsky Tests of Motor Proficiency—Tests for sensory motor dysfunctions.

Roswell-Chall Diagnostic Reading Test of Word Analysis Skills—A reading diagnosis test.

Stanford Diagnostic Tests—Diagnostic tests of reading and mathematics.

Woodcock Reading Mastery Tests—Reading diagnosis tests.

Tests such as these are used mainly in diagnosing learning disabilities. Learning disabilities, along with behavioral disabilities, are the main areas of concern for regular teachers. Other types of handicap are diagnosed through observation by specialists, as in the case of behavioral handicap and mental deficiency, or by medical personnel, as in the case of orthopedic, health, visual, and auditory disabilities.

Diagnosis can be technical and lengthy. As such, it may worry regular teachers. They need not be concerned, however. The diagnoses for handicapped children will be conducted by specialists provided by the school districts. Those specialists will keep teachers informed about each child's specific difficulties and the provisions that should be made to overcome them.

Annual goals

The IEP calls for a statement of educational progress that can be reasonably anticipated for the student during the year. These goals, by nature, are imprecise. They are global targets, loosely defined. Examples might be the following.

Make 4 months' growth in overall reading ability.

Control own behavior sufficiently to remain in the regular classroom at least half of each day.

Make significant progress in speaking clearly, with as little stuttering as possible.

These annual goals are like a compass. They set the direction you will follow; but they do not tell you how close you are getting to your destination, nor do they tell you when you have arrived.

Short-range objectives

Short-range objectives state exactly what the student is to become able to do. They may also state the levels of acceptable performance. Experienced teachers will recognize these short range objectives as "behavioral statements." That is, they state specific observable behaviors that students will perform, as a result of the instruction they receive. Since these behaviors must be observable, objectives such as "understand," "appreciate," and "enjoy" are not acceptable. They may be fine goals. But we cannot see what a person does when understanding, appreciating, or enjoying; therefore they are not acceptable statements for objectives.

We can hear people speak, see them move, and observe work they have produced. Acceptable short range objectives might be:

Spell the thirty-two service words correctly.

Read three books and score at least 80% on tests of comprehension over their contents.

Increase on-task behavior by at least 50%, as documented through teacher observation and recording.

Several short-range objectives are needed to specify behaviors and steps that lead to the annual goals. These objectives state exactly what the student is to do. As each is reached and verified, it leaves a clear record of progress.

Specific educational services

The IEP must describe the educational services to be provided for the handicapped student. Included among educational services are regular instruction, special equipment and materials, instruction from specialists, therapy, attention to health needs, and transportation.

Instruction. Regular instruction must attend to needs identified through expert diagnosis. It must be aimed at the stated goals and guided by the short-range objectives. To meet these requisites it will usually have to be provided in individualized format.

Providing this instruction is the duty of the regular classroom teacher. The IEP is planned by teacher, specialist, and parent, and it is the guide that teachers follow. It is implemented best in diagnostic-prescriptive format, which will be discussed in a later section.

Materials. Special equipment and materials may be needed for individual instruction in both the regular classroom and the special classroom. *Equipment* refers to items such as wheelchairs, crutches, braces, hearing aids, magnifiers, tachistoscopes, tape recorders, and so forth. *Materials* refer to items such as braille writing, maps and rulers, books written in very large print, remedial materials for reading and mathematics, worksheets, puzzles, and the like.

Specialists. Specialists are involved with instruction in four ways. (1) They help diagnose special needs and weaknesses related to learning. (2) They help plan the IEP for each handicapped student. (3) They observe and provide assistance to the teacher in the regular classroom. (4) They provide direct instruction to students who attend special classes for part of the day.

Instruction by specialists is to be provided only when students can profit more from the special classroom than they can from the regular classroom. That is often the case for students with severe physical handicaps, with strong emotional or behavioral problems, with profound mental retardation, and with severe speech handicaps such as those that accompany lifelong deafness.

Therapy. Therapy is a routine part of the lives of students with speech defects and crippling conditions. It is provided outside the regular classroom by trained personnel. It can correct certain disabilities, such as some vocal articulation problems. For other disabilities such as muscular atrophy, arthritis, amputations, and spasticity therapy can reduce the severity of the effects.

Health needs. Health needs, which do not figure into the lives of most people, must receive attention in some forms of handicap. Such is the case for students who are diabetic, who experience strong allergic reactions to substances in their normal surroundings, and who are subject to frequent grand mal epileptic seizures. These students will already have undergone medical diagnoses. They may require drugs or other medications in order to function. The school nurse will ordinarily dispense medication required during school hours. Some older students may administer their own medication, in accord with their physician's instructions.

Transportation. Transportation is basic to equal access to education. Students who are unable to walk, who are in wheelchairs or on crutches, who are blind, or who have other disabilities that make normal ambulation impossible are provided free transportation to and from school. The nature of this transportation, together with procedures for movement around the school, are stipulated in the IEP.

Appropriate evaluation

The law requires that each IEP specify appropriate procedures and devices for testing, evaluating, and placing the individual student. These procedures and devices must be nondiscriminatory regarding culture or race.

This requirement has many implications. In the first place, no devices or procedures may be used that permit the handicapping condition to falsely color other abilities. For example, care must be taken to be sure that the influence of profound deafness does not lead, by itself, to one's being diagnosed as mentally retarded, or that emotional behavior brought on by allergic reactions is not interpreted to be behavioral handicap or learning disability.

To avoid mislabeling, precautions are taken to use a variety of diagnostic procedures and to have group deliberations by experts and parents.

To assess academic progress, criterion measures have come strongly into vogue. There is little value in using standardized achievement tests to measure learning for many handicapped students. Since specific short-range objectives are included in the IEP, it is far more appropriate to use tests and observations related directly to those objectives. That is precisely what criterion measures do, as contrasted with standardized tests which attempt to measure small samples of knowledge selected randomly from a very large body.

In short, IEPs must specify evaluation that is accurate. False diagnoses and assessments are to be avoided at all costs.

INDIVIDUALIZED INSTRUCTION

PL 94-142 requires individualized instruction for handicapped students. The term is included several times in the law, and of course the IEP is a specific plan for individualized instruction.

The IEP is merely a plan, however. It is not, itself, individualized instruction. That can be provided only by teachers in their daily work with handicapped students.

Percentage-wise, not many regular teachers use individualized instruction. Some do not espouse it philosophically, believing that grouped instruction reaches the broad goals of education more efficiently for most students. Many do not have a clear handle on how to go about individualizing. Many who know how to individualize do not feel the results are worth the effort required. Many find that levels of motivation can be kept higher in groups than in individual work. Some teachers are completely sold on individualized instruction, and they individualize the major part of their program. All in all, however, probably fewer than one teacher in twenty individualizes instruction most of the time.

That must change. To meet legal requirements, teachers have to individualize instruction. The requisite skills are few in number*; it takes more preparation and more detailed record keeping. When under way, however, it permits giving much more personal attention to students. Many teachers like it for that reason alone.

In a nutshell, here is what you need to do to individualize instruction.

1. Appraise the abilities and special needs of your students.
2. Decide which of the following instructional elements you will vary for your students—contents, objectives, activities, time, and supervision. Notice that these five elements make a comfortable acronym: COATS.
3. Decide on the delivery system you prefer. The following are in common use: diagnostic-prescriptive teaching, commercial programs and materials, special teacher-made programs, modularized instruction, learning centers, and open experience. For mainstreaming handicapped students, diagnostic-prescriptive teaching is most appropriate.
4. Organize the management details for your delivery system. These details include: (1) preassessment of student abilities and needs; (2) selection of instructional activities and materials; (3) scheduling; (4) giving directions; (5) tutoring and instructing; (6) monitoring; (7) postassessment and evaluation of student growth; (8) record keeping and reporting.

Let us see how each of these four aspects of individualized instruction relates to the IEP requirements for handicapped students.

Abilities and needs

Individualized instruction does not make sense unless it builds on special abilities and attends to special needs of individual students. Otherwise, normal total group instruction would serve just fine.

In regular classrooms, very precise appraisal of strengths and weaknesses is seldom made. The process is done informally through day-to-day observations and judgments by the teacher, supplemented by evidence such as samples of student work and occasional standardized test scores. The evidence obtained in this way provides a profile of strengths and weaknesses upon which quality individualized programs can be based.

When handicapped students are involved, the picture changes. To be identified as handicapped means that one has special needs that go well beyond the ordinary. Precise identification of these special needs must be made before the most effective instruction can be planned. These needs are not simply a lack of knowledge, which is often the case for regular students. Instead, there may be difficulties in perceptual processes, in mental organization, in thought processes, in

*For detailed explanations of various methods of individualizing instruction, see Charles, C. M.: Individualizing instruction, ed. 2, St. Louis, 1980, The C. V. Mosby Co.

physical abilities, in communication skills, and self-control, and so forth. These special needs call for materials, activities, and teaching techniques that may be unfamiliar to regular classroom teachers.

The diagnostic devices and procedures that are useful in making these assessments fall into the jurisdiction of special educators. Regular teachers seldom have responsibility for them. For the present let us note that rather precise information is needed as a beginning point for working with handicapped children. This information is called for on the IEP, and it provides the foundation upon which the individualized program is built.

COATS variations

You individualize instruction when you have different students in the class working at different *contents*, *objectives*, or *activities*, or when you allow them different amounts of work *time*, or when you use a different type of *supervision* for them.

Contents. Contents refers to the subject matter being learned. Contents are varied when different topics are being studied by different students at a given time.

Objectives. Objectives are the specific, observable, short-range goals toward which student work is directed. Different students may work toward different objectives within the same content area or subject. This is the case when significant differences exist in student levels of ability.

Activities. Activities are the learning tasks provided to students to help them attain the objectives toward which they are striving. Different activities are appropriate to different contents and objectives. Even when working toward the very same objectives, students may be assigned different activities. This is often done, especially in modularized instruction, as a means of allowing students to use their own preferred styles of learning.

Time. Time refers to the length of work, in minutes, hours, days, or weeks, that students are allowed for completing assigned tasks. It is well known that, even among students of equal ability and intelligence, some work much faster than others. Research evidence shows that, if given sufficient time, slower students can reach mastery level as well as faster students. Some teachers very time allotments so that faster students remain engaged on the task at hand until completed, then move on to something else. Slower students, meanwhile, are allowed the time needed to do their best work.

Supervision. Supervision refers to the direct attention the teacher gives students, in aspects of motivation, guidance, monitoring, and follow-up conferencing. Some students work very well on their own. They need little attention from the teacher. Others require teacher proximity, urging, and support in order to progress satisfactorily.

COATS and IEP

Individualized instruction is necessary for handicapped students. Some aspect of their physical, intellectual, behavioral, or sensory functioning has to be quite different from the norm for them to be identified as handicapped. That difference calls for adjustments in teaching.

Contents (subject matter) must be adjusted for students who are intellectually handicapped. In some cases the same is true for students with motor and sensory handicap. This simply means that these students will work at specially selected subject matter, at least part of the time.

Objectives will be varied in one way or another for most handicapped students. This may be because their achievement levels are lower or because they have special needs in motor skills and communication.

Activities must be varied for most handicapped students. Because of their handicapping condition they may not be able to read, write, speak, move, pay attention, or understand in the way that normal students do.

Time allotments will usually be varied, too. Physically handicapped students may perform motor activities such as writing quite slowly. Visually impaired students often read slowly. Learning-handicapped students can seldom remain on task for long. It is essential that they have adequate time, that they not be rushed beyond their capabilities.

Supervision may be done somewhat differently for some categories of handicap, but not for all. Emotionally handicapped students require close surveillance and much teacher attention. Hearing-impaired students need to see the teacher up close to speech read. The physically handicapped may need special assistance. The learning-handicapped require close monitoring, to be sure they are progressing and not practicing errors. After a short time, teachers recognize different students' supervision needs, and they provide them with little special effort.

In short, teachers can expect to vary contents, objectives, activities, time, and supervision for their handicapped students. The IEP calls for such variations. They are not difficult to provide. They merely take some advance preparation and a few adjustments by the teacher.

Delivery systems

The most popular systems for delivering individualized instruction are (1) diagnostic-prescriptive teaching (DPT), (2) commercial programs and materials, (3) teacher-made programs, (4) modularized instruction, (5) learning centers, (6) and open experience. Of these six systems, the first three—DPT, commercial, and teacher-made—are best suited to working with handicapped students.

Diagnostic-prescriptive teaching. Diagnostic-prescriptive teaching (DPT) is a very structured, detailed, and specific approach to teaching. Because it is so precise, it is a preferred method of instructing handicapped students. Its components also match, more closely than any other system, the legal requirements for the IEP.

DPT begins with a list of objectives, which cover large segments of the curricular area under consideration—reading, math, physical education, and so forth. They are the targets toward which instruction is aimed.

Given the large set of objectives, *diagnosis* is the first step in DPT. Traditionally, diagnosis is more of an assessment. Its purpose is simply to see which of the target objectives the student can already reach and which still require instruction. In special education, diagnosis probes deeper, seeking error patterns and special difficulties in processing information.

When diagnosis is completed, the next step in DPT is to prepare *prescriptions*. These prescriptions are instructional activities that are selected for each student individually. The prescriptions are aimed at objectives on the master set that the student has not reached, as revealed by the diagnosis. The prescribed activities are usually given as individual work. Often, more than one student receives the same prescription at the same time. Then they may either be taught in a small group or work independently.

The third step in DPT is to check the student once more after the prescriptions have been completed. This process determines which additional objectives have been met on the master list. A new prescription is given, based on this assessment.

You can see how well DPT matches IEP requirements. IEPs must include assessment of present levels of functioning, short-range and long-range objectives, individually prescribed learning activities, and clearly stated procedures for evaluation of learning; DPT includes most of these elements.

Commercial programs and materials. Commercial programs and materials are more often used than DPT for individualizing instruction in regular classrooms. A plethora of excellent materials exists, often packaged as attractive kits, with instructions, tests, and record-keeping devices included. Examples include the familiar SRA kits in reading, mathematics, and other areas, the Scholastic reading kits with their collections of books, and the Peabody kits for developing language skills.

Such kits have many advantages, among which are carefully organized and precisely controlled activities, excellent management systems, proven effectiveness, and ease of use, storage, and mobility. The disadvantages of the kits are: (1) They are expensive; this prohibits extensive use in regular classrooms, but not in special education, which has extra money for materials. (2) The commercial kits are aimed at hypothetical students with hypothetical abilities and disabilities. They are not always best suited to a real individual who has unique needs. (3) They suffer from a fact of teaching life: whatever teachers have a hand in developing, they use to best advantage. The commercial materials come ready-made, and many teachers just cannot get enthusiastic about them.

Kits are not the only type of commercial material for individualizing instruction. There are the large, computer-based programs such as PLAN, IPI, and IGE. The last, Individually Guided Education, has enjoyed wide popularity across the country. These large-scale programs do not seem to be efficient for working with handicapped students, however.

There are mountains of small programs and duplicator materials for individualizing instruction. While attractive to teachers in regular classroom, these small programs and materials do not appear to lend themselves easily to working with the handicapped.

Teacher-made programs. Teacher-made programs make up a loosely defined approach to individualizing instruction that enjoys the most widespread use of all. This type of individualized program cannot be defined in terms of its components or procedures, which vary extensively. These programs can best be understood through the following illustration: Suppose a teacher wants to individualize instruction, but for only a portion of the curriculum, for part of the day, with selected students. DPT seems too highly structured for the purpose in mind. Money is not available for purchasing kits or other ready-made materials. Perhaps more than anything else the teacher just wants to experiment, but on a limited scale.

In this situation, large numbers of teachers devise their own programs. They usually start very small. If successful, they expand, including more topics for more students for more of the day. Here and there you can find teachers who use an almost completely individualized approach to teaching, one which they have put together themselves.

These programs do not have a common format. They use all sorts of materials. They run the gamut from tightly to loosely organized. The thing they have in common is that individual teachers put them together, solely for their own use. The act of putting them together seems to be the key to their success. Those things we have a hand in developing usually work well for us.

While teacher-made individualized programs have been popular and effective, they do not promise so much for working with handicapped students in regular classrooms. That is because the IEPs are very explicit as to what must be included. They do not permit instruction that simply suits the fancy of individual teachers.

The other three delivery systems commonly used for individualizing instruction are modularized instruction, learning centers, and open experience. These systems have little to offer in IEP preparation, but they can be very useful in the education of the gifted.

Modularized instruction. Modularized instruction is all preplanned. It has its objectives set for the entire class. It does permit alternative activities for reaching those objectives, and it allows flexibility in working time. IEPs, however, must be planned for individual students who have special needs; thus preplanned modules of instruction are not appropriate.

Learning centers. Learning centers have become widely popular for individualizing small portions of the curriculum. They allow students to work on their own, at materials and activities made available in an attractive place in the classroom. While greatly flexible, they are not sufficiently structured nor efficient for meeting the clearly defined needs of most handicapped students. Handicapped students can use them profitably and enjoyably along with other students in the class, but they are not suitable for meeting most IEP requirements.

Open experience. Open experience is also widely used across the country. It has provided an avenue for student selection of learning tasks, with attendant self-direction, responsibility, pursuit of special interests, latitude, and enjoyment. Open experience is provided in the following manner. The teacher, perhaps assisted by the students, brings into the classroom a variety of materials, games, etc., in which the students are especially interested. These materials are placed at suitable working areas in the room. For a designated amount of time each day, students are permitted to choose what they want to do, using what is available in the room. They are not allowed to be disruptive or to damage the materials. Otherwise they get involved with what they want to do, and they work at their own pace. The teacher does not intervene unless asked for help or to correct misbehavior.

This approach, popularized by Herbert Kohl in *The Open Classroom,* is now used, in varying degrees and formats, by a large percentage of teachers.

Open experience, however, does not meet most of the specific needs of students identified as handicapped. At most it could supply an occasional instructional activity leading toward self-direction, self-control, or greater involvement. Otherwise, the very lack of structure that is its strength disqualifies it for use in IEP.

Management details

Previously, we saw that three elements were essential for individualizing instruction. The first was deciding which of the *COATS* (contents, objectives, activities, time, and supervision) were to be varied for each individual. The second was deciding on a *delivery system* that would lead most effectively to the goals of the program. The third, which is addressed in this section, has to do with clarifying the *management details* necessary to make the program work.

Most programs of individualized instruction require attention to the following management details: (1) preassessment of student abilities and needs, (2) selection of instructional activities and materials, (3) scheduling, (4) giving directions, (5) tutoring and instructing, (6) monitoring, (7) postassessment and evaluation of student growth, and (8) record-keeping and reporting. Let us examine each of these briefly.

Preassessment of student abilities and needs. This first group of details is highly important for both regular and handicapped students. As indicated earlier, it is done differently for the two groups.

Regular students are preassessed to find levels of performance, strengths, weaknesses, and special problems. Levels of performance refer to student abilities in academic areas, such as reading, mathematics, language, and so forth. Preassessment is done through (1) daily teacher observation, (2) examination of products—compositions, art work, worksheets, etc.—that students do in class activities, (3) oral and written tests given by the teacher, and (4) standardized achievement tests, which are given once every year or two in most grades.

Strengths and weaknesses are preassessed in the same way as levels of performance—low levels show weaknesses, high levels show strengths. Exceptional weaknesses call for further diagnosis. Exceptional strengths may be seen in academic areas, or they may appear as unusual aptitudes in music, athletics, art, science, and so forth.

Special problems of regular students may be obvious, as in speech irregularities, poor eyesight, poor health, or chronic misbehavior. Sometimes diagnosis is required to bring them to light. This is the case for many health problems, as well as some difficulties in reading, language, and mathematics, which are sometimes influenced by perceptual and intellectual dysfunctions.

Selection of instructional activities and materials. Following preassessment, teachers who individualize instruction must attend to a second group of management details—the selection of activities and materials needed for instruction.

Preassessment will have shown strengths, weaknesses, and special needs of each student. All three should receive attention. Students should have the opportunity to build upon their strengths, to pursue them as fully as time permits. If strengths are in academic areas, more advanced materials may be called for. If strengths are in specialized areas, such as music, art, athletics, or science, special instruction and facilities may be needed.

Areas of weakness should receive strong attention, too. If weaknesses are academic, excellent materials are available for remedial instruction in mathematics, reading, and spelling. If weaknesses are in affective areas, such as attitude or self-concept, specially designed activities are available to strengthen them. Examples are seen in the work of Simon, Howe, and Kirschenbaum (1972), and Felker (1974). If weaknesses are behavioral, strategies are available, such as behavior modification and intervention measures suggested by Glasser (1969), Ginott (1972), and Kounin (1970). Suggested activities for improving self-concept and social behavior are discussed in detail in Chapter 5.

Special needs overlap with areas of weakness, especially regarding social behavior and self-concept. For handicapped children, additional needs are evident, including special apparatus for defects in vision, hearing, and sensory-motor processes, and/or special seating, medication, exercises, therapy, or transportation.

Instructional activities and materials must be selected to meet such strengths, weaknesses, and special needs. The task of providing these things seems formidable at first, but in actuality it is not very difficult. Individualized programs have at hand a variety of suitable activities and materials. Preassessment simply indicates which of those things available are most appropriate for each student.

Scheduling. Deciding who should be doing what, and when, requires some deliberation. If contents are varied for students, different topics will be pursued during a specified time by different students. This arrangement is easy to make. Students work individually for a portion of the day or period, then work together in group activities for the remainder of the time. Those who finish early are allowed to read or do other quiet activities.

When activities are varied, each student must be provided with assignments and materials. Younger students may be given their materials, which are set out on work tables in advance or are passed out quickly. Older students can obtain their materials from designated storage areas in the room.

When time limits are varied, schedules must be posted so that different individuals and groups know (1) how much time they have for working at a given task, and (2) what they are supposed to do when their time allotment has run out.

The purpose of scheduling is twofold: (1) it lets students know what they are supposed to do and when they are supposed to do it; (2) it cuts down on the confusion that occurs between instructional activities. This saves valuable time for learning and removes many of the conditions that produce misbehavior.

Giving directions. Giving directions is a management detail that pays off handsomely with a minimum of effort. Students need to know precisely what they are expected to do, how they are to do it, where to get materials, what to do with completed work, how to tidy up and return instructional materials, and what to do when they have finished.

Such directions should be kept as few in number as possible. They should be clear. Procedures through which instructions will be given should be discussed carefully. For example, they may be given orally; they may be posted on a chart in the room; they may be written on the instructional materials; they may be inherent in the materials and activities themselves, as in procedures for using SRA Reading Labs—once you learn the procedure, no further directions are needed.

Oral directions should be given only once. Tell the students, "Listen, I'm going to give these directions one time." After giving the directions, a student may be called on to repeat them, as a check on understanding. If students are allowed to ask for repetitions, they will get into the habit of not listening carefully.

Tutoring and instructing. Tutoring and instructing are essential components of any individualized program. In only a few cases do the materials themselves provide sufficient guidance with sufficient clarity. For that reason, personal instruction is necessary on a regular basis.

This instruction is normally provided in two ways. One way is through tutoring, working one-to-one with a student. Such tutoring can be provided by the teacher, an aide, an adult volunteer, a cross-age tutor (a student from a higher grade), or more advanced students helping less advanced students in the same class.

The second way is through small group instruction. By means of diagnosis or observation, the teacher determines that several students need help in a given topic, for example, the steps in long division. The teacher will call those students together in a group and go over the long division algorithm. This approach, when possible, is much more efficient than individual tutoring.

Monitoring. Monitoring is a management procedure of observing students at work individually. It allows the teacher to keep tabs on progress, to note errors that need correcting, to detect obstacles that can be removed, and to show interest, concern, and helpfulness.

Teachers should station themselves so that they can observe the entire class, even when talking with individuals or working with small groups. They should circulate among students as much as possible. This provides physical nearness, which effectively motivates students while suppressing their inclinations to waste time or get into trouble.

Postassessment. Postassessment of learning is done on both a short-range and long-range basis. Short-range assessment checks for progress toward specific objectives. It reveals errors, difficulties, and misunderstandings. It notes work output, student interest, and efficiencies and inefficiencies in classroom management.

This short-range assessment is done through observation, analysis of daily work completed by students, notation of amount of work done, and success on teacher-made tests.

Long-range assessment checks for progress toward the larger goals of instruction. It is done through compilations of short-range assessments and the use of standardized achievement tests. These tests mark student achievement levels in comparison with other students of their age or grade across the country. Pretesting and post-testing with these instruments show growth over a period of time, such as one school year.

A second kind of test, a "criterion test," is becoming more and more popular for assessment in individualized instruction. Items on the test relate directly to specific objectives of instruction. The test reveals student progress in attaining those objectives. Attention is given to which objectives the student has and has not reached. Concern is for individual progress against goals, not for how the individual compares to other individuals, which is what standardized tests show.

Postassessment is done primarily to examine student growth in areas of strength and weakness. It is also done as a means of examining the effectiveness of instructional materials and procedures.

Record keeping and reporting. Record keeping and reporting are essential in individualized instruction. If not done conscientiously, adequate records will not be available for planning instruction and for reporting to parents.

Many teachers balk at individualized instruction because they have seen systems that overwhelmed them with paperwork. Such record keeping is not needed. All your records need to do is allow you to accurately portray the following about each student:

1. Beginning ability and goals for the year
2. Present level of working ability
3. Plans for correcting weaknesses and building on strengths
4. Specific materials and activities being used at the present time

All this information can be put on index cards stapled into a file folder kept for each student. The folder should contain a few samples of that student's work, which reveal information useful for conferencing with student and parents and for planning future work.

The information should come mostly from teacher observation and analysis of student work. Graphs are very useful. Older students can keep their own, charting their progress. Handicapped students' IEPs can be kept in their folders.

Remember, masses of information are not needed. Records are sufficient if they permit teachers, at a glance, to talk sensibly about a given student's specific strengths, weaknesses, goals, achievements, and future needs. Simple, clear documentation, in the form of objectives, scores, checkmarks, graphs, and work samples, facilitates this commentary. It also portrays the teacher as professionally informed, while not a slave to forms and data.

A SECOND WORD ABOUT DIAGNOSTIC/PRESCRIPTIVE TEACHING

At various points in this chapter, mention has been made of diagnostic-prescriptive teaching, commonly referred to as DPT. This approach is a highly structured means of individualizing instruction. Because it individualizes, and because its elements so closely parallel the contents of the IEP, it is especially appropriate for use by teachers who work with handicapped students. For that reason, it is discussed here once more.

DPT begins with an assessment that consists of two parts. One part determines the functional educational level of the student, in any curricular or behavioral area. That is, we first find out what the student *does* and is *presently capable of doing.* The second part of this assessment consists of a genuine diagnosis, which probes into areas of knowledge or behavior considered weak or lacking. It attempts to identify the *underlying cause* of the weakness.

Following the diagnosis, goals and short-range objectives are specified for the student. These objectives are selected as specific thrusts for propelling the student along most rapidly in learning. The objectives may be selected from a large master list of already established objectives, or they may be compared just for the student under consideration.

Once the desired objectives are specified, activities and materials are selected. These are called *prescriptions.* They comprise the instructional interventions believed to move students most rapidly to the attainment of the stated objectives.

After the student has completed the assigned prescriptions, a postassessment is conducted. In actuality, this is an ongoing procedure, repeated at regular intervals throughout the year. This postassessment reveals whether and to what extent the student has reached the stated objectives.

The steps in DPT can be summarized as follows:

1. Assess-diagnose
2. State objectives (short-range, behavioral)
3. Provide prescriptions (learning activities and materials)
4. Postassess (determine whether objectives have been reached)

You can see how closely these DPT steps correspond with what is to be included in the IEP. That correspondence is what makes DPT a teaching tool of highest value for teachers of handicapped students.

RESUMÉ OF INDIVIDUALIZED INSTRUCTION

This concludes the overview of the nature and requirements of individualized instruction. It was described as consisting of the following:

1. Appraising abilities, weaknesses, and special needs of individual students
2. Deciding on the contents, objectives, activities, time, and supervision (COATS) indicated by the initial appraisal of each student
3. Deciding on the delivery system most effective for the COATS variations that were selected; handicapped students, the most effective systems are usually diagnostic-prescriptive teaching (DPT), commercial programs and materials, or special teacher-made programs
4. Organizing management details, to include (a) preassessment, (b) instructional activities and materials, (c) scheduling, (d) giving directions, (e) tutoring and instructing, (f) monitoring, (g) postassessment of student progress, and (h) record-keeping and reporting

Teachers who use individualized instruction devise means for streamlining these elements. Thus, individualizing instruction becomes a pleasant instructional system, easy to apply, and not at all the formidable ogre it might appear at first glance.

SUGGESTED ACTIVITIES

1. Practice filling out IEP forms, such as that from Anchorage (Fig. 1). Use fictional data or data supplied by the instructor.
2. Compose an ideal IEP form, one that is ultra-efficient and streamlined, but one that also provides all necessary information.
3. Interview a teacher in special education. Find out how IEPs are prepared in that person's school system.
4. Locate a diagnostic prescriptive program for students in reading, math, or other areas. Check with local schools and/or college library. Discuss the format, record-keeping procedures, teacher duties, and so forth.
5. Devise an individualized approach to acquiring the material presented in this chapter. Keep the contents the same for everyone, but vary the objectives, activities, time, and instructor supervision.
6. Interview a teacher or psychometrist in special education concerning the tests and testing procedures used for diagnosing learning abilities. Explore how those tests and procedures are nondiscriminatory.

SUGGESTED READINGS

Charles, C. M.: Individualizing instruction, ed. 2, St. Louis, 1980, The C. V. Mosby Co.

Felker, D.: Building positive self-concepts, Minneapolis, 1974, Burgess Publishing Co.

Ginott, H.: Teacher and child, New York, 1972, Macmillan Publishing Co.

Glasser, W.: Schools without failure, New York, 1969, Harper & Row, Publishers.

Kounin, J.: Discipline and group management in classrooms, New York, 1970, Holt, Rinehart and Winston.

Simon, S., Howe, L., and Kirschenbaum, H.: Values clarification: a handbook of practical suggestions for teachers and students, New York, 1972, Hart Publishing Co.

CHAPTER 5

Acceptance, integration, and group process

Regular teachers worry about having handicapped students in their classrooms. Part of their concern is negative. It comes from uneasiness about disruptions, unforeseen problems, and changes in organization and teaching procedures. But much of their concern is thoroughly positive. They want handicapped students to learn. They want them to succeed. They want them to feel at home in the class, be accepted, and have the opportunity to make genuine contributions.

This chapter deals with these aspects of positive concern. It provides information and suggestions for establishing an air of acceptance and for helping handicapped students find profitable niches in the social-intellectual milieu of the classroom.

You will find virtually nothing here that applies solely to the handicapped— this material applies to all students, all classrooms, and all teachers. Everyone needs to feel accepted. Everyone needs to take part in class activities. Everyone needs to find success. In these ways, the handicapped are no different from anyone else.

The material presented in this chapter is divided into four major sections. The sections are arranged in a sequence that should facilitate understanding of the self, of the self in relation to others, of interactions that enhance the self and others, and of means for maintaining a climate of self-enhancement in the classroom.

THE SELF, ITS NATURE AND MECHANISMS

We must recognize five facts about the self, about the "I," the "Me," the "Yours truly" that comprise our unique individualities.

First, the self is very fragile, but at the same time very resilient. It is crushed as easily as a buttercup. Yet the stuff remains to bring it quickly to flower again.

Second, many defense mechanisms protect the delicate self. It fears hurt as fully as nature abhors a vacuum. When dangers threaten, it throws up an array of defense mechanisms as buffers against possible harm.

Third, the self is buoyed by a compelling urge to grow. It seeks to expand, to find new horizons, to realize its highest potentialities. Threat can hold back this urge but rarely kills it.

Fourth, the self, while unique, is composed of two elements. One element is innate; you are born with it. The other element is experience, the feedback that comes from interacting with natural and social environments. Experience combines chemically with the innate potentialities, to produce the unique self. This self, dependent on experience, can and does change throughout life.

Fifth, selected experiences can feed the growth of the self. They can provide a hotbed, rich with nutrients, that pushes growth toward security, sense of competence, sense of autonomy, and general fulfillment. Such experiences can be provided in the classroom.

Let us explore in more detail each of these five facts about the self.

Fragility and resiliency

Of all earth's creatures, none is so succeptible to hurt feelings as humans. We hold a monopoly on certain cutting emotions. True, you can hurt a dog's feelings, or a chimpanzee's, but you have to act pretty mean to do it, and they get over their hurt quickly. People, on the other hand, can be tremendously hurt by the slightest word, spoken in the kindest voice.

It is interesting that hurt feelings result from what other people do or say. We never hurt our own feelings. Nature doesn't hurt our feelings, either. Only other people do. Here is an example to illustrate the point: In the gymnasium there is a climbing rope, fastened to a beam high overhead. Some of us do not have the upper body strength to climb that rope, never have, never will. Whole-hearted attempts do not get us 3 feet off the floor. We can accept that perfectly, as a fact of nature. We may be disappointed, but our feelings are hurt not at all. Now suppose Johnny sees our fruitless efforts. He says to his companions, "Hey, look, he can't even get off the floor." We are hurt. We were just fine until Johnny spoke.

That shows you two things. First, it is other people who hurt our feelings, not ourselves or our experiences that do not involve others. Second, we are hurt when we feel others ridicule us or express disapproval. It does not matter whether they really do so or not. It does not matter whether what they say is true or false. The only thing that matters is what we think they have done.

You may say, so what? A little hurt feelings now and then never wrecked anybody's life.

Occasional hurt feelings are acceptable. They even help us learn to roll with the punches. But a steady diet of hurt can be most damaging to our fragile selves. It can produce a pervasive sense of inferiority, which stifles initiative. It can call up an array of defense mechanisms, which interfere with our ability to deal with reality. It can cause us to be retiring, awkward, and ill at ease among others. It can ruin self-concept, that private view of ourselves that is tied in with self-assurance, feeling of capability, and willingness to take risks.

Many of us shrug off the few hurts that come to us each day. Many others, however, are so overwhelmed with personal hurts that their ability to function normally is curtailed. Schoolrooms are places where much hurt can occur. At the same time, they can be places of positive exhilaration, where much good is done for students' selves. Later we will see how classrooms can be given this positive aura.

Before moving into a consideration of the healthy, fully functioning self, let us take a moment to review some of the mechanisms that selves us as protections against hurt.

Defense mechanisms

Hurt feelings produce great distress. That distress is so unwelcome that people unwittingly throw up barriers against personal hurt. Those barriers have been identified by psychoanalysts in their work with people whose selves have been so damaged that they have difficulty coping with the requirements of daily life. The barriers, called "defense mechanisms," are used, at one time or another, by all of us when we feel threatened. They are generally considered to be learned behaviors. They are so consistent among people, however, that they may be inborn traits, rather than learned ones, waiting like blood cells to repel harmful infections.

We should remember that these defense mechanisms, employed to a limited degree, fulfill useful functions. They protect us from hurt that would otherwise impair adequate functioning. Continual threat, however, calls forth the defense mechanisms so strongly that they become counterproductive, causing us to avoid responsibility, receive distorted views of reality, and persist, in immature behavior.

Nine defense mechanisms are presented here. They fall naturally into three categories, which we might call "denial mechanisms," "escape mechanisms," and "self-modification mechanisms."

Denial mechanisms pretend the problem is not there, assign it to someone else, or make excuses about it. They include *denial of reality*, *rationalization*, and *projection*.

Escape mechanisms help the individual get away from the threat. They include *fantasy* and *withdrawal*.

Self-modification mechanisms attempt to remake the self, modifying it so as to remove imminent threat. They include *internalization*, *regression*, *displacement*, and *compensation*. Here are brief descriptions of each of these nine mechanisms.

Denial of reality. We refuse to acknowledge the threatening situation; we pretend that it does not exist. This mechanism protects us from worry and hurt, but can also cause us to avoid responsibilities, fail to act on positive criticism, and fail to take precautions against still greater hurt.

Rationalization. Through rationalization we make excuses for our inabilities and failures. We think of a thousand socially acceptable explanations for them. Sometimes we may have genuine excuses, but resorting to rationalization can lead to lack of initiative and a general attitude of "sour grapes."

Projection. Through projection we lay our own faults and shortcomings on other people. We say Sally Jones is lazy, irresponsible, and inept. We say George Smithers is an arrogant back-biting gossip-monger. We are describing ourselves in their bodies. This mechanism helps us tolerate our own faults, but it prevents us from acting to correct them.

Fantasy. When threats are strong and we are unable to deny them, we find ways of escaping. One such way is through fantasy, slipping into make-believe worlds where we do fine, exciting acts. We may fantasize within our own thoughts, or we may escape into TV soap operas, glamour magazines, or novels, where we find marvelous characters with whom to identify. We all fantasize, but when done as escape, it prevents our taking positive steps to improve our lots in the real world.

Withdrawal. When confronted with threatening situations, we withdraw like snails into our shells. We take no risks, do not get involved, withhold our affection. This passivity reduces the chances of getting hurt, but within it we stagnate. We cannot withdraw from the world and remain able to function in normal ways.

Internalization. Threats sometimes cause us through internalization to modify our personal selves, so as to incorporate or build upon the threat. When around people who threaten us, we may adopt some of their personality traits. We figure we "can't lick 'em," so we join them. If they are harsh and abusive, we become harsh and abusive to someone lower in the pecking order. This mechanism is especially evident among school-age children. It is highly counterproductive.

Regression. Through the self-modification mechanism of regression, we revert to earlier stages in life. Threats cause us to show dependence on an authority figure, and perhaps engage in childish quarreling, complaining, and crying. It reduces threat by showing that one is "little," hence not to be attacked. It has no positive aspect that can be built upon.

Displacement. In a manner similar to projection, through displacement we unload on other people. Instead of merely attributing our own faults to others, however, we threaten them directly. We become oppressors. Often we oppress people near to us, such as family members, who are not likely to retaliate. Passing along the threat lightens the burden temporarily, but it hurts innocent others, which soon compounds the problem.

Compensation. To fend off the hurt associated with a personal defect, we build great strength in another area of our self through compensation. If not carried to extremes, this mechanism has positive effects. People with physical handicaps often show it. They become especially good at something, which builds their self-concept while drawing attention away from the handicap.

The urge to grow

Up to this point we have concentrated on personal hurt, the damage it can do to the self, and the defense mechanisms we employ to reduce the threat of hurt. We should remember, however, that the self is also resilient. It continually bounces back, alway tries to grow. Given half a chance, it will put its defense mechanism into storage and get on with the business of seeking optimal growth.

This section discusses aspects of that powerful urge to grow. The ideas reported were put forth by some of the great "third force" psychologists, notably Gordon Allport, Abraham Maslow, Carl Rogers, Earl Kelley, and Arthur Combs. These men helped spearhead a rebellion against a psychology of man based only on behaviorism and Freudian psychodynamics. They believed that a strong, healthy, personal "self" was at the core of human personality, and that its natural urge to grow best explained human behavior. Their rebellion became a strong new movement in itself. Today it is subsumed under the label "humanism."

Abraham Maslow (1962) laid out some basic propositions concerning this self. Here are some of those propositions.

1. Each of us has an inner nature that is unique, inborn, and essential.
2. This inner nature persists throughout life. It has a force of its own, which may be seen as a will to grow, to be healthy, and to allow us to function more fully.
3. This self cannot reach health and full functioning unless it is accepted and respected by others. If the self is frustrated, denied, or suppressed, psychological illness results.
4. The main path to health and self fulfillment is through need gratification. Maslow earlier postulated a "hierarchy of needs." He said that "lower order" needs that allowed fuller, more human functioning. The hierarchy is as follows:

MASLOW'S HIERARCHY OF NEEDS

Higher	Self-actualization
	Esteem
↑	Love and belonging
↓	Safety
Lower	Physiological needs

5. Complete absence of frustration is not good for the self. Small amounts of frustration build frustration-tolerance, which allows the self to function strongly during adversity.
6. The self presses toward growth. Growth brings pains as well as pleasure. It requires risk and relinquishment of some things that are comfortable.

7. As it pushes toward the upper limits of growth, the self begins to actualize, to reach a state of harmony and integration. Self-actualized people are self-directing and secure in themselves. Work and play tend to fuse, as do duty and pleasure, consciousness and unconsciousness, and self and all else.
8. Self-actualizing people enjoy frequent "peak experiences," those experiences that make life supremely worthwhile.
9. The growing self brings the future clearly into one's life, in the form of ideals, hopes, goals, and unrealized potentials.

How the self grows

Humanistic psychologists stress that each of us is born with an inner nature. That inner nature consists of a complex of potentialities, plus a persistent drive toward growth.

Life brings us a tremendous number and variety of experiences. Our innate drive toward growth causes us to reach out for those experiences, not shy away from them. As we reach out and interact with the world, we experience pleasure, pain, excitement, frustration, success, and failure. Our inner cores, our selves, result from this interplay of potentialities and experiences, always motivated by our drive toward growth.

The growth of the self—ideally, it never stops growing—can be healthy or unhealthy. It is healthy if it makes us more capable, competent, confident, and caring. It is unhealthy if it makes us defensive, passive, fearful, or intolerant. Healthy growth occurs when we enjoy support, care, encouragement, and adequate protection from crippling harm. Unhealthy growth occurs when normal needs are frustrated, as when we live in constant fear, find no belongingness, and are permitted no outlets for normal functioning.

This healthy growth that results from acceptance, success, and freedom to explore can lead to self-actualization. In this state, the individual is able to function in accord with highest capabilities, often enjoying peak experiences.

Unhealthy growth, on the other hand, brings lack of fulfillment, cynicism, defensiveness, and a pervasive sense of inferiority. One feels incapable of dealing with the world, impotent, and without direction. These effects can be very debilitating. They take all pleasure out of life. For practical and humanitarian reasons, we should do what is in our power to promote healthy growth in all people around us.

Building the self

The self grows out of the continuing interaction between innate potentialities and experiences. Its nature can be influenced markedly by those experiences.

Experiences are valuable if they provide success, competence, meaningful work with others, and wide opportunity to explore and pursue personal interests. Such experiences are valuable because they promote capability, confidence, and a view of oneself as a part of society and all other things. The individual becomes more calm and accepting, yet confident and able to act.

Experiences are counterproductive if they provide constant failure, frustration, conflict with others, and narrow horizons. Such experiences produce insecurity, hostility, cynicism, and a sense of incapability. The individual becomes reticent, complaining, and lacking in self-direction. Defense mechanisms burst into evidence.

It is within our personal grasp to *make* ourselves much as we would like to be. Abraham Heschell (1973) reflected on that point in his last interview before his death. "Remember," he said, "to live your life as though it were a work of art." Just as we have power over ourselves, so do teachers have power over their students. They can provide the experiences that lead to success, recognition, confidence, and sense of belonging. They cannot work miracles overnight, but they can redirect the current, so that the river of student behavior slowly makes a new and better channel for itself.

There is no lack of suggestions for ways of building the self. Carl Rogers (1962) outlines the directions we should follow:

1. Increase openness to experience. This direction begins to remove barriers through acknowledgement of what is happening to oneself. The experience can be verbalized. It is objectified, seen as something apart from the self; we become an impartial observer. This process reduces inhibition and removes the need for defense mechanisms.
2. Think of life as a process of becoming. We change constantly, always on the way to becoming something different from what we are. We do not remain the same. We can influence, somewhat, the direction we wish this change to follow.
3. Trust in ourselves. When we are truly open to experience, and when we recognize that we are always in a process of becoming, we can place confidence in what our total being senses as right and proper behavior for ourselves.

Earl Kelley (1962) stresses that the self grows as one comes to think better of oneself, a view that accompanies self-acceptancce and a feeling of ability to cope with daily experience. As one thinks better of oneself, he begins to accept others, think well of them, and see his life as interdependent with theirs. This process builds further, so that one comes to hold human values that guide life without subterfuge and deceit.

Don Hamachek (1978) makes practical suggestions for developing the self:

1. Make self-other understanding a personal goal. Hamachek mentions Goethe's advice for knowing ourselves and others: To know others, look within ourselves—there we find fears, aspirations, and uncertainities. To know ourselves, look at others—there we find flaws, self-deceptions, and prejudices that we hold in ourselves but are unable to see.
2. Practice social feeling or empathy. This involves the attempt to see, feel, and hear from another person's point of view, to get inside his skin, to "walk a mile in his shoes."
3. Practice honesty and self-disclosure. This means sharing freely our fears, faults, and other inner feelings. Doing so reduces personal defensiveness and helps develop closeness with others.
4. Practice being a total listener. We tune in and respond to other peoples' feelings as well as their words. Our responses are reflections or commentaries, and are nonjudgmental and noncritical.

• • •

These suggestions reflect some of the more global notions about the self and how it can be enhanced. The section that follows reflects further on the roles that "others" play in the growth of the self.

OTHERS

Other people strongly influence the growth of the self. They do so in three major ways: (1) they provide many of the experiences that produce growth; (2) they feed evaluative information back to us, which we use for making judgments about ourselves; and (3) they provide the frame of reference that allows us ultimately to see the interrelationships that exist among all people and all things.

Experiences

Human interactions can be spontaneous or contrived. Spontaneous interactions are those that occur naturally, without preplanned effort, in the course of daily life. Contrived interactions are those that follow a conventional form and are provided for a special purpose.

Spontaneous interactions occur as part of life. They cannot be avoided, unless one chooses to be a recluse. They cause each of us to observe others, communicate with them, and do a variety of other acts such as cooperate, help, resist, or squabble.

Spontaneous experience is very powerful. It teaches us most of our social behavior. It teaches us to communicate. It teaches the group's system of values. It builds the concept of self and others. And according to the Swiss psychologist, Jean Piaget, it is absolutely essential for adequate intellectual development.

Contrived interactions are specifically arranged, in advance, to foster certain kinds of desired behavior. Examples of this kind of experience include school lessons, religious training, ceremonies of all types, and the social graces of manners, etiquette, and protocol.

Contrived experience occupies a smaller portion of one's life than does spontaneous experience. Its effects, though, are equally powerful. It tends to develop precise ways of thinking and doing—attitudes, thought processes, skills, knowledge, and manners that enable people to function at their best.

The self grows out of both spontaneous and contrived experiences. Spontaneous experience can cause good growth or bad growth; usually it results in a mixture of the two. Contrived experience can do the same, with still greater efficiency. It has the additional power to greatly increase the quality of the self. That quality, of course, is one of the ends toward which schooling is aimed.

Evaluative feedback

The growth process of the self is constantly influenced by the evaluative feedback we receive from others. Their words and actions tell us whether they think we are doing right or wrong, well or poorly. They tell us when they think we are intelligent or stupid, successful or failures, able or incompetent. We know ourselves in large part by the way others see us.

This evaluative feedback does two things. First, it promotes growth. Second, it determines to a great extent our self-concept, what we believe to be true about ourselves. What we *believe* to be true about ourselves is often as important as what really *is* true.

Most evaluative feedback is unsolicited. We do not often ask people directly what they think of us. We do, of course, have many clever ways to draw compliments. Usually, though, people's looks of pleasure, admiration, and disappointment—their "oohs," "ahs," and "ughs"—tell us amply about their opinions.

Interrelationships

When the self grows healthy, it becomes supremely aware of its relationship to everything else. During babyhood, we first begin to develop a sense of self. We see that the world consists of our individual self, which is at the center of things, and of all other things and people, which resolve around us.

This self view can follow one of three paths to maturity. If the growth of the self is very negative, the result is a sense of inferiority, isolation, incompetence, and unworthiness. If the growth of the self is neutral, because positive and negative growth patterns balance each other, self-centeredness remains. The result is a self that is demanding, authoritarian, and rigid. If the growth of the self is positive, the result is tolerance, belongingness, and openness. Above all is the realization that the self's importance is heightened through a merging with people and the natural environment. We see ourselves as an important part of an important whole.

Without the presence of other people, this positive view of the self is not possible. Nor is it possible unless we find, in others who are significant to us, an acceptance, a concern, a caring. Even when we have great confidence in our abilities, it is impossible to function to the fullest when all others belittle and reject us.

Of all social groups, school classrooms have the greatest potential for encouraging this view of self as interrelated with all else. The family and religion have played roles in this view, as well, but the influence of both appears to be declining.

INTERACTIONS

We have seen that others play key roles in our personal growth. We have also seen that contrived experience has great potential for fostering positive growth. This section draws attention to specific kinds of contrived experiences with others. These experiences are called interactions, and when used well they bring about efficient, positive growth of the self.

Interactions may be thought of as active mutual influences. Objects, of course, can interact. Bodies in space draw each other. Magnets attract and repel each other. Salt dissolves in water. Dust blows in the wind.

The interactions receiving attention here are active mutual influences between people. People interact when they talk, discuss, work together, argue, fight, and so forth. Implied is the notion that both parties are active. If one person is active, but the other is passive, there is little or no interaction.

Four kinds of interactions have strong potential for aiding personal growth: (1) communication, (2) working together, (3) group process, and (4) conflict resolution. These four kinds of interaction are discussed in the paragraphs that follow.

Communication

Communication occurs whenever one person sends a message and another person receives it. Receiving is essential. Mere sending is not enough. The sending can be done orally, in writing, graphically (pictures and designs), or behaviorally (body movements). The message may be transmitted by direct sound or sight, or by means of telephone, radio, video, printed material, pictures, and the like.

But unless someone receives the message, and can make sense of it, communication does not occur.

Receivers do not always interpret the message just the way the sender intended. They may misunderstand, misconstrue, or misinterpret. They may think something was meant that in fact was not. They may find connotations in the words that the speaker was unaware of.

All in all "there's many a slip between the lip and the ear"—or between the hand and the eye, as the case may be.

This point is worth belaboring because communication has as much to do with personal growth as any experience you can name. Probably it is the most influential of all. That being the case, it is clear that communication should be accurate, supportive, and tactfully honest. It should expand horizons, provide a testing ground for ideas, and provide an avenue for self-expression.

Applied to the classroom, these ideas imply (1) considerable class discussion, (2) a drawing out of each individual for self-expression, (3) carefully selected teacher talk, for best motivation, encouragement, support, and feedback, (4) instruction and practice for students in reacting positively and supportively to others, and (5) conducting sessions for the purpose of discussing and resolving problems related to work in the class.

Some of the best advice along these lines comes from Ned Flanders, Thomas Gordon, Haim Ginott, and William Glasser. The following are brief summaries of what they have had to say.

Flanders on interaction analysis. Ned Flanders (1965) is famous for his work in interaction analysis, a technique for analyzing and improving the talk that occurs within the classroom. He found that students tended to learn more and like school better when they had increased opportunity to talk in class discussions. This opportunity, as well as the effectiveness of student talk, was greater when teachers drew students out and accepted what they had to say. The teachers in Flanders' research drew students out by asking open questions that required answers several words in length. Such questions call for descriptions, explanations, conclusions, and opinions. Those teachers accepted students' responses by encouraging, praising, and helping give positive redirection to their comments.

Gordon on teacher effectiveness. Thomas Gordon (1974) became nationally recognized for his work in Parent Effectiveness Training, which he reported in his book of the same title. Later, he adapted his ideas to the classroom. He explained them in *Teacher Effectiveness Training*, a book that has had considerable impact on teaching and teacher training.

Gordon advises teachers to practice four things when talking with students:

1. Listen actively.
2. Reflect back their feelings when they want to talk out a problem.

3. Use I-messages rather than You-messages. These messages tell how I (the teacher) am affected; they do not tell what you (the student) is doing wrong.

4. Use the no-lose approach in settling conflict. Help disputants collaborate in finding a solution that is agreeable to both.

Gordon also has much to say about "roadblocks to communication"—ways people talk that almost stifle communication or bring hostile responses. These roadblocks include such things as ordering, threatening, preaching, criticizing, blaming, ridiculing, probing, and humoring others.

Ginott on congruent communication. Haim Ginott (1972) like Thomas Gordon, first caught wide attention through a book written for parents, *Between Parent and Child*. He, too, followed shortly with a book for teachers, *Teacher and Child*, which contains many important suggestions for teachers when talking with students.

Ginott placed major emphasis on what he called "congruent communication," which is authentic in that the words fit the feelings of the speaker. Yet those words are carefully chosen so that they do not hurt the other person. Such hurt is counterproductive. It produces avoidance, deviousness, and hostility, rather than positive responses that lead to growth.

Ginott's work, built around this basic idea of congruent communication, stresses many points. A few of them are:

1. Use *sane messages*. When misbehavior occurs, sane messages address the situation (too much noise, impolite behavior, work not done on time, etc.). They do not address the character of the student (you are lazy; that is irresponsible of you; you have been bad).

2. *Invite cooperation*. Give students choices instead of demanding that they do a certain thing.

3. *Accept and acknowledge*. Students grow in self-esteem when the teacher pays attention to what they say. (If what they say is inappropriate, acknowledge it positively and return immediately to the topic.)

4. *Do not label* students. Labeling is disabling, Ginott says. Talk to students as if they were guests in your home.

5. *Correct by directing*. When you must correct students, do so by giving them positive suggestions rather than by berating them.

Glasser on the reality approach. William Glasser (1969), first known for his book on psychotherapy, *Reality Therapy*, has made three great contributions to education. All three are explained in his book, *Schools Without Failure*:

1. Failure is the most debilitating experience that students can have in school. Of the various kinds of failure, failure to find love from others is the worst.

2. Behavior is a matter of choice. We choose to act the way we do. Good behavior is synonymous with good choices; bad behavior is synonymous with

bad choices. Teachers have the prime responsibility for helping students make good choices.

3. Good communication is the key to providing acceptance, recognition, and love. It reduces conflict and solves problems. Teachers should speak sincerely, without sarcasm. They should hold classroom meetings as a regular part of the curriculum. These meetings allow students to air concerns and seek solutions. All comments must be positive. Students are not allowed to backbite, find fault with people, or assign blame.

Working together

We have seen that the sense of self grows out of interactions with other people. Self-concept results in large part from feedback others give to us about our behavior and appearance. The basic needs for acceptance, belongingness, esteem, and love can be provided only by others. Others provide the models and influences that shape our social behavior. The higher growth of the self is dependent on deep relationships with other people who are significant in our lives.

We have examined communication as one kind of human interaction that influences growth. A second influential interaction is that of working together, of pulling as a group toward a common goal.

Group activities provide great opportunity for communication, discussion, argumentation, cooperation, esprit de corps, sense of purpose, and sense of oneness with others. They have also been viewed as essential by two of the most influential figures of this century, Jean Piaget and John Dewey.

Piaget, a Swiss psychologist, has developed a compelling theory of how the intellect grows. He describes various processes that account for that growth. One of the major processes depends on social interaction, on talking, arguing, and working with others.

John Dewey, the great American psychologist and philosopher, saw the school as the major force for developing and maintaining a democratic society. He thought schooling should include large amounts of group work, in which students could practice the functions and duties of citizens in free societies.

People are social creatures. They are not like some animals that live lives of isolation except at mating time. People want to be together most of the time, to live in groups, to work together, to play together, to plan and strive together.

Given this fact, it is natural that schools should enhance togetherness. Classroom activities can do much to teach individuals how to form groups, establish effective work procedures, stimulate the give and take of ideas, and foster the trust, acceptance, and mutual support that constitute the best in human relations.

Group process

Many writers have described research and put forth suggestions about group work.

Mary Bany and Lois Johnson (1975) remind us that effective groups must have cohesiveness, interaction, structure, goals, and norms.

Cohesiveness. Cohesiveness refers to the bonds that hold the group together. Factors that promote cohesiveness include charisma of the leader, sense of being special, sense of important purpose, and awareness of the contributions each person can make.

Interaction. Interaction refers to verbal and behavioral give and take among group members. Factors that promote interaction include openness to ideas, absence of threat, encouragement of contributions, practice in problem-solving techniques, and positive approaches to resolving conflict.

Structure. Structure refers to the pattern of positions held by members of the group, that is, their formal and informal statuses. Formal structure includes official roles, such as selected leaders, work groups, recorders, and so forth. Informal structure refers to the lines of personal persuasive power that exist within the group. Factors that influence structure include peer relations, group size, and purpose of the group.

Goals. Goals are the ends toward which the group is striving. They supply one of its main reasons for existing. These ends may be academic, social, recreational, performance, or problem solving. Group structure and function are set so as to lead most efficiently to the attainment of established goals.

Norms. Norms refer to the codes of behavior that are acceptable and unacceptable for group members. They stipulate what is expected of members. Norms may be established through discussion, as in rules of class behavior, or they may develop naturally as "understood," though never specified, codes of behavior. Many norms grow in this spontaneous way. However, group morale and effectiveness are usually improved when the norms are spelled out clearly.

Stages in group development. Richard and Patricia Schmuck (1974) describe stages through which effective groups progress. Three of those stages are:

1. Establishing feelings of inclusion and membership. Students must feel themselves important, contributing members of the group.
2. Establishing the channels for collaborative decison-making. This involves establishing roles that permit leadership that is strong, yet guided by group interest, and "followership" that is allowed to express its desires, yet willing to abide by majority decision.
3. Actively pursuing academic and personal goals. In this stage the group works cooperatively toward goals it has set.

Stimulating belongingness. Schmuck and Schmuck also provide suggestions for stimulating sense of group belongingness. One of their suggestions is to provide skill training in verbal communication. Schmuck and Schmuck say this training should include such skills as *paraphrasing* (repeating in one's own words what someone else in the group has said), and *describing own feelings* (telling frankly how one feels in the discussion).

Other authorities have suggested that it is fruitful to use exercises such as:

Agree-disagree—When given statements to which they usually have mixed reactions, students are asked to agree or disagree with each statement. They exchange reasons, opinions, and reactions.

Brainstorming—Students are given a practical problem to solve. An example might be "How can we show other students that we like them?" Students are encouraged to toss out ideas, all of which are accepted and listed on the board. When ideas are exhausted, students make judgments about the ideas, in terms of usefulness, practicability, and value.

Role-playing—Students are assigned roles to play in hypothetical situations involving manners, conflict, job interviews, conversation topics, and so forth. They play their roles as realistically as possible. The class then discusses the exercise.

Conflict resolution

Conflict is disagreement strong enough so that emotions affect behavior. It can involve individual students, groups of students, or teacher and students. During conflict, both sides become upset. Neither wants to give in. Each tends to react hostilely toward the other.

Classroom conflict is often counterproductive, accomplishing little. It results in impasses, leaving hurt feelings and smoldering animosities.

Yet conflict affords a surprisingly good opportunity for intellectual, social, and emotional growth. It has potential for clarifying thought, presenting new ideas, and opening new vistas. It can help one to learn to relate better with others, to maintain calm equilibrium in the face of aggression, and to think clearly in the midst of turmoil.

In order for conflict to lead to these desirable ends, it must be dealt with in positive ways. It must be resolved so as to assuage hurt feelings. Disputants must feel their concerns have been understood and that positive steps have been taken to attend to them.

When possible, conflict resolution should lead to cooperation between the disputants. Each should contribute. Each may have to modify original stances. They can then take positive action in reaching a state of affairs acceptable to both.

Useful suggestions for dealing positively with conflict have been developed by Thomas Gordon, William Glasser, and Haim Ginott, all of whom received attention earlier in this chapter. Eric Berne and Thomas Harris have also contributed with their work in transactional analysis. Here are some of their ideas and suggestions.

Gordon's no-lose approach. Thomas Gordon (1974) made two especially helpful suggestions: (1) using door openers and active listening, and (2) implementing the "no-lose" approach.

Door openers are comments that a person makes to help another speak his mind, for example, "Sounds like you are upset," and "Would you like to say more about that?" Active listening helps people express themselves more fully and clearly. It consists mainly of reflecting back, in nonjudgmental ways, what the speaker is saying. Door openers and active listening open up communication, and help make behavior more rational. They clear the air, let people get things off their chest; they reduce hostility. Sometimes the disputants resolve on the spot the condition that is producing conflict.

The no-lose approach is a strategy for resolving conflict so that neither disputant comes out the loser. This result is very important, not only as an end in itself, but also for feelings of success and for training in positive ways of dealing with future conflict. This no-lose approach aims at a solution that is satisfactory to both disputants. Small efforts usually lead to surprisingly effective results. The approach includes these six steps:

1. *Clarify the problem.* Try to specify observable behaviors that reflect the desires and frustrations of each side.
2. *Jointly suggest possible solutions.* Each side makes suggestions that would solve the problem. It is helpful to list the suggestions.
3. *Jointly evaluate the suggestions.* Each item on the list is scrutinized. It is eliminated if not acceptable to both parties.
4. *Decide on one of the solutions.* Pick a solution that is acceptable to both. If there are none, list more possibilities.
5. *Decide exactly how to put the solution into effect.* Specify who will do what, and when.
6. *Evaluate the success of the solution.* If it has not worked, select another. One of the great strengths of this approach is that it causes disputants to become collaborators. Divisiveness is turned into cooperation.

Glasser's classroom meeting approach. William Glasser (1969) has made a strong case for classroom meetings as workshops for conflict resolution. He advocates three types of meetings, conducted as regularly scheduled parts of the curriculum as follows.

1. *Social problem-solving meetings,* which deal with problems and difficulties that arise in working and getting along with other people
2. *Open-ended meetings,* in which any topic of concern is admissible
3. *Educational diagnostic meetings,* whose purpose is to seek solutions to difficulties encountered in dealing with subject matter

Classroom meetings, in order to be most effective, should be conducted in ways consistent with the following guidelines:

1. Students and teacher sit in a close circle.
2. The tone is kept positive. Harping and blaming are not allowed. Problems are explained as clearly and rationally as possible.
3. Positive, constructive suggestions are sought for solving the problems described.
4. The teacher's duties are to establish and maintain a positive climate, start the discussion, participate little, be nonjudgmental, point out alternatives and options, and keep the discussions on tract.
5. Students' duties are to participate, remain positive, and attempt to find solutions.
6. The meetings should ordinarily be no shorter than 15 minutes, no longer than 45 minutes.

One special strength of classroom meetings lies in their total group involvement in conflict resolution, with attendant relationality, free expression, and helpfulness.

Ginott's views. Haim Ginott (1972) gave most of his attention to reducing conflict between teacher and students. He stresses that it is primarily the teacher's responsibility to reduce conflict. This is done through verbal communication that:

1. Addresses the situation, not the personality of the student
2. Accepts and acknowledges the student's contributions, comments, and feelings
3. Corrects misbehavior by directing students toward acceptable behavior
4. Never uses sarcasm
5. Never labels students
6. Uses brief, succinct statements; does not belabor or harangue
7. Encourages cooperation through providing acceptable options
8. Is always genuine, never phony

Berne's ego states. Eric Berne has identified "ego states" that come into play during conflict resolution. Thomas Harris advises how to adjust those ego states to produce positive results.

Berne (1964) identified the ego states that people use during conflict as "parent," "adult," and "child." Here are Berne's characterizations of each state:

Parent—When using this ego state we talk to others as our parents did to us when we were little. We try to control, admonish, advise, and correct, using an authoritarian stance.

Adult—We think and talk in rational ways. We use logic and reason. We dispassionately consider facts, possibilities, and probabilities.

Child—We revert to childlike behavior. We behave emotionally, act on impulse, defer to authority. We get our feelings hurt easily, and we may act like brats, kicking and screaming to get our way.

The most positive conflict resolution, that which leads to personal growth, occurs when both disputants use the adult ego-state, that is, when they remain calm, reasonable, and reliant on facts. Children can use the adult ego-state, just as adults can use the child ego-state.

Harris's transactional analysis. Harris (1967) picked up on Berne's theme and elaborated it in his book *I'm OK—You're OK*. He determined that serious communication casts people into one of four possible postures:

I'm not OK—You're OK
I'm not OK—You're not OK
I'm OK—You're not OK
I'm OK—You're OK

Positive conflict resolution can occur only when disputants use the fourth posture, which is synonymous with Berne's adult states. To use any other posture is ineffective because it depicts one or both sides as unworthy and subservient. Harris suggests that we learn to identify these ego-states within ourselves and become aware of what we do when we use each of them. Then we should always strive to use our adult state. It should be in charge because it is open, reasonable, and nondefensive; it is flexible enough to allow positive change to occur.

SUSTENANCE AND MAINTENANCE

So far we have considered several aspects of personal relations. We have concentrated on individual growth, acceptance, and integration into the group. Those aspects have included the nature of the self, how the self defends against threat, how the self grows, the roles that others play in self-development, and the growth effects of interactions such as communication, cooperation, group processes, and conflict resolution. These considerations have explained numerous facts and theories about the self, especially in relation to groups.

In this final section, we consider five specific teaching strategies that promote growth, acceptance, and integration: (1) living by the "Golden Rule," (2) humanizing education, (3) teaching through modeling, (4) providing ongoing communication, and (5) maintaining a sense of purpose. These strategies should be incorporated into ongoing teaching practice. They should become a normal and essential part of the social milieu of the classroom.

Let us explore these five strategies briefly, in order to see what they mean and how they are used.

Living by the "Golden Rule"

Beginning with the first day of school, and continuing daily through the year, the Golden Rule (Do unto others as you would have them do unto you) should be the principal guide to classroom behavior and should be discussed every week. It should be understood when class rules are composed. It should be referred to whenever students begin to show untoward behavior.

Discussions about the Golden Rule should be concrete, not abstract. They should call on students to reflect on specific acts in specific situations. These can be of the negative sort, such as laughing when someone makes a mistake, making snide comments about physical disabilities, interrupting when another is speaking, and crowding in instead of taking turns. The negative situations lead, through discussion, to positive ones, for example, helping others who are having difficulty, speaking courteously, showing self-control in lives and group activities, and using best behavior even when the teacher is not present.

Humanizing education

"Humanize" is a term that suffers from vague definition. It is important nonetheless, well worth our attempting to understand it.

Generally speaking, to humanize is to provide conditions that promote self-understanding and self-growth. In schools, this must be done in group settings. Self-understanding implies exploration of natural traits, aptitudes, and tendencies of humans. Emphasis is placed on what one is capable of becoming under the best conditions, on how the fully functioning person sees himself, relates to others, and adjusts to change. Self-growth refers to the process of moving ever closer to the state of full functioning. It implies steadily increasing self-acceptance, absence of defensiveness, openness to experience, pursuit of aptitudes and interests, and security in recognizing personal potentialities and limitations.

Teachers humanize education through attending to both individuals and groups. They attend to individuals through acceptance, providing opportunities for significant student contributions, allowing self-direction and responsibility, and continually finding ways to show they care about the student. They never belittle students. They are tolerant and flexible, conveying constant optimism about what the student can become.

Teachers attend to groups through providing for purposeful collaboration, assigning significant roles, maintaining standards of conduct that protect the integrity and rights of individuals, sharing decision-making with students, and maintaining clear and open channels of communication.

The success of efforts to humanize education can be seen in resulting student behavior, which will tend toward greater self-expression, more efficient cooperation, improved ability to deal positively with conflict, more open-mindedness, less defensiveness, greater self-direction, and greater willingness to accept responsibility for one's own learning and behavior.

Teaching through modeling

It has been estimated that upwards of 80% of our total learning is acquired through imitation. We see what others do; we imitate them. This process accounts for almost all of our social learning, especially during the formative years from birth through adolescence. It is the process through which we become socialized, through which we learn customs, manners, and language.

In schools, much learning comes from interaction with printed materials and concrete objects. Even there, imitation learning stands at the forefront. It accounts for much of our attitudes, toward learning, toward school, toward other people. It is by far the most efficient means of learning physical skills: we see someone do the act correctly and we follow suit. It is very efficient, too, in teaching process learning, the "how-to" aspect that provides practical ability.

When formalized into educational practice, we use the term "modeling" as the label for the process. Modeling means teaching through example and learning through imitation.

The key to effective modeling is the model. Teachers are especially powerful models. Students imitate their behavior to a surprising degree. Students who have prestige in the group are powerful models, too.

The traits we wish to develop in fully functioning persons are heavily dependent on modeling. We best teach openness through being open, acceptance through accepting, courtesy through being courteous, responsibility through being responsible. Students are more likely to do as teachers do, rather than as teachers say.

Providing ongoing communication

Much has been presented earlier in the chapter about communication. Teachers who are willing, open, and clear in communicating with their students have fewer behavior problems to deal with. Their students come to feel more in charge of their educational lives, more responsible, more self-directing, more able to deal with others.

Classroom meetings, as suggested by Glasser, provide one of the best vehicles for maintaining open communication. These open forums give all students the opportunity to air feelings. They serve well to solve and forestall problems.

Regarding the actual wording that enhances communication, we do well to remember Ginott's advice about congruent communication, sane messages, and the language of acceptance. We should also be mindful of Gordon's views on active listening and the kind of talk that stifles communication.

Maintaining sense of purpose

Here is a fact of human nature: if we see a clear and desirable purpose in what we do, we will work our tails off in its pursuit. Never mind the hours needed. Never mind if we skip lunch. The sense of importance and direction that accompanies strong purpose carries us along, transcending time and effort.

The reverse of the coin is equally notable. When we see no purpose in what we do, you can hardly get us to do it. We are bored, listless, given to procrastination. Worse yet, we look for ways to entertain ourselves, and some of those ways are less than desirable.

These facts show how important it is to find purpose in all school learning. That is more easily said than done, as every teacher knows. It is hard to motivate the learning of parts of speech, or algebra (because we will need it for higher math), or Spanish (because we may go to Mexico someday).

Purpose can be found, however, genuine purpose that students understand. If not inherent in the topic, it can be built out of competition, displays, performances, chances to show off (humbly) and have parents be proud of us. It can grow out of joyous group work. It can exist in the opportunity to earn privileges.

Purpose in school is the tonic, the vitamins, the elixir that vitalizes self-growth. It provides goals, incentives, directions, the desire to cooperate. It can provide the need for positive relations with others, for communication, for productive compromise. It is the essential ingredient that supports all class efforts toward personal growth and toward the acceptance and integration of individuals into the group.

SUMMARY

This chapter has dealt with the processes that can be manipulated to improve acceptance and integration of individuals into the group, and to help groups function efficiently and well.

The self, as related to the group, received first consideration. The self was depicted as highly susceptible to hurt but also quite resilient. Defense mechanisms the self uses for protection against hurt were described. The self shows a persistent urge toward growth. Mechanisms by which the self grows were described, and suggestions for building the self were presented.

Other people, that is, the group, provide the environment for personal growth, through interpersonal experiences, evaluative feedback, and various kinds of interrelationships.

Teachers can make good use of many contrived experiences to promote acceptance, integration, and efficient group functioning. Such experiences include communication, working together, and conflict resolution.

Exemplary personal relations can be sustained through group living by the "Golden Rule," humanizing the educational process, providing ongoing communication, and maintaining a strong group sense of purpose.

SUGGESTED ACTIVITIES

1. Make assignments for reading the following books. Report to the class and allow discussion of provocative ideas:
   Perceiving, Behaving, Becoming (1962 ASCD Yearbook)
   Teacher and Child (H. Ginott)
   Schools Without Failure (W. Glasser)
   Freedom To Learn (C. Rogers)
   Teacher Effectiveness Training (T. Gordon)
   I'm OK—You're OK (T. Harris)
   The Open Classroom (H. Kohl)
2. Conduct your own classroom meetings, following the guidelines presented by William Glasser.
3. Discuss procedures teachers should follow to (a) forestall and (b) correct students who are cruel, discourteous, or disruptive to others.
4. Make a list of things teachers can do to show acceptance of students. Should you accept everything students do?
5. Describe the personal experience, encounter, or influence that contributed most to your own personal growth.

SUGGESTED READINGS

Bany, M., and Johnson, L.: Educational social psychology, New York, 1975, Macmillan Publishing Company.

Berne, E.: Games people play, New York, 1964, Grove Press, Inc.

Flanders, N.: Teacher influence, pupil attitudes, and achievement, Washington, D.C., 1965, United States Government Printing Office.

Ginott, H.: Teacher and child, New York, 1972, Macmillan Publishing Company.

Glasser, W.: Schools without failure, New York, 1969, Harper & Row, Publishers.

Gordon, T.: Teacher effectiveness training, New York, 1974, Perer H. Wyden/Publisher.

Hamachek, D.: Encounters with the self, ed. 2, New York, 1978, Holt, Rinehart, and Winston.

Harris, T.: I'm OK—You're OK, New York, 1967, Harper & Row, Publishers

Kelley, E.: The fully functioning self, Washington, D.C., 1962, ASCD Yearbook.

Maslow, A.: Some basic propositions of a growth and self-actualization psychology, *Perceiving, Behaving, Becoming,* 1962, ASCD Yearbook.

Rogers, C.: "Toward Becoming a Fully Functioning Person," *Perceiving, Behaving, Becoming,* 1962, ASCD Yearbook.

Schmuck, R., and Schmuck, P.: A humanistic psychology of education, Palo Alto, CA, 1974, National Press Books.

Stern, C.: Abraham Joshua Heschell: last words, Intellectual Digest, June, 1973.

CHAPTER 6

Behavior management

MISBEHAVIOR, TEACHERS' GREATEST FEAR

Teachers' greatest concern is classroom control. It makes them or breaks them. With good control fine learning is possible; without it learning declines and teaching becomes a bad dream, even a nightmare. That is why teachers fear and detest student misbehavior. The behavior bugaboo plagues them more and more each year. Kids, like the times, just are not what they used to be. Automatic respect for the teacher has vanished along with the saber-toothed tiger.

With control already their number one nemesis, it is no wonder so many teachers blanch when they hear the word "mainstreaming." Speak of special education and teachers automatically think of behavior problems. It is not the deaf student they worry about, nor the blind, nor the student in the wheelchair; it is the behaviorally disabled student who leaps to mind. They know from bitter experience how a single disruptive child can turn the class topsy-turvy.

WHAT IS MISBEHAVIOR?

Asking what misbehavior is seems a silly question; you'd think everybody knew. They may know, but they do not agree. For example, teachers may hold views quite different from those held by others who work with the young. You can see this difference clearly if you compare teachers' views with those of psychologists. Ask psychologists to list student behaviors they consider most serious and you will get a list that looks something like this:

1. Withdrawal
2. Severe depression
3. Resentfulness
4. Cruelty
5. Suspiciousness

Teachers do not consider these behaviors admirable, but neither do they dread them. Class can continue just fine when you have a couple of students who are withdrawn or depressed.

Ask teachers what they consider to be serious misbehavior. Their list will look more like this:

1. Disobedience
2. Rowdiness
3. Impertinence
4. Aggressive hostility
5. Cheating

In short, teachers may think suspiciousness and resentfulness undesirable, but they certainly do not *fear* those behaviors. What they fear are hostility, unruliness, and disobedience, which disrupt classes. They are what classroom teachers fear most from handicapped students.

CONTROL IN THE REGULAR CLASSROOM

These facts about teachers' concerns, real and imagined, might cast a pall over the thought of teaching behaviorally handicapped students, but they shouldn't. Useful and practical methods exist for controlling disruptive behavior. To understand those methods and how they are used, let us first review the control techniques normally used in regular classrooms.

Most teachers use control techniques that fall into three major methods: the *intimidation method*, the *laws-crimes-punishment method*, and the *behavior management method*. The labels do not sound flattering. Please keep in mind they are not the devices of ogres, sadists, and child haters, but the survival devices of humane, caring teachers.

Intimidation method. The intimidation method holds that kids behave best when they fear the teacher. They are afraid to misbehave, to face the teacher's sure wrath. In this approach the teacher gets in the first licks, scowling, talking in a mean voice, laying down the law, and tying into the first student who steps across the line. It works fairly well, and is most frequently used at the upper elementary and junior high levels.

Laws-crimes-punishment method. The laws-crimes-punishment method follows law enforcement procedures. Laws (class rules) are laid down by the teacher. Students know the laws and are expected to live by them. They are told what the punishment will be if they break the class law. When they do, the teacher deals out the punishment. Rarely is this punishment physical. It usually consists of students' staying in, doing extra work, or losing certain privileges. This method is used through all levels of schooling, from primary grades through university.

Behavior management method. The behavior management method operates with an eye to improving student behavior; by contrast, the intimidation method intends to suppress bad behavior, and the laws-crimes-punishment method intends to give transgressors their just reward. Those methods both assume that students know exactly how to behave. When they misbehave they are doing so out of orneriness, not ignorance.

The behavior management method attempts to teach good behavior. It attempts to make good behavior something students know and choose because, all in all, it seems more desirable to them.

BEHAVIOR MANAGEMENT IN REGULAR CLASSROOMS

Behavior management is used a great deal in regular classrooms. The conviction is growing that we should teach students how to behave and help them want to behave in appropriate ways. Several different approaches are in vogue for teaching and reinforcing good behavior. The thrusts for these approaches have come mostly from the work of Fritz Redl and William Wattenberg, Jacob Kounin, Albert Bandura, William Glasser, Haim Ginott, and B. F. Skinner.

Redl and Wattenberg

Fritz Redl and William Wattenberg (1959) have viewed behavior management as a three-pronged approach. They suggest *preventive* measures, *supportive* measures, and *corrective* measures.

Preventive control refers to what is done to prevent behavior problems from arising. It includes rules, organization, and careful planning that prevents boredom, frustration, and slack times during instruction.

Supportive control includes what is done to help students stay on task and maintain self-control. Redl and Wattenberg mention such techniques as eye contact, physical proximity to students, encouragement, and change of pace when necessary.

Corrective control refers to measures the teacher takes when misbehavior does occur. Included are such steps as authoritative verbott (saying, "no, that won't do; stop it."), restitution (making right that which was done wrong), and the loss of privileges.

Kounin

Jacob Kounin (1970) has done more research into actual classroom discipline than anyone else. He has identified several techniques and traits common to teachers who maintain good class control. Among those techniques and traits are what Kounin calls *withitness*, *overlapping*, and the *ripple effect*.

Withitness means that teachers know what is going on at all times in the classroom. They are aware of every single student. Nothing goes unnoticed. Teachers have eyes in the back of the head.

Overlapping means that teachers can attend to two or more things at the same time, for example, work with a reading group while simultaneously directing seatwork for the rest of the class.

The *ripple effect* is a phenomenon used by teachers skilled in control. If one student is corrected properly, the "ripples" from that correction will affect other members of the class. Publicly praising a student's good behavior, for example, will usually produce better behavior in other class members, too.

Bandura

Albert Bandura (1971) has been responsible for producing the theory of social learning called *modeling*. It has been estimated that as much as 85% to 90% of all learning occurs through this process.

Modeling can be thought of as teaching by example and learning through imitation. All of us imitate others; that is how we learn to speak, to use a fork, and to dress appropriately. Bandura and others have shown that we tend to imitate people who have power and prestige.

Because teachers have power and prestige, students often imitate their behavior. That makes modeling an effective method of behavior management. Over the long haul, students tend to behave in ways similar to their teacher. If the teacher is always courteous, attentive, and good-mannered, students tend to become the same.

Setting good examples day after day can be thought of as informal modeling. Used as a specific teaching technique, modeling is even more effective. We can think of this approach as formal modeling.

In formal modeling the teacher teaches specific behaviors by demonstrating a behavior and having students imitate it. Teachers themselves can present the model, or they can select students to be the models. In either case the desired behavior is clearly shown. Then members of the class replicate that behavior.

The formal modeling procedure is very effective for teaching such things as good manners, treating other people with courtesy and respect, keeping on task in learning situations, and relating with students who have special needs, learning difficulties, or behavior problems.

Glasser

William Glasser (1966) has gained widespread recognition for his work with recalcitrant learners. Good behavior, Glasser asserts, is simply a matter of making good choices instead of bad ones. All students choose the behavior they exhibit. School gives students the opportunity and incentive to make good behavior choices, choices that can bring them success and recognition. These good behavior choices result in a personal success identity that leads to further success instead of failure.

The student's responsibility is to make better choices, here and now. The teacher's responsibility is to do everything possible to help students make good choices. This teacher role is key in Glasser's view of behavior management. Teachers must operate in the present, with an eye to the future. They must focus on what the student is doing right now, at this moment. At the same time they must be thinking of how they can help students behave more acceptably in the future.

The "now" focus represents Glasser's strong opinion on effective therapy. He expressed it as the central core of his book *Reality Therapy*. The past doesn't count, he said, only the present. It's what you do here and now that matters.

Teachers therefore should not excuse bad behavior just because students come from poor backgrounds. That reality does of course affect their behavior, but it doesn't prevent their choosing to behave in successful ways.

When students misbehave, Glasser would first call on them, gently and positively, to state what it is they are doing. He would then ask them whether this behavior is helping the class, the school, or themselves. Finally, he would ask them to identify a behavior that would help, that is, to choose a more desirable behavior. If the student can think of none, Glasser would suggest two or three possibilities and ask the student to choose one of them.

This procedure causes students to doubt the value of their misbehavior, to see that they are empowered to select better behavior, and to see that they are ultimately responsible for their own behavior.

Teachers should also do their best to help students make strong commitments to improved behavior and to stick by their commitments. Again, the teacher never accepts excuses for students' failing to live up to their commitments. Instead, the teacher persists in helping students resolve to behave in successful ways and stick by that resolve.

As vehicles for discussing success, success behavior, and problems that interfere, Glasser advocates using regularly scheduled classroom meetings.

Classroom meetings are discussion periods held three to five times a week. Students may talk about problems of interpersonal relations, classroom learning, or other things of intellectual or behavioral significance. The meetings last 15 to 45 minutes, depending on the age of the students. They are conducted in a tight circle, with the teacher playing a relatively passive role. Problems are identified and possible solutions are explored. Students are not allowed to cast blame or verbally attack others. Positive problem-solving is the hallmark of the classroom meetings.

Ginott

Haim Ginott wrote three books that have become classics in education and psychology: *Between Parent and Child* (1965), *Teacher and Child* (1972), and *Between Parent and Teenager* (1968). All three of these books present Ginott's ideas about working positively and profitably with children and adolescents.

Ginott's view of behavior management is best summed up in his assertion that good discipline is a series of little victories that gain students' trust. Behavior management is not a single intervention nor a single skill. It is a continual, ongoing procedure of treating students in ways that show you have genuine concern for them, their progress, and their behavior.

Ginott says teachers have a hidden asset. They should always side with it. That asset is letting students know that you want to be helpful, helpful right now. That posture disarms misbehaving students, calms them, shows them that you care.

This sense of caring is heightened by encouraging student cooperation. Students like to receive private messages that ask for assistance. They like to get notes, mailed to their homes. They respond to being asked for help in private conferences.

Ginott recognizes that misbehavior is bound to occur despite teachers' best efforts at preventing it. He suggests a number of strategies that correct misbehavior while strengthening the bond of trust between teacher and student.

First, teachers should always send "sane messages," which address the situation, not the character of the students involved. If there is too much noise, the teacher might say, "It is so noisy I can't do my work," rather than "James, I've told you three times to stop talking. Can't you get it through your head?"

Second, the best way to correct misbehavior is to suggest more appropriate behavior. One of Ginott's catch phrases is "Correcting is directing." Let students know what you would rather they do. If they say they are sorry, remind them that being sorry means you intend to behave in a better way, that you have made an inner decision to do so.

For misbehavior serious enough to warrant teacher comment, Ginott suggests the use of laconic language and long words. Laconic language is very sparse and to the point. "No hitting." "We never use sarcasm." Long words give laconic language even greater impact. "I am appalled. I am aghast. I am chagrined."

Ginott's book *Teacher and Child* is a compendium of advice for improving student behavior in positive ways. Teachers find the advice practical. Ginott's writing style is elegantly simple. This combination places *Teacher and Child* near the top of teachers' preferred books.

Skinner

Whenever behavior management is mentioned, the name B. F. Skinner leaps immediately to mind. Recognized as the world's premier psychologist, Skinner has had profound influence on matters related to teaching, learning, and general behavior.

Skinner's work ranges from the experimental-theoretical (*The Behavior of Organisms*, 1938) to the practical (*Walden Two*, 1948, and *The Technology of Teaching*, 1968) to the highly philosophical (*Beyond Freedom and Dignity*, 1971). All of it hinges on a single key principle—the principle of reinforcement. This principle holds that behavior is shaped in accord with the reinforcing stimuli that follow it. In layman's terms, we work for that which brings us pleasure.

This principle was not formalized by Skinner. Edward L. Thorndike (1932) used it earlier as an element in his theory of learning. He called the principle the "law of effect," which held that behaviors followed by a state of satisfaction for the organism tended to be repeated.

Skinner developed the concept to its present level of power. Using rats and pigeons he showed how reinforcers, usually food, could be used to teach the animals very complex chains of behavior. He argued persuasively that human behavior is shaped in just that same way. His *Walden Two* was a novel about a utopian society based on principles of reinforcement. His *Beyond Freedom and Dignity* argued that the concepts of freedom and dignity, considered so uniquely human and so essential to a democratic society, were meaningless in light of present knowledge about human behavior. Man is not free, he said. Everyone controls and is controlled. In light of that fact, the question becomes one of how to build, for everyone, those behaviors that promote the greatest individual and collective good.

That very question lies at the heart of behavior management systems that use Skinnerian principles of reinforcement. In educational circles, Skinnerian principles are systematized into a procedure called behavior modification.

Behavior modification attempts to produce better, more desirable student behavior. This behavior includes learning, comportment, effort, and attitude. Its key element is providing reinforcers (think of them as rewards) following a desired student act. The student does what we want; we supply a reward. The reward can be anything the student seeks. It can be attention, praise, marks, privileges, or tokens. Ultimately, we hope that virtue will be its own reward, that students will behave appropriately because they find inherent satisfaction in doing so.

For classroom management, the rules-ignore-praise (R.I.P.) paradigm is widely used. Rules are established that state appropriate behavior; when students exhibit inappropriate behavior, they are ignored; when they exhibit appropriate behavior, they are praised. The praise reiterates the desired act: "Thank you, Shirley, for raising your hand before speaking."

Practitioners in behavior modification offer two important suggestions. The first is "Catch 'em being good." Find students who are behaving desirably and praise them. This has a positive effect on other students, including those who are not behaving so well.

A second suggestion is to use "desist" instead of "ignoring" if a misbehaving student does not respond to praise received by others. You might say, "Stop talking please, right now. Thank you, Jason, for not talking."

Some teachers still look askance at behavior modification. They consider it to be a form of bribery. Many feel it teaches students to work only for the rewards, subverting the true aims of education.

Whatever your opinion, there is no denying the power of reinforcement. It works. It causes students to behave in more acceptable ways, and it makes life more tolerable for teachers.

CONTINGENCY MANAGEMENT

Behavior modification has become a household word in teaching. Such is not the case for contingency management. Few teachers can tell you what contingency management means. Yet, it is a sibling of behavior modification, a clone really, impeccably attired. It is the behavior management system preferred by teachers whose specialty is working with behaviorally disabled and learning disabled students.

Skinner is responsible for the term. He described how behavior shaping is "contingent" upon reinforcement, that is, how behavior is dependent upon and affected by reinforcement. Contingency management deals very precisely with selecting reinforcers and applying them most effectively. When one manages contingencies of reinforcement, one selects the most appropriate reinforcers for an individual and a behavior. One then supplies those reinforcers in the dosages, frequencies, and schedules that most effectively bring about the desired behavior.

Compared to behavior modification, contingency management shows greater organization, skill, and accuracy. It is very efficient. It takes some know-how, but it is the most effective means known for shaping behaviors in students who do not respond well to the techniques advocated by Glasser, Ginott, and Redl and Wattenberg.

A PRIMER OF CONTINGENCY MANAGEMENT

The following terms and principles are basic in behavior modifications and contingency management.

Reinforcer—A stimulus supplied *after* the individual performs an act that increases the likelihood of that act's being repeated. (Commonly thought of as a reward.)

Reinforcement—The act of supplying reinforcers.

Target behavior—The end, the desired behavior toward which instruction is aimed.

Shaping—The act of building toward the target behavior, through progressive reinforced steps.

Schedules of reinforcement—Refers to when and how often reinforcement is supplied. At first, all improvements, however small, should be reinforced. Later, greater improvements can be required before reinforcement is

given. To maintain desired behavior, intermittent reinforcement (reinforcement given occasionally) is used.

Contingencies of reinforcement—The conditions under which reinforcement
effectively occurs.

Contingency management—A highly organized, precise system for shaping behavior, calling for target behaviors, approximations (improvements), and procedures and schedules for supplying various types of reinforcers.

CONTINGENCY MANAGEMENT IN THE CLASSROOM

Any program of contingency management must specify three things: (1)
desired student behaviors (in observable terms), (2) the reinforcers that will be
used to promote the desired behaviors, and (3) the ways the reinforcers will be
managed—that is, how, to whom, and for what they will be dispensed. For total
class contingency management the reinforcement categories most often used are
(1) social reinforcers, (2) graphic reinforcers, and (3) tangible reinforcers.

Social reinforcers. Social reinforcers include recognition, praise, activities, and
special privileges. Recognition and praise are reinforcers mentioned earlier in
conjunction with behavior modification. In a true contingency management program, they are administered systematically in an attempt to shape specific behaviors.

Activity reinforcers. Recognition and praise can be administered with relatively
little advance preparation. Privilege and activity reinforcement requires greater
planning. Privilege reinforcers allow individual students to do things not normally
allowed. Advance preparation must be made for awarding and following through
on such privileges. Examples of privileges include such things as:

For children and adolescents

Getting a free period
Putting on a show for another class
Seeing a film
Having a party
Going out to recess early
Having a longer or extra recess
Having a class art display in the hall or library
Watching television
Listening to music
Going on a field trip
Playing games in class
Having class outdoors
Competing with another class

For children only

> Putting on a puppet show
> Having a policeman or fireman visit
> Being entertained by older students
> Being cafeteria helpers
> Being hall and yard monitors

For adolescents

> Having a rap session
> Changing the "due date" for an assignment
> Getting to go home early—having class cancelled for the day
> Having the teacher entertain in class
> Being treated to a party or outing by the teacher
> Choosing and working on a class project
> Having a social affair during class time

Special activity reinforcers allow students to earn, as a class, activities they prefer. Privilege reinforcers are supplied to individuals; activity reinforcers are supplied for total group effort. They are made contingent in a way that David Premack calls "Grandma's Rule"—first you do what I want you to do, then you can do what you want to do. Examples of class activity reinforcers include:

ACTIVITY REINFORCERS
Individual

For children and youth

> Playing a game
> Getting to sit where you want
> Choosing the game
> Being in a skit
> Having extra time at lunch
> Taking care of the class pet
> Helping set up equipment
> Working at a learning center
> Having dinner with the teacher
> Being ball monitor
> Taking the class pet home for the
>   weekend
> Being called on to answer first
> Working on special projects or
>   hobbies
>
> Free reading
> Going to the library
> Being hall monitor
> Being team captain
> Being group leader
> Being on safety patrol
> Going first
> Having free choice
> Going to an assembly program
> Tutoring younger students
> Decorating classroom
> Being class officer
> Visiting the teacher's home

For children only

> Sitting near the teacher
> Leading the flag salute
> Getting to draw a picture

Helping clean up
Reading or performing for the principal
Bringing a pet or toy to school
"Snoopy" or other pet toy gets to sit at your table
Having your art or classwork displayed in the hall
Being teacher's helper
Choosing songs to sing
Being paper monitor
Getting to share first

For adolescents

Being excused from a test
Studying with a friend
Being class representative
Making your own work schedule
Having a teacher write a complimentary letter to your parents
Having your picture in the office as "student of the week"
Getting to "cut" class
Choosing alternate assignments
Demonstrating special skills
Having a teacher sponsor you

Group

For children and adolescents

Getting a free period
Putting on a show for another
    class
Seeing a film
Having a party
Going out to recess early
Having a longer or extra recess
Having a class art display in
    the hall or library
Watching television
Listening to music
Going on a field trip
Playing games in class
Having class outdoors
Competing with another class

For children only

Putting on a puppet show
Having a policeman or fireman visit
Being entertained by older students
Being cafeteria helpers
Being hall and yard monitors

For adolescents

> Having a rap session
> Changing the "due date" for an assignment
> Getting to go home early—having class cancelled
> Having the teacher entertain in class
> Being treated to a party or outing by the teacher
> Choosing and working on a class project
> Having a social affair during class time

In programs that use privilege and activity reinforcement, class members must know in advance exactly what is expected of them. Reinforcement is supplied only if and when students reach expectations. They are never reinforced for substandard behavior, for that defeats the whole purpose.

It is important to keep requirements low at first, so even small improvements can be reinforced. Later, requirements can be increased.

Graphic reinforcers. "Graphics" refers to marks, graphs, charts, pictures, and so forth. Teachers have found that graphic reinforcers can be very useful in shaping behavior. Especially effective are checklists, stars and faces, numerals, grafitti, and graphs.

Checklists show names of students down the side and activities or behaviors across the top. As students progress, they are checked off. These devices were once used widely. Presently, they may violate students' right to privacy if kept in public view. Such devices should be cleared with the school principal before use.

Stars and faces are used everywhere for reinforcement. Teachers draw them or buy inexpensive stick-ons that can be put on students' work or clothing.

Numerals, to indicate quality or points earned, are also widely used. Point systems can assign values to work completed, work quality, good behavior, and so forth. Points can later be used to buy privileges, treats, or items students bring from home for class auctions.

Grafitti are the personal marks teachers use to show improvement, quality, or poor work. Commonly used are checks, plusses and minuses, comments, cartoons, and interjections such as *Wow!*, *Fantastic!*, or *On the beam!*

Graphs, when used to chart individual student progress, are both motivating and reinforcing. In addition, they provide accurate records that can be used when conferencing with students and parents. They are best used to show individual progress against that person's own past records. When this graphing is done systematically, it is called "precision teaching," an approach that experimentation has shown to be effective in shaping student behavior rapidly.

A graph of the type used in precision teaching, followed by samples of other reinforcers, is presented in Fig. 2. It can be duplicated for use in teaching.

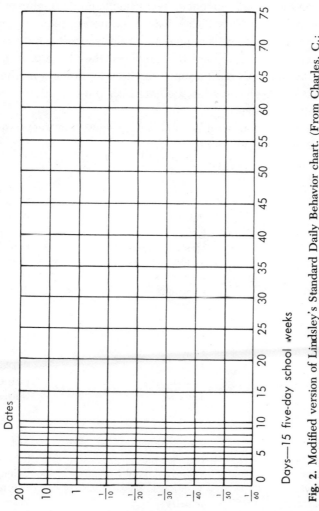

Fig. 2. Modified version of Lindsley's Standard Daily Behavior chart. (From Charles, C.: Individualizing instruction, St. Louis, 1979, The C. V. Mosby Co.)

Tangible reinforcers. Tangible reinforcers are objects that can be held, collected, and saved; some can even be eaten. They are considered to be a more powerful class of reinforcers for most students. What they gain in power, however, they lose in convenience.

In order to conduct a management system using tangible reinforcers, one must first purchase or make the objects. They have to be stored, then dispensed. Often this means the teacher has to walk around with reinforcers in hands, pockets, or a container. As students begin to earn the tangibles, they have to have a place to keep them. Finally, teachers must arrange a system for doing something with the reinforcers earned. Usually they let students cash the objects, in exchange for privileges, activities, or toys.

Here is a listing of various tangible objects that have been successfully used in contingency management programs:

TANGIBLES AND PLAY MATERIALS

For children and adolescents

Records	Toys	Dolls
Comic books	Puzzles	Books
Playing cards	Notebooks	Key chains
Games	Sports equipment	Pencils
Pens	Magic Markers	Model kits
Real money	Toothbrushes	Combs
Art print	Figurines	

For children only

Clay	Kites	Toy soldiers
Coloring books	Crayons	Jacks
Balloons	Marbles	Blocks
Legos	Toy animals	Picture books
Badges	Toy cars	Noisemakers

For adolescents

School decals	Address books	Tickets to concert
Tickets to sports event	Cassette tapes	School T-shirts
School pennants	Paperback books	Calendars
Tickets to movie	Motorcycle magazines	Fan magazines
Hot rod magazines	Jewelry	Posters
Cosmetics	Stationery	

If you want to implement a contingency management system using tangibles, here are points to keep in mind:

1. Clear the plan with the school principal.
2. Collect or make the reinforcers.

3. Decide what it takes to earn them—what achievement, improvement, behavior.
4. Establish rules for handling the tangibles—for example, no trading, keep in container, no counterfeiting.
5. Plan times and procedures for cashing in the tangibles.
6. Explain the program to the class. Go over all details.
7. Write a letter to parents, explaining the program.
8. Plan to run the program for at least 2 months, to allow students to adjust to it.

Rewards and punishments. Up to this point nothing has been said about the role of punishment in behavior management. That is because punishment has undesirable side effects. It often causes student resentment, evasion, lying, cheating, and overt hostility. It also reinforces the notion that might makes right.

Nevertheless, punishment effectively suppresses unwarranted behavior. It can be used when the totally positive approach fails. You just have to remember the side effects it produces and weigh them against its benefits.

Regular classroom teachers are often shocked when they see special teachers working with behaviorally disabled students. The special teachers use a highly systematic program of behavior management. For difficult cases they combine lavish positive reinforcement with mild punishment. You might see them lightly slap students' hands or legs to stop inappropriate behavior. They might loudly say, "No! Stop that!" They might isolate students in small enclosures.

These punishments seem contrary to the tenets of behavior management. Though neither harsh nor hurtful, they seem negative instead of positive. However, they are used because certain students do not respond to the positive reinforcers.

One-to-one management. What regular classroom teachers fear most is the behaviorally disabled student, one who is loudly disruptive, hyperactive, or hostilely aggressive. They know that one such student can ruin learning for the entire class.

If assigned such a student, the teacher may need to set up a one-to-one behavior management program. The other class members may be managed in the usual ways. They are informed that Alex needs special help from all of them, and that the treatment he gets from the teacher will be of a different kind that will help him most.

The teacher then sets up a carefully designed management program for Alex. A special teacher can help arrange the program. Alex will begin earning rewards for such things as staying in his seat, not blurting out, not pushing or hitting, and getting his work done and helping others.

The rewards (reinforcers) are of several varieties. They include praise from the teacher and other students, tangibles, certificates, and charts showing improvement. They include letters of commendation for Alex to take home to his parents.

Alex suffers the consequences when he behaves inappropriately. He will not be reinforced. He can be isolated in a part of the room, denied participation in class activities, or even taken home. These consequences are only given for very disruptive behavior. Alex can always redeem himself by behaving as he should.

To strengthen Alex's resolve further, the teacher may decide to use a behavior contract, a form that Alex and the teacher sign as a mutual agreement. (Sample forms are presented at the end of this chapter.) It stipulates what Alex is realistically expected to do. It may also indicate what he will earn if he abides by the contract. It will be helpful to have Alex's parents sign as witnesses. Their interest in Alex's program will be keen, and their support can help greatly.

Remember that one-to-one contingency management must be very well planned. It requires:

1. Specifying the behavior(s) to be modified
2. Counting the frequency of misbehavior and appropriate behavior, to use as baseline data
3. Specifying desired terminal behavior and the small steps that lead to it
4. Deciding on the combination of social, graphic, and tangible reinforcers that will be used
5. Deciding how and when to provide reinforcement
6. Informing other class members and enlisting their help
7. Setting up a contract between student and teacher, with parent involvement
8. Graphing student improvement against the baseline data

Most regular classroom teachers have not been trained to set up and carry out one-to-one behavior management programs. They can count on strong assistance from special teachers. They will be pleasantly surprised to find that these programs allow them to continue class as usual while contributing significantly to the disabled student who so badly needs their help.

SUMMARY

This chapter dealt with the positive management of student behavior in the classroom, so as to assist purposeful on task behavior, reduce disruptive behavior, and maintain an efficient working environment in the classroom.

Student misbehavior was called the classroom teacher's greatest concern. Types and causes of misbehavior were discussed. The traditional control techniques of intimidation, laws-crimes-punishments, and behavior management were examined. Behavior management was judged to have the most value for controlling behavior while maintaining positive purposeful relationships.

Several established models of classroom management were described. They were the models of Redl and Wattenberg, Kounin, Bandura, Glasser, Ginott, and Skinner.

Much attention was given to contingency management, based on the reinforcement principles proposed by Skinner. Reinforcement, reinforcers, schedules, and contingencies effective in the classroom were described. Different types of reinforcers received further attention: social reinforcers, activity reinforcers, graphic reinforcers, and tangible reinforcers.

Graphic illustrations of effective reinforcers follow at the end of the chapter. They may be reproduced for use in the classroom.

SUGGESTED ACTIVITIES

1. Read *Teacher and Child*. Letter his catchy phrases on strips of tagboard. Discuss their meanings and applications in class.
2. Conduct classroom meetings in your college class, as suggested by Glasser. Review the suggestions for seating, topics, teacher role, and student restrictions.
3. In triads, role-play behavior modification techniques. One person plays the teacher and the others are students. Remember to "catch 'em being good." Practice a variety of social reinforcers, both verbal and nonverbal. Remember the rules-ignore-praise approach.
4. Devise a token economy system for a grade or class of your choice. Use plastic disks of different colors and values. Describe how to set up and conduct the program. Refer to the list of suggestions on pp. 104-105.
5. Assume you have a student (select age 6, 9, 12, or 15) who is very disruptive in class— blurting out loudly and walking around. Plan a one-to-one contingency management program to improve those behaviors. Follow the outline presented on p. 106.

SUGGESTED READINGS

Bandura, A.: Social learning theory, New York, 1971, General Learning Corporation.

Ginott, H.: Between parent and child, New York, 1969, Macmillan Publishing Company.

Ginott, H.: Between parent and teen-ager, New York, 1969, Macmillan Publishing Company.

Ginott, H.: Teacher and child, New York, 1972, Macmillan Publishing Company.

Glasser, W.: Schools without failure, New York, 1969, Harper & Row, Publishers.

Kounin, J.: Discipline and group management in classrooms, New York, 1970, Holt, Rinehart, and Winston, Inc.

Redl, F., and Wattenberg, W.: Mental hygiene in teaching, New York, 1959, Harcourt Brace Jovanovich, Inc.

Ritholz, S.: Children's Behavior, New York, 1959, Bookman Associates, Inc.

Skinner, B. F.: The behavior of organisms, New York, 1938, Appleton-Century-Crofts, Inc.

Skinner, B. F.: Walden two, New York, 1948, Macmillan Publishing Company.

Skinner, B. F.: The technology of teaching, New York, 1968, Appleton-Century-Crofts, Inc.

Skinner, B. F.: Beyond Freedom and Dignity, New York, 1971, Alfred A. Knopf, Inc.

Thorndike, E.: The fundamentals of learning, New York, 1932, Teachers College Press.

Accoutrements for behavior modification*

FINAL REWARD

This is to recognize Debbie's outstanding contribution to the lowering of the noise level in room B.

Congratulations!!

CONTRACT

I, Debbie Jones agree to try my best to abide by the rules below.

1. Talk at appropriate times, e.g., at recess, free time or when called on.
2. Refrain from speaking during films, quiet time, when others are speaking or whenever it is appropriate.

In doing this I will be assisted by Beth Farmer .

x *Debbie Jones*

x *Beth Farmer*

*Courtesy of Dr. David K. Gast, San Diego State University.

EXAMPLES OF PRIVILEGE OR ACTIVITY CARDS THAT CAN BE EARNED. A POINT SYSTEM.

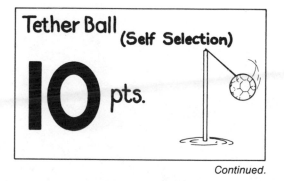

Continued.

Simple tokens teachers can make

SOME TOKEN IDEAS

"Money" tokens

Contract for behavior modification

I've Got An Offer You Can't Refuse

If ___Jane Voelker___ can learn up through her sixes by Friday, Oct. 24 and finish the rest **by** ___Oct 29___

Then ___she may attend the party___ on Oct. 29

___10-20-80___ _____ _____ ___Miss Feldman___

date   student   witness   teacher

Teaching the special students

CHAPTER 7

Teaching students with behavior disorders

Chapter 6 stressed three points: (1) classroom control makes or breaks a teacher; (2) teachers are more distressed by student misbehavior than by anything else in teaching; and (3) many excellent techniques are available for controlling student behavior, all of which work part of the time, but none with 100% effectiveness.

When it comes to working with mainstreamed students, regular teachers especially fear one category of disability. That category is the emotionally disturbed child, whose overt behavior is so often disruptive and resistant to available techniques of control.

This chapter deals with teaching emotionally disturbed students in the regular classroom. Instead of using the label "emotionally disturbed," as is specified in PL 94-142, we will use the term "behavior-disordered" to refer to this category of handicap; this is a more useful term because it directs attention to the problem with which teachers must deal, namely, the overt behavior of the student.

THE TROUBLE WITH DEFINITIONS

Authorities have not been able to agree on a single definition of "behavior disorder." Common to most definitions are the expressions "inappropriate behaviors," "antisocial dealings," "fears," "unsatisfactory interpersonal skills," "disturbed functioning," and "unacceptable conduct." But these terms present problems in interpretation. "Unacceptable conduct" raises questions: Unacceptable to whom? In what context, in what environment? For example, suppose a profile were to be developed of an individual who exhibited very anxious behaviors, paced back and forth, twisted his hands, stared out the window for long periods of time, returned to pacing, had sweaty palms, cried occasionally, at the sound of a siren ran to the window, fixated on the sound, and attempted to track it as it diminished, then returned to pacing back and forth, twisting his hands and so on. Most teachers would classify this individual as "disturbed," "behavior-disordered," or maybe even "crazy."

Any teacher would be in a quandary as to how to teach this student. The most enlightened might rearrange the classroom to dimish distractions, and might try to provide more individualized on task teaching. This approach would address itself to the overt behaviors that were most troublesome.

Other information would have to be collected, however, in order to develop good programs of instruction and behavior management. The age of the individual would matter greatly, as would the situation and environment in which the behavior occurred. If the individual were a 2-year-old child, the behavior management plan would be quite different than if the person were 10, 35, or 80 years old. The judgment that the person is "disturbed" or "crazy" would change if the individual behaved that way in a hospital cardiac unit awaiting a transplant or in a maternity ward awaiting a delivery.

AGE-APPROPRIATE AND CONTEXT-APPROPRIATE

With age and context information, "crazy" behaviors can be considered for a particular situation. This same application of age-appropriate and situational-appropriate observations should be made for students in the regular classroom. This requires that the teacher be aware of what is appropriate behavior for a specific age. A temper tantrum from a 2-year-old child is a normal behavior, manifested in a typical power struggle. A temper tantrum from a 42-year-old adult is not "normal," not an age-appropriate means to express a power difficulty.

Observations of context, the specific situation existing in the classroom, provide additional information for situation-specific behaviors. For example, suppose a student suddenly withdraws or exhibits "acting-out" behavior. No stress situation exists in the classroom; the behavior seems entirely unwarranted. Stress may exist within the child, however. Further probing may reveal a separation or pending divorce in the family. This knowledge presents a context in which the manifested behavior can be understood. Rather than being "abnormal," this withdrawn or acting-out may be a very "normal" way of coping with the situation at home. True, it may not change the instructional program established for the child, but it may help in the development of a more appropriate behavior management program.

FREQUENCY, DURATION, DEGREE, AND SOURCE

You can see that teacher awareness of age-appropriate and context-appropriate behavior is important. It helps to be aware of other aspects of the behavior, too, especially its frequency, duration, degree, and source.

Frequency refers to how often the behavior occurs. Suppose a teacher pinpoints a specific behavior problem, such as "out-of-seat behavior." It is important to determine how often this behavior occurs. This determination can be made easily by tally marks recorded during the day. Now let us say that the behavior in question occurred thirty times that day, twenty of them in a 1-hour period. This information provides a basis for implementing an effective behavior management program. The marking of time period occurrences facilitates zeroing in during specific activity periods.

Sometimes a frequency count will show that the behavior is not a problem. If that out-of-seat behavior occurred only twice a day, it might be better to leave well enough alone. It is just as important to know when *not* to intervene as it is to know when to intervene.

Duration refers to how long the specific behavior lasts. Using the same out-of-seat behavior example, it may be found that in the thirty times the student was out-of-seat, each occurrence lasted 2 to 3 minutes. By contrast, another student might have exhibited out-of-seat behavior only three times, but the duration for each was several minutes. Again, this specific information helps the teacher to decide if the behavior warrants attention, and if so, what kind of management technique would be most useful.

Degree refers to how much the behavior impairs the student's functioning in the classroom, both socially and academically. For some students, being out of their seats does not keep them from functioning at the level established by the teacher. For others, such behaviors impair their ability to complete assignments, to interact effectively with peers, or keep up with other members of the class.

The behavior in question may also impede other students in the class. When a behavior is having a detrimental effect on the class, it calls for immediate intervention. The key question is whether the behavior is keeping the student and/or other students from learning.

Source refers to the context or stress situation that provokes the behavior. Crises in the family environment, such as divorce, separation, sibling conflicts, or the death of a pet present frequent problems. The student's way of dealing with the problem may result in behavior that is "unusual" for that student. Recognizing this fact gives the classroom teacher a handle on placing the behavior in context, to understand its manifestations, and to determine appropriate interventions for dealing with it.

MENTAL CHECKLIST

Utilizing these factors of age, context, frequency, duration, degree, and source of the behavior, teachers can prepare a "mental checklist" for use in dealing with misbehavior. The checklist also helps communicate concerns to special teachers and consultants. For example, if a behavior occurs often and for long periods of time, is keeping the student from attending, is disrupting the other members of the class, and is an attention-getting tactic, both teacher and specialist will feel secure in acting quickly and accurately.

These factors do not provide a generic definition of behavior disorders. They do, however, provide individual points to consider when attempting to objectively determine "appropriate" and "inappropriate" behaviors.

The line between normal behavior and behavioral disorders is, as you can see, a fuzzy one. This fuzziness leaves teachers unsure as to whether they need to call for help in dealing with behavior problems. Kauffman (1977) helped with the following commentary on behavior disorders:

Children with behavior disorders are those who chronically and markedly respond to their environment in socially unacceptable and/or personally unsatisfying ways but who can be taught more socially acceptable and personally gratifying behavior. Children with mild and moderate behavior disorders can be taught effectively with their normal peers (if their teachers receive appropriate consultative help) or in special resource or self-contained classes with reasonable hope of quick reintegration with their normal peers. Children with severe and profound behavior disorders require intensive and prolonged intervention and must be taught at home or in special schools, or residential institutions.

Kauffman's definition does not key on specific behaviors. Yet when the factors mentioned previously are coupled with his commentary, the result is an in-class management system and referral framework for special services.

SOURCES OF BEHAVIOR DISORDERS

Kauffman's definition took into account the planning and programming needs of educators. Other definitions of behavior disorder have been proposed by professionals outside of education to meet their respective programming needs. These definitions are of interest to teachers. They are based on the factors that relate to the cause of behavior disorders.

Rhodes and Tracy (1972) presented a comprehensive review of the models, definitions, and etiologies of child variance. These models, formulated to serve as "explanatory systems" of behavior disorders, are reviewed in the sections that follow.

Biophysical basis of behavior disorders

The perspective within this model is that a physical disorder exists within the individual exhibiting the deviant behavior. The intervention becomes a diagnosis of cause, followed by subsequent "cure." The factors that determine this "cause and cure" include:

1. *Genetic* factors, or a predisposition to disturbances of behavior and pathology
2. *Developmental* factors, such as clear lags in social and emotional growth
3. *Arousal* factors which provide a regulation or misregulation of sensory input (for example, the hyperactive child's arousal system is thrown into a state of imbalance when distracting objects, noises, etc., are introduced)
4. *Perceptual* factors, which include disturbances in the processes of attention, sensory reception, speech, and movement
5. *Neurological* factors, which suggest that there exists some brain disorder that is precipitating or maintaining the behavior disorder
6. *Biochemical* factors, which reveal chemical imbalances in the body, par-

ticularly the brain; chemical processes influence brain functioning, which in turn influences behavior; recently, the diet of children, particular their sugar intake, has been found to affect activity level

Behavioral basis of behavior disorders

The behavioral basis of behavior disorder contends that behavior is a learned phenomenon. By a systematic schedule of various types of reinforcements any behavior can be taught. By the same token, behaviors can be unlearned. The notion of rewarding desired behaviors and not rewarding undesired behaviors is common to educators and parents. In using this approach, observation plays an important role. In order to determine how or why a particular observed behavior is being maintained, three key observations must be made.

1. *Antecedants.* These are the circumstances, environmental or psychological, that preceded the behavior. For example, the behavior of "fighting" may have followed a verbal altercation, which in turn was preceded by "innocent" name-calling. This information provides an entry point for treating a subsequent behavior problem.

2. *The behavior.* Careful observation will enable teachers to state in objective terms *who* is doing *what*, to *whom*, *where* and *when*. Stating that a child is "lazy," "daydreams," or is "aggressive" provides no specification of the behavior to be changed. An objective description would state that "Sally hits Suzie in the arm, every noon, while in the cateferia line." The more specifically a behavior can be stated, the more readily it can be dealt with effectively.

3. *Consequences.* By observing the effects of the pinpointed behavior, one can detect the rewards that are maintaining that behavior. For example, a child who is engaging in "attention-getting" behaviors will maintain this behavior if peers are laughing and providing attention. The point of intervention then becomes the peer group. The rewards they provide are shut off.

Not only can the ABCs (antecedents, behaviors, and consequences) provide valuable information for initiating, maintaining, and following through on a behavior management program, they can also be used as a problem-solving method for individual students. For example, suppose it is pointed out to a student that hitting the student behind was a result of a broken pencil lead, and that the pencil could have been sharpened; however, taking a pencil from the other student started a fight. This verbal "playing back" of circumstances, events, misbehavior, and consequences provides feedback to the student that helps in future decision-making. Older students can specify the ABCs of their own behavior when they misbehave.

As desired and undesired behaviors become specific, a plan for behavior change can be built. The behavior change can be brought about in the following three ways.

1. *Increasing behavior.* Reinforcements can be given to increase the likelihood of a desired behavior being repeated. Reinforcements, such as peer (buddy system, working with friend), activity (free time, listening to tapes or slides, movie viewing, fieldtrips), tokens (chips, stamps, candy, points), nonverbal (smile, pat, touch, nod of head), and verbal ("good going," "great work") are effective in increasing behavior.

2. *Decreasing behavior.* An undesired behavior can be suppressed in three ways: through punishment, ignoring, and reinforcement of incompatible behaviors. *Punishment* can be the removal of positive reinforcement, or it can be the application of consequences undesirable to the student. *Ignoring* is the withdrawal of attention from the student who is misbehaving. This removes the rewards that were sustaining the behavior. *Reinforcing incompatible behavior* draws attention to desired ways of behaving. When the teacher says "Thank you, Johnny, for raising your hand," students who have been blurting out answers will tend to raise their hands.

3. *Creating new behaviors.* Several techniques exist to develop new behaviors in students. The most effective of these techniques is *modeling.* Bandura (1963) defines modeling as an observer copying responses that he has not made heretofore. We all learn much of our behavior by watching what other people do. Teachers are powerful models for their students. They teach new behaviors through example, demonstrations, and verbal description.

Within the behavioral view, a problem remains about the behaviors to be increased, decreased, or created. Appropriate behavior for one teacher is inappropriate for another. Problem-solving, decision-making, and intervention are, in the final analysis, matters for each individual teacher, aimed at the unique needs of the specific classroom, while respecting differences in individual students.

Psychodynamic basis of behavior disorders

The psychodynamic view of behavior takes into account the conscious and subconscious mind forces that affect personal behavior. It sees the individual student as a conglomeration of influences that follow a distinct developmental sequence. Each sequence consists of a variety of developmental tasks that must be mastered if a student is to move on in his/her social and emotional learning.

Many great psychologists and psychiatrists have espoused this view. The position was put forth by Sigmund Freud, whose work stirred great controversy and stimulated much research. His concepts of id, ego, superego, fixations, and defense mechanisms have become part of western culture.

Later work by Erik Erikson (1950) has been of more benefit to teachers. Erikson sees humans as going through eight stages of development. He calls them "Eight Ages of Man." For purposes of this discussion, the first five stages are reviewed. They bracket the ages of birth through 18 years. Erikson's theory is developmental and sequential—developmental, in that key tasks have been isolated that must be resolved within each stage, and sequential in that the stages are built upon one another. The overlap in Erikson's stages can be depicted in this manner:

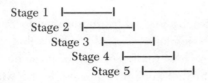

This depiction shows that development issues are being presented and resolved continuously, while development continues.

Trust versus mistrust. Erikson's first developmental stage occurs between birth and approximately 2 years of age. The developmental task at this stage is to acquire a sense of basic trust while overcoming a sense of basic mistrust. The child at this time is helpless. Trust must be developed that others will nurture, protect, feed, and reassure the child. If these needs are met in a consistent manner the child will develop the basis for a trusting attitude. If the needs are not met, the child will develop a mistrusting attitude.

If this developmental task has been mastered and the child has developed a sense of basic trust, specific adaptive behaviors can be observed later in school. The student is comfortable within the classroom, self-confident, curious to explore, and trusting of others.

A student who has not mastered the task will exhibit "mistrusting" behaviors, be apprehensive, unwilling to explore, upset at change, and withdrawn. Behavioral management techniques for this child focus on establishing predictability in the environment, maintaining routines, and adhering to class schedules and expectations. Opportunities to experience success should abound.

Autonomy versus shame and doubt. In Erikson's second stage, approximately ages 2 to 4, the child is attempting to acquire a sense of autonomy while overcoming a sense of shame and doubt. The critical task is to develop the ability to make choices for onself.

Students who have been unsuccessful in this task are dependent, lethargic, hesitant, and reticent. They go along with group opinion, being easily influenced. They show little initiative and often have poor self-concepts. Classroom management techniques provide a gradual experiencing of autonomy, through decision-making activities. The student is made aware he or she is making choices. The social environment encourages students to stand on their own feet when provided situations for choice and self-direction, but at the same time protect against experiences that produce shame and doubt.

Initiative and responsibility versus guilt. Erikson's third stage, from approximately ages 4 to 6, involves the task of acquiring a sense of initiative and responsibility while overcoming a sense of guilt. Having established a sense of trust in the environment, children exhibit very purposeful behavior. They begin to view themselves as "counted-upon" individuals in the family and school. They are required to assume responsibility for self, toys, chores, siblings, and school. Erikson feels that failure to perform this task comes from unnecessary punishment, which causes the child to experience resignation and guilt. These feelings in turn form a basis for giving up, coupled with feelings of unworthiness in adult life.

School students who never mastered this task adequately can be helped by encouraging them to volunteer for special duties, participate in extracurricular activities, and do more than required on assignments. Teachers should encourage the initiation and follow-through of activities, with attendant responsibility.

Industry versus inferiority. Between the ages of 6 and 12, students are functioning in Erikson's fourth stage. The main task there involves acquiring a sense of industry while overcoming a sense of inferiority. School provides a fertile ground for producing feelings of both industry and inferiority.

The sense of industry is developed when the student is provided worthwhile things to do in school, is encouraged, motivated, and supported, and finds much success.

A sense of inferiority will develop if the student is overwhelmed, unsuccessful, punished, or ridiculed. A sense of inferiority can establish a vicious circle: "When I try, I fail, so I won't try and I won't fail." It can also produce diversion from the "feared" activity and verbal physical attacks on the assignment.

Identity versus identity confusion. Erikson's fifth stage brackets the adolescent years between 13 and 16. Its prime task is establishing a sense of identity while overcoming a sense of identity confusion. At this stage the youth is searching for a sense of self-identity. Erikson suggests that the task of settling on a single identity is so hard and anxiety-producing that adolescents often over-identify with heroes and idols. The adolescent is struggling with "trying on many hats" to determine which are comfortable and viable. A resulting behavior in the classroom might show a student arriving at school one day dressed as a popular television personality, only to show up the next day attired as a street gang member. Corresponding to the attire, of course, are the appropriate mannerisms for that particular identity.

Management of the behaviors that occur while the student is attempting to acquire a sense of identity include teacher acceptance, tolerance, and a continual willingness to talk about students' quests, trials, and tribulations.

Sociological and ecological bases of behavior disorder

The sociological view of behavior disorder relates to the social contexts within which the individual is functioning. Components of the theory include labeling, rule breaking and rule following, and the dynamics of forces within the environment (DesJarlais, 1972).

Labeling. Labeling poponents emphasize that one does not become a deviant by breaking rules. One must be labeled a deviant first, then the social expectations that define deviancy become activated (DesJarlais, 1972). For example, students are placed in special education classes only after being labeled. This label then conjurs up myths and specific expectations for the student. Complying with the "self-fulfilling prophecy," the student eventually lives up to the expectations that accompany the label.

Rule-breaking. Labeling theory also defines the relationship between rule-breaking and deviance. Lemert (1962) differentiates between primary and secondary deviance. Primary deviance is the initial breaking of social rules. Secondary deviance is the rule-breaking that occurs *after* one is perceived as a "rule breaker."

Social forces. Social forces include a variety of dynamics that exert themselves on individuals. They come from family, school, peers, and significant others. These forces combine to foster "disorganization." Disorganization is the breakdown of orderly ways of interacting within the community. The community is the place where social-psychological needs are met. In "disorganized areas" social institutions fail to provide for needs.

Ecosystem disturbances. Related to sociological bases of behavior disorder are those called "ecological." Ecology refers to interactions between the environment and the child. The central concept of ecological theory is the "ecosystem" which is defined as the "interaction system comprising living things together with their nonliving habitat" (Evans, 1956).

When students are mainstreamed from special education classes to regular classes, their ecosystem changes. They now must function within a new ecosystem.

Rhodes and Tracy (1972) point out that human ecologists do not speak about emotional disturbance or behavior disorders. They speak of a disturbance within the ecosystem which, paraphrasing Sells (1966), is a mismatch between circumstances and individual, a lack of "goodness-of-fit." Faegans (1972) suggests that the disturbance is not centered within the individual as suggested in biophysical and psychodynamic theories, or even within the environment as behavioral and socio-logical theory suggest. Rather, it is the interaction between the idiosyncratic individual and his unique environment, which together have a high probability of producing a disturbance.

Ramifications for students in the classroom are many. An example would be a hyperactive student placed in a classroom with many distractions, other overly active students, or even a hyperactive teacher. The student needs calm and struc-ture, but the ecosystem provides overstimulation. The result is inevitable dis-turbance.

Behavior management techniques within the classroom focus on restructuring the disturbing situation. This restructuring is coupled with management of stu-dents' surface behaviors. Ultimately, a "goodness-of-fit" will occur between student and environment.

EDUCATIONAL IMPLICATIONS OF THE MODELS

Specific teaching strategies exist that are consistent with the various models of behavior disorder just presented.

Treatment of biophysically caused disorders

Biophysically caused behavior disorders are corrected through communication and planning with parents and other professionals. The most common biophysical behavior disorder is seen in what we call the hyperactive student. Medical man-agement helps correct the behavioral manifestations. So does reducing physical distractions in the classroom. Instruction is improved by structuring assignments so they are clear, with a step-by-step progression. The teacher plays a key role in providing feedback to parents and medical professionals.

Treatment of learned behavior disorders

Implied in the learned behavior view of behavior disorders is that behavior can be both learned and unlearned. Using this view, teachers deal with misbehavior through collecting data, selecting reinforcers, and arranging conseqences. When formalized, these procedures take the form called contingency contracting.

Contingency contracting. Contingency contracting is an agreement developed between teacher and student or parent and student. It specifies behavior to be shown or work to be accomplished. Specific timelines, responsibilities, and con-sequences are included. The contract may be written and signed by all parties. If the contingencies are met as stipulated, the rewards follow. But if the contin-gencies are not met, the stated consequences are implemented or the contract is renegotiated.

Homme (1970) identifies ten basic rules for setting up a contingency contract:

Rule 1. The contract payoff (reward) should be immediate. Initial contracts should demand a small bit of behavior, then a progress check to see whether the behavior was executed to the contract's specifications. Then the reward should be offered immediately.

Rule 2. Initial contracts should call for and reward small approximations. The initial performances requested from the student should be small, simple-to-perform approximations of the final desired performance. For example, a contract to read an entire book would reward the reader chapter by chapter.

Rule 3. Reward frequently with small amounts. It has been demonstrated that frequent, small reinforcements are far more effective than a few large ones.

Rule 4. The contract should call for and reward accomplishments rather than obedience. Reward for accomplishment leads to independence. Reward for obedience leads to continued dependence on the teacher.

Rule 5. Reward the performance after it occurs. To be most effective, rewards have to be given after the performance, not before or during it.

Rule 6. The contract must be fair. The terms of the contract, on both sides, must be of relatively equal weight. A student completing one hundred homework assignments for a comic book is not an example of a fair contract. Nor is "Writing ten spelling words for one comic book" fair.

Rule 7. The terms of the contract must be clear. This means that the terms on both sides of the agreement must be explicitly stated. The "trust me" syndrome of "you do a few problems, and I'll give you something" is not appropriate in contingency contracting. A more clearly stated contract would specify, "Do ten arithmetic problems correctly and you will receive 10 minutes of free time." The student must know how much performance is required, and what to expect as a payoff.

Rule 8. The contract must be honest. An honest contract is one which is carried out immediately, according to the terms specified.

Rule 9. The contract must be positive. An appropriate contract should not say, "I will not do X, if you do Y." The terms of the contract should contribute something to the student's experience, rather than take something away.

Rule 10. Contracting as a method must be used systematically. Perhaps the most difficult thing to learn about the laws of reinforcement is that they go on working all the time. Once contracting has been established as a motivation-management procedure, it should be maintained, and care should be taken not to reward undesirable acts.

Homme concludes by stating that the payoff for teachers "is a kind of joy in their activities, they seem to have a feeling of delight in their willingness and conscious accomplishment and their well deserved rewards. Observing and participating in this kind of learning is, in turn the greatest reward teachers or parents can experience."

Engineered classroom. Contingency management is based on principles of reinforcement. Another system based on reinforcement is the *engineered classroom,* which uses applications of behavior modification. Frank Hewett developed this classroom application for emotionally disturbed learners. His scheme includes behaviors he considers necessary for learning. Kameya (1972), in a reveiw of Hewett's model, suggests that a child can make progress in learning if a suitable educational *task* provides meaningful, appropriate *rewards* in an environment which provides the *structure* necessary for efficient application of resources, and which defines the relevant task-reward contingencies. This triangle of learning could be depicted as in Fig. 3. Hewitt further proposes a hierarchy of educational goals. The hierarchy consists of a student first *attending* to a task, then making a purposeful *response, ordering* subsequent behaviors, *exploring* the nature and parameters of learning, seeking and gaining social *approval, mastering* the task at hand, and receiving intrinsic reinforcement in the form of *achievement.* This hierarchy is depicted in Fig. 4.

Hewett describes appropriate tasks, rewards, and structure in his engineered classroom design (1968). The classroom is divided into three areas:

1. The *attention-response-order* center, which includes activities focusing on participation, direction-following, and task completion.
2. The *exploratory-social* center, which includes science, art, and communication areas. At the center would be a variety of "exploratory" types of equipment such as microscopes, calculators, tape-recorders, videotapes, and other audiovisual machinery. Students would proceed to this area following completion of work at the attention area, or as a reward. Peer involvement and interaction are encouraged in this area.

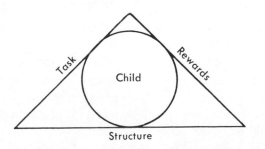

Fig. 3. Hewett learning triangle. (From Frank M. Hewett, The emotionally disturbed child in the classroom. Copyright © 1968 by Allyn and Bacon, Inc., Boston. Reprinted with permission.)

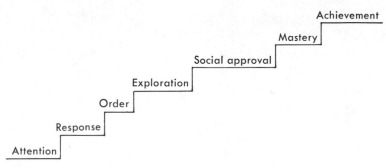

Fig. 4. Hewett hierarchy of learning. (Adapted from Frank M. Hewett, The emotionally disturbed child in the classroom. Copyright © 1968 by Allyn and Bacon, Inc., Boston. Reprinted with permission.)

3. The *mastery and achievement* center includes the desks of the students and teacher as well as "offices" or cubicles.

Kameya (1972) describes a typical engineered classroom. The class is conducted by a teacher and an aide. The day is divided as follows: 2 hours for reading, writing, and arithmetic; 1 hour for exploratory activities; and 1 hour for recess and physical education. The remaining time is used for ancillary activities. Each child picks up a work record card and keeps it through the day. The card can have checkmarks placed on it. These checkmarks are earned for showing good behaviors and working on tasks.

The engineered classroom (Fig. 5) provides a physical structure in which behaviorally disordered students can function. It offers regular rewards and allows students to accumulate points for coming to class, picking up their folders, beginning assignments, maintaining attention on task, completing assignments, and so forth.

Treatment of psychodynamically caused disorders

Behavior disorders that result from psychodynamic factors can be dealt with in ways suggested within each of Erikson's stages.

Stage 1. Trust versus mistrust. Students who did not succeed earlier in this stage need a predictable environment. They need routines and structure. They need a class schedule and they need to know exactly what is expected of them. The teacher should show (model) trusting behavior. As students begin to imitate this behavior they should be rewarded systematically.

Stage 2. Autonomy versus shame and doubt. Decision-making, independent work, and problem-solving are key tasks for students who did not succeed in this stage. In attempts at asserting autonomy, the student must be made aware of consequences of behavior. Limit-setting helps the student discover which be-

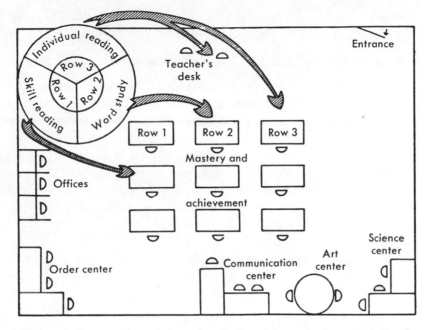

Fig. 5. Floorplan of an engineered classroom. (Adapted from Frank M. Hewett, The emotionally disturbed child in the classroom. Copyright © 1968 by Allyn and Bacon, Inc., Boston. Reprinted with permission.)

haviors are acceptable and which are unacceptable. The teacher must be very consistent in enforcing limits.

Stage 3. Initiative/responsibility versus guilt. The classroom teacher must help the student exhibit purposeful and responsible behavior. Small increments in purposeful behavior can be rewarded systematically. Giving students responsibilities in the classroom will help, as will making assignments that require individual problem solving.

Stage 4. Industry versus inferiority. Students become more industrious as they become more competent. Teachers can help them toward greater competence by providing worthwhile activities that lead to rapid learning. Furthermore, they can encourage leadership with peers, emulation of selected models, involvement in sports and other physical activities, and involvement with peer groups, gangs, clubs, and secret societies.

Stage 5. Identity versus identity confusion. Physical and psychological changes prompt adolescents to ask the question of identity: "Who am I?" Allowing the student to explore multiple aspects of self with and through others will be helpful and satisfying. It will provide valuable information for piecing the many "selves" into one. Providing opportunities in the classroom to come into contact with others, personally or vicariously, will broaden selection from which the student will choose the components of personal identity.

Treatment of socially and ecologically caused disorders

Behavior disorders that result from ecological factors suggest changes in the interaction between student and classroom environment. One of the best conceived programs for improving these interactions is Self-Enhancing Education, proposed by Randolph and Howe (1966).

Self-Enhancing Education. Self-Enhancing Education is designed to provide two-way communication, involvement of the student, stronger motivation, higher achievement, socially productive behaviors, and expanded self-esteem. It is also intended to modify perceptions of teachers and pupils so they are more able to accept individual differences. This approach should help the child develop the skills necessary for self-direction and self-control.

Randolph and Howe's twelve processes. Randolph and Howe propose twelve specific processes for raising self-esteem and increasing motivation and achievement:

1. Problem solving
2. Self-management
3. Changing negative reflections to positive images
4. Building bonds of trust
5. Setting limits and expectations
6. Freeing and channeling energy
7. Overcoming unproductive repetitive behavior
8. Changing tattling to reporting
9. Developing physical competencies
10. Making success inevitable
11. Self-evaluation
12. Breaking curriculum barriers

These twelve processes enhance interactions between the teacher and learner. They provide a cooperative learning atmosphere that results in improved confidence, self-direction, and self-esteem.

BEHAVIORAL IMPLICATIONS OF THE MODELS

All behavior springs from an underlying purpose. That is another way of saying that all behavior is directed toward some goal. Teachers do not always know what students' goals are; students do not always know, either. That makes their behavior difficult to understand at times.

Goals of misbehavior

Dreikers and Grey (1972) have concluded that student behavior in all its myriad forms is really directed at only four different goals: *attention, revenge, power,* and *warding off inadequacy.*

Attention. Attention is a popular goal for everyone. All individuals in some way seek attention and consequently engage in attention-getting behaviors. In classrooms it is evident that some students seek and gain attention in positive ways, while others do so in negative ways. Attention-getting behaviors include much "fronting behavior," excessive showing off, clowning, and being highly interruptive. Other forms of attention-getting include pencil-tapping, tapping fingers on the desk, wandering around the classroom, and bashfulness.

Classroom teachers' reactions to these behaviors usually show annoyance. They feel that too much of their time is spent reminding students to do their work. When they respond, however, the attention-getting ploy has worked.

Behavior management involves ignoring the negative acts, or suppressing them if they are outrageous. Meanwhile, attention should be given in adequate amounts when appropriate behavior is shown.

Revenge. Revenge is often sought when students feel slighted or hurt. They want to get even; they feel they can do so by misbehaving. Students "getting even" with other students on the playground or after school occurs frequently. Teachers returning to classrooms may find pencil shavings scattered on the desk, glue on the blotters, and tacks on the chair. Other revenge behaviors include stealing, viciousness, defiance, and sullenness. The resulting teacher reaction is hurt, outrage, even retaliation.

Behavioral interventions attempt to prevent hurts from occurring. Manners, courtesy, and gentleness are practiced by teacher and students alike. Consequences rather than punishments are applied for strong misbehavior. Peer group encouragement for good behavior is stressed. Reality statements such as "You must have been really mad at me to have put tacks on my chair" can be made. The simple airing of the act is a relief to the student who is carrying the fear of being found out.

Power. Power seeking is a reality in all walks of life. In the classroom, power rightly belongs to the teacher. Students generally accept that, so long as the power is exercised consistently and fairly. Occasionally, however, students will vie with the teacher for power. Power struggles typically involve arguing, bossiness, temper tantrums, lying, disobedience, destruction of work, and defiance.

Management techniques focus on problem-solving with the student, providing choices, specifying consequences to behaviors, and following through consistently. The student should be treated with respect, allowed face-saving escapes from the confrontation, and subsequently treated as if nothing had happened.

Warding off inadequacy. Warding off inadequacy is the true goal of much of the behavior of each of us every day. Students will do almost anything to avoid feelings of inadequacy and inferiority. Yet their escape behaviors often wind up as feelings of hopelessness, "stupid actions," and even worse, inferiority complexes. To avoid feelings of inadequacy, students will give up easily, state that they cannot do the work, or even get sick on the spot.

Behavior management takes care to see that students are given sufficiently easy tasks with strong support. Encouragement, prompting, task assistance, and peer support enhance feelings of worthiness, as do stressing the students' strength and giving praise when genuine attempts are made.

SUMMARY

The term "behavior disorder" is hard to define. Different classrooms show a wide range of behavior. Different teachers tolerate different behaviors.

Exhibited behaviors within their environmental and developmental context can be analyzed. Frequency, duration, degree of debilitation, and the source of the problem provide guidelines for referral and behavioral intervention. Different authorities see behavior rising from biophysical, behavioral, psychodynamic, sociological, and ecological causes. These causes, when seen in conjunction with frequency, duration, degree, and source, provide a framework for dealing with behaviorally disordered students.

The educational implications for behavior-disordered students suggest a range of specific behavior management techniques.

Many of these techniques were discussed, such as behavior modification, success structuring, and the removal of disruptive influences. It helps to recognize the major goals of misbehavior, which are attention, revenge, power, and warding off inadequacy. When the cause of misbehavior can be determined, an appropriate and consistent intervention can follow.

SUGGESTED ACTIVITIES

1. Make individual lists of the kinds of behaviors you would find hardest to accept from students. Rank the behaviors in order. Compare them in class.
2. Discuss positive steps you could take for dealing with the misbehaviors. Take into account their possible sources.
3. Discuss the circumstances under which you would tolerate certain kinds of misbehavior.

Under what circumstances would you squelch the misbehavior immediately?

4. Examine Erikson's stages. Which of the five included was most difficult for you to resolve? How have you remained affected by it?
5. Describe all the factors in the classroom ecosystem you can think of that might contribute to misbehavior. How could you change those factors for the better?

SUGGESTED READINGS

American Psychiatric Association: Diagnostic and statistical manual of mental disorders, ed. 2, DSM-II, Washington, D.C., 1968, American Psychiatric Association.

Anderson, C. M.: Classroom activities for modifying misbehavior in children, New York, 1974, The Center for Applied Research in Education, Inc.

Axline, V.: Play therapy, Boston, 1947, Houghton Mifflin Co.

Ayllon, T., and Roberts, M. D.: Eliminating discipline problems by strengthening academic performance, J. Applied Behavior Analysis 7:71-76, 1974.

Bandura, A., and Walters, R. H.: Social learning and personality development, New York, 1963, Holt, Rinehart & Winston.

Bettelheim, B.: Love is not enough, New York, 1950, Macmillan Publishing Co., Inc.

Bettelheim, B.: Truants from life; the rehabilitation of the educable child, Glencoe, IL, 1955, The Free Press.

Blackham, G.: The deviant child in the classroom, Belmont, CA, 1967, Wadsworth Publishing Co., Inc.

Bower, E. M.: Early identification of emotionally handicapped children in school, ed. 2, Springfield, IL, 1969, Charles C Thomas, Publisher.

Bower, E., and Lambert, R.: In-school screening of children with emotional handicaps. In Long, N., Morse, W., and Newman, R., editors: Conflict in the classroom, Belmont, CA, 1976, Wadsworth Publishing Company, Inc.

Burbaum, E.: Troubled children in a troubled world, New York, 1970, International Universities Press.

Burke, D.: Counter theoretical interventions in emotional disturbance. In Rhodes, W. C., and Tracy, M. L., editors: A study of child variance. Vol. III, Interventions, Ann Arbor, 1973, University of Michigan Press.

Buss, A.: Psychopathology, New York, 1966, John Wiley & Sons, Inc.

Caldwell, B. M.: The rationale for early intervention, Exceptional Child. 36:717-727, 1970.

Catterall, C. D.: Taxonomy of prescriptive interventions, J. School Psychol. 8:5-12, 1970.

Clarizo, H. F., and McCoy, G. F.: Behavior disorders in children, New York, 1970, Thomas Y. Crowell Company, Inc.

Cohen, D. H., and Stern, V.: Observing and recording the behavior of young children, New York, 1958, Columbia University Teachers College.

Coloroso, B.: Strategies for working with troubled students. In Gearheart, B. R., and Weishahn, N. M., editors: The handicapped child in the regular classroom, St. Louis, 1976, The C. V. Mosby Company.

Cooper, J. O.: Measurement and analysis of behavioral techniques, Columbus, OH, 1974, Charles E. Merrill Publishing Co.

Coopersmith, S.: The antecedents of self-esteem, San Francisco, 1967, Freeman.

Csapo, M. G.: Utilization of normal peers as behavior change agents for reducing the inappropriate behavior of emotionally disturbed children in regular classroom environments, Dissertation Abstracts International 32:4, 1971.

DesJarlais, D. C.: Mental illness as social deviance. In Rhodes, W. C., and Tracy, M. L., editors: A study of child variance, volume I: conceptual models, Ann Arbor, 1972, The University of Michigan Press.

Despert, J. L.: The emotionally disturbed child—then and now, New York, 1965, Brunner/Mazel, Inc.

Dreikurs, R., and Grey, L.: Discipline without tears, New York, 1972, Hawthorne Publishing Company.

Dupont, H., editor: Educating emotionally disturbed children: readings, New York, 1969, Holt, Rinehart & Winston.

Easson, W. M.: The severely disturbed adolescent, New York, 1969, International Universities Press.

Erikson, E.: Childhood and society, New York, 1950, W. W. Norton & Company, Inc.

Erikson, E.: Identity, youth and crisis, New York, 1968, W. W. Norton & Company, Inc.

Evans, F. C.: Ecosystem as the basic unit in ecology, Science 123:1127-1128, 1956.

Faas, L. A., editor: The emotionally disturbed child; a book of readings, Springfield, IL, 1970, Charles C Thomas, Publisher.

Fagen, S. A., and Hill, J. M.: Behavior management: a competency-based manual for in-service training, Washington, D.C., 1977, Psychoeducational Resources, Inc.

Fagen, S. A., Long, N. J., and Stevens, D. J.: Teaching children self-control, Columbus, OH, 1975, Charles E. Merrill Publishing Company.

Feagans, L.: Ecological theory as a model for constructing a theory of emotional disturbance. In Rhodes, W. C., and Tracy, M. L., editors: A study of child variance: volume I: conceptual models, Ann Arbor, 1972, The University of Michigan Press.

Fink, A. H.: Teacher-pupil interaction in classes for emotionally handicapped, Exceptional Child. 38:469-474, 1972.

Gallagher, P. A.: Teaching students with behavior disorders: techniques for classroom instruction, Denver, 1979, Love Publishing Company.

Grossman, H.: Nine rotten lousy kids, New York, 1972, Holt, Rinehart & Winston.

Hammer, M.: Teachers' guide to the detection of emotional disturbance in the elementary school child, J. Learning Disabil. 3:29-31, 1970.

Haring, N. G., and Phillips, E. L.: Educating emotionally disturbed children, New York, 1962, McGraw-Hill Book Co.

Hewett, F. M.: A hierarchy of competencies for teachers of emotionally handicapped children, Exceptional Child. 33:7-11, 1966.

Hewett, F. M.: Exceptional engineering with emotionally disturbed children, Exceptional Child. 33:459-467, 1967.

Hewett, F. M.: The emotionally disturbed child in the classroom, Boston, 1968, Allyn & Bacon, Inc.

Hewett, F. M.: Educational programs for children with behavior disorder. In Quay, H. C., and Werry, J. S., editors: Psychopathological disorders of children, New York, 1972, John Wiley & Sons, Inc.

Hobbs, N.: Helping the disturbed child: psychological and ecological strategies, Am. Psychol. 21:1105-1115, 1966.

Hobbs, N.: The re-education of emotionally disturbed children. In Bower, E. M., and Hollister, W. G., editors: Behavioral science frontiers in education, New York, 1967, John Wiley & Sons, Inc.

Homme, L.: How to use contingency contracting in the classroom, Champaign, IL, 1970, Research Press.

Hunter, M.: Reinforcement theory for teachers, El Segundo, CA, 1967, Theory into Practice Publications.

Kameya, L. I.: Behavioral interventions in emotional disturbance. In Rhodes, W. C., and Tracy, M. L., editors: A study of child variance: volume II: interventions, Ann Arbor, 1972, The University of Michigan Press.

Kanner, L.: Emotionally disturbed children: a historical review, Child Dev. 33:97-102, 1962.

Kauffman, J.: Characteristics of children's behavior disorders, Columbus, OH, 1972, Charles E. Merrill Publishing Co.

Kessler, J. W.: Psychopathology of childhood, Englewood Cliffs, NJ, 1966, Prentice-Hall, Inc.

Knoblock, P.: Open education for emotionally disturbed children, Exceptional Child. 39:358-366, 1973.

Knoblock, P.: Critical factors influencing educational programming for disturbed children. In Jones, R. L., editor: Programs and issues in the education of exceptional children, Boston, 1971, Houghton Mifflin Co.

Knoblock, P., editor: Intervention approaches in educating emotionally disturbed children, Syracuse, NY, 1966, Syracuse University Press.

LaBenne, W.: Differential diagnosis and psychoeducational treatment for the emotionally disturbed, Psychol. School 4:366-370, 1967.

Ledermen, J.: Anger in the rocking chair; gestalt awareness with children, New York, 1969, McGraw-Hill Book Co.

Lemert, E.: Paranoia and the dynamics of exclusion, Sociometry 25:2-20, 1962.

Long, L., Morse, W. C., and Newman, R.: Conflict in the classroom; the education of emotionally disturbed children, Belmont, CA, 1976, Wadsworth Publishing Co., Inc.

Long, N. J., Alpher, R., Butt, F., and Cully, M.: Helping children to cope with feelings, Childhood Educ. 45:367-372, 1969.

Maes, W. R.: Identification of emotionally disturbed elementary school children, Exceptional Child. 32:607-609, 1966.

Malian, I. M.: Regular classroom teachers and

administrators and children with exceptional needs, Sacramento, 1979, California State Department of Education.

Meichenbaum, D. H., and Goodman, J.: Training impulsive children to talk to themselves, J. Abnorm. Psychol. **77**:115-126, 1971.

Morse, W. C., Cutler, R. L., and Fink, A. H.: Public school classes for the emotionally disturbed; a research analysis, Washington, D.C., 1964, The Council for Exceptional Children.

Moustakas, C. E.: Children in play therapy, New York, 1953, McGraw-Hill Book Co.

Nelson, C. M.: Techniques for screening conduct disturbed children, Exceptional Child. **37**:501-507, 1971.

Patterson, G.: An empirical approach to the classification of disturbed children, J. Clin. Psychol. **20**:326-337, 1964.

Peterson, D. R., Becker, W. C., Shoemaker, D. J., Luria, Z., and Hellmer, L. A.: Child behavior problems and parental attitudes, Child Dev. **32**:151-162, 1961.

Quay, H. C.: Children's behavior disorders; selected readings, Princeton, NJ, 1968, Van Nostrand Reinhold Co.

Quay, H. C., Morse, W. C., and Cutler, R. L.: Personality patterns of pupils in special classes for the emotionally disturbed, Exceptional Child. **32**:297-301, 1966.

Randolph, N., and Howe, W.: A program to motivate learners: self enhancing education, Palo Alto, CA, 1966, Educational Development Corporation.

Redl, F.: When we deal with children, New York, 1966, The Free Press.

Redl, F.: The concept of a therapeutic milieu, Amer. J. Orthopsychiatry **29**:721-736, 1959.

Redl, F., and Wineman, D.: Children who hate, New York, 1951, The Free Press.

Redl, F., and Wineman, D.: Controls from within, New York, 1952, The Free Press.

Reinert, H. R.: Children in conflict: educational strategies for the emotionally disturbed and behaviorally disordered, St. Louis, 1976, The C. V. Mosby Co.

Rhodes, W. C.: A community participation analysis of emotional disturbance, Exceptional Child. **36**(5):309-314, 1970.

Rhodes, W. C.: The disturbing child: a problem of ecological management, Exceptional Child. **33**(7):449-455, 1967.

Rhodes, W. C., and Tracy, M. L.: A study of child variance: volume I: conceptual models, Ann Arbor, 1972, The Universty of Michigan Press.

Rhodes, W. C., and Tracy, M. L.: A study of child variance: volume II: interventions, Ann Arbor, 1972, University of Michigan Press.

Rosenthal, R., and Jacobson, L.: Pygmalion in the classroom, New York, 1968, Holt, Rinehart & Winston.

Ross, A. O.: Psychological disorders of children, New York, 1974, McGraw-Hill Book Co.

Rubin, R., and Balow, B.: Learning and behavior disorders; a longitudinal study, Exceptional Child. **38**:293-299, 1971.

Russ, D. F.: A review of learning and behavior theory as it relates to emotional disturbance in children. In Rhodes, W. C., and Tracy, M. L., editors: A study of child variance: volume I: conceptual models, Ann Arbor, 1972, University of Michigan Press.

Sagor, M.: Biological bases of childhood behavior disorders. In Rhodes, W. C., and Tracy, M. L., editors: A study of child variance: volume I: conceptual models, Ann Arbor, 1972, The University of Michigan Press.

Saunders, B. T., editor: Approaches with emotionally disturbed children, New York, 1974, Exposition Press, Inc.

Sells, S. B.: Ecology and the science of psychology, Multivariate Behav. Res. **1**(2):131-141, 1966.

Shea, T. M.: Teaching children and youth with behavior disorders, St. Louis, 1978, The C. V. Mosby Co.

Thomas, E. C.: Emotionally disturbed children and their school related perceptions, Exceptional Child. **36**:623-624, 1970.

Vacc, N.: Long term effects of special class intervention for emotionally disturbed children, Exceptional Child. **39**:15-22, 1972.

Vorrath, H. H., and Brendtro, L. K.: Positive peer culture, Chicago, 1974, Aldine Publishing Co.

Weissman, H. W.: Implications for the education of children with emotional and social disturbances, J. Learning Disabil. **3**:502-508, 1970.

Whelan, R. J.: The emotionally disturbed. In Meyen, E. L., editor: Exceptional children and youth: an introduction, Denver, 1978, Love Publishing Company.

Whelan, R. J.: In Kauffman, J. M., and Lewis, C. D., editors: Teaching children with behavior disorders: personal perspectives, Columbus, OH, 1974, Charles E. Merrill Publishing Co.

Whelan, R. J.: The relevance of behavior modification procedures for teachers of emotionally disturbed children. In Knoblock, P., editor: Intervention approaches in educating emotionally disturbed children, Syracuse, NY, 1966, Syracuse University Press.

CHAPTER 8

Teaching students with learning disabilities

Public Law 94-142 describes specific learning disability as "A disorder in one or more of the basic psychological processes involved in understanding or in using language—spoken or written—which may manifest itself in an impaired ability to listen, think, speak, read, write, spell or do mathematical calculations."

You can see that the term refers to difficulties in processing language intellectually. It does not include learning problems which result from visual, hearing, or motor handicaps, emotional disturbance, mental retardation, or environmental, cultural, or economic disadvantages. To be classified as learning disabled in some states, students must display the following conditions: (1) failure to achieve commensurate with their age and ability levels in at least one of the academic areas listed below; *and* (2) show an association between that academic deficit and at least one of the conditions listed under "learning handicap."

A. Areas of *academic* deficit:
   1. Reading, specifically word recognition, including word attack skills and comprehension, including listening comprehension.
   2. Mathematics, specifically reasoning and calculation.
   3. Written expression.
B. Areas of *learning* handicap:
   1. Sensory motor, specifically auditory processing, visual processing, and haptic (sense of touch) processing.
   2. Perceptual motor, specifically fine motor, and gross motor development.
   3. Behavioral problems, with attention to the severity of the problem as well as the frequency, duration, and nature of the disruptive behavior.
   4. Limited intellectual functioning, with attention to the discrepancy between present level and that expected for the student's age.

Classroom teachers regularly have experience working with children whose achievement is far below what they seem capable of. Such students challenge and frustrate teachers, especially those who do not recognize the nature of learning disability. It is difficult to pinpoint their problems. The students may have difficulty in one or two, but not all, subject areas. The pattern of their academic difficulties may vary. These difficulties often cause teachers to consider such students "underachievers," "clumsy," "short attention spans," "hyperactive," "daydreamers," "unmotivated," "messy," "poor or low self-concept," "reluctant learners," "don't remember," "bad handwriters," and, of course, "lazy." These descriptors mask specific types of learning disabilities, which may be (1) perceptual processing; (2) visual perception, including figure-ground discrimination and visual discrimination; (3) auditory perception; (4) spoken language; (5) expressive language; (6) reading disabilities; (7) arithmetic disabilities; and (8) written language disabilities. The natures of these different disabilities, together with educational and behavioral manifestations, are described in the following sections.

PERCEPTUAL PROCESSING

The Dictionary of Special Education and Rehabilitation defines perception as an "awareness of one's environment through sensory stimulation. [It] is an important part of cognition and understanding. A child who has faulty perception may have difficulty in learning." Perceptual disorders suggest "difficulties or deficiencies in using the sense of sight, touch, smell, taste, or hearing to correctly recognize the various objects or situations within the environment. Such disorders may become apparent in a student's poor performance in activities such as drawing, writing, and recognizing forms, sizes, or shapes" (Kelly and Vergason 1978).

VISUAL PERCEPTION

Visual perception can strongly affect behavior and classroom learning. It is the process by which objects and situations are apprehended by the mind, through the mechanics of the eye. Considerable research has explored the relationship of visual perception to the process of reading. It has been found that the skills of visual perception are strongly related to reading achievement and to a lesser extent to general test intelligence.

Educational manifestation

Various types of visual perception problems affect learning in the classroom. For example, form perception, or the ability to perceive shapes and sizes, affects word recognition. If a student cannot perceive differences in the shapes of letters and words, difficulty in reading will occur. This difficulty also shows itself in handwriting. The formation of letters, consistency in size, and upper and lower levels of letters may be affected. Mathematical calculations may be confusing for the student when

$$1 + 2 \qquad \text{and} \qquad \begin{array}{r} 1 \\ + 2 \\ \hline \end{array}$$

are perceived as different problems.

Figure-ground discrimination. Figure-ground discrimination consists of the ability to distinguish and focus upon selected foreground figures and screen out irrelevant stimuli in the background. This difficulty manifests itself in failure to focus on the essential elements of problems and situations. Students have difficulty in following along in reading activities and in pinpointing lines in specific paragraphs or specific words within lines. Other behavioral manifestations may include inattentiveness and disorganization, since attention switches from one distraction to another.

Visual discrimination. Kelley and Vergason (1978) define visual discrimination as "one's ability to use the sense of sight to determine whether things appear to be the same or different." Difficulties in visual discrimination affect reading most strongly. Students who cannot discriminate similarities and differences in letters, words, and geometric forms will experience difficulty and frustration in all aspects of learning.

Educational implications

The teacher must use materials and assignments that circumvent or accommodate the visual weaknesses; for example, rather than presenting twenty items or problems, present two or three at a time. This will help the student and perceive consistency in the assignment. These short-term instructional revisions can also be provided through commercially prepared materials available from publishers.

Behavioral implications

When students are frustrated, they misbehave. Frustration can be avoided by capitalizing on students' areas of strength. For example, if a student is a good listener or can carry out verbal directions well, the teacher can use auditory rather than visual materials. This is an example of the educational principle of teaching through the strength areas to remediate the weak areas.

AUDITORY PERCEPTION

Auditory perception involves the central processing of sounds. Individuals with auditory perceptual difficulties may hear perfectly well, that is, their ears may function perfectly, but still be unable to correctly interpret what is heard. Students reflect these disabilities in many ways. They may be unable to associate a sound with what makes it. They may be unable to blend isolated sounds into complete words. They may be unable to discriminate between sounds and between spoken words. They may not perceive that a series of words constitutes a sentence or command. They may have difficulty selecting the word that keys an appropriate response. They may be unable to make any sense of what they hear. They may have poor auditory memory. All these effects make it difficult for the student to respond in a manner consistent with the intended communication.

Educational implications

Students with auditory perceptual difficulties will have trouble selecting and attending to relevant auditory stimuli. They will have difficulty focusing their attention on the teacher's directions, particularly if the classroom is noisy or distracting. Their inability to hear similarities and differences in sounds causes confusion in carrying out directions. In accordance with the principle of teaching to strength, teachers can use visual or behavioral procedures for instructing and giving directions.

Behavioral implications

Students with auditory perception problems have trouble following verbal directions. Coupled with their disability one often finds an auditory memory deficit. The student may remember only one of a series of verbal directions, or perhaps through confusion, none. This condition is especially noticeable in students at the secondary school level. Their failure to comply with auditory commands is often seen as antisocial or defiant behavior.

Teachers can do several things to help these students learn, while reducing the incidence of behavior problems. Giving instructions in a specific order and asking the student to follow them one by one provides not only sequencing activities, but gives the instructor an informal check as to the patterning of difficulties. For example, does the student follow only the first direction given, the first heard? Or does he/she follow the last direction given, the last heard? Verbal directions and instructions can be reinforced with written directions. Tape recorders can be used to play back initial instructions. They can be used by the student to record the sequence of directions and activities that were carried out. This could provide, upon playback, a documentation of consistency or inconsistency in following through on assignments. Always include auditory discrimination activities, such as asking if "tap and cap" are the same or different; these activities can be incorporated into instructional sessions.

RECEIVING SPOKEN LANGUAGE

This section describes a separate aspect of auditory perception—the ability to receive and understand spoken language. Individuals with difficulties in this area usually hear what is said, but they are unable to comprehend the meaning of what they have heard.

Educational implications

The understanding of words is the basis for most academic work. Students with receptive language problems respond best to simple, concrete words. These words can be related to their classroom and home experiences. They are not as easily misinterpreted as are abstract, ambiguous words.

Behavioral implications

Miscommunications within auditory receptive language occur regularly between teacher and student. What the teacher intends to communicate becomes something else for the student. Idioms and colloquialisms add to ambiguity and confusion. For example, the teacher may say "Put your pens and pencils up." The students could have pens and pencils in the air by the time the teacher was ready to go on to the next command. Teachers attempting to speed the class along might be heard saying "Step on it," at which point assignments may be "footprinted." If by chance, in a moment of desperation, a teacher should exclaim, "I'm so mad I could hit the ceiling" it would not be inconsistent to have students look toward the ceiling in anticipation of the flight. Directions that teachers consider very specific may be very general and abstract to the student.

To avoid receptive language difficulties as well as miscommunication and misinterpretation, teachers can use activities that involve:

1. Simple commands and instructions
2. Analyzing, with the student, the task to be completed
3. Checking out the student's interpretation of what *was* actually intended
4. Rephrasing what was said
5. Modeling, to show in behavioral terms what is intended

USING EXPRESSIVE LANGUAGE

Some students are poor at using spoken language as a means of communication; this disability is usually categorized as an expressive language disorder. Students with difficulties in expressive language hear and understand what is said to them, but they have problems in planning thoughts or organizing words and phrases to express those thoughts

Educational implications

A speech clinician will usually be the multidisciplinary team member who will have primary responsibilities for students with specific and severe language and speech difficulties. That person will suggest four general approaches for implementing regular classroom work with expressive disorders.

1. The phonetic approach to language, which stresses a step-by-step system of involving a student with letter identification, sound identification, syllable sounds, words, phrases, and ultimately sentence expression.
2. Auditory perception activities to develop, strengthen, and remediate areas of weakness.
3. The concept formation approach, in which specific meanings, concepts, ideas, and communications are emphasized. This approach focuses on daily experiences and practical communication patterns.
4. The grammatical approach, which seeks to improve word usage and basic sentence structure and transformations.

Behavioral implications

Expressive language difficulties frustrate students and teachers alike. However, there are specific tactics that teachers can use to reduce this frustration. Wood (1969) suggests the following measures.

1. Work with the students at their own level of speech and language.
2. Allow the students to say what they are attempting to say without being too specific or demanding.
3. Translate gestures into simple concrete words.
4. Allow the students to show you what they mean, if unable to express ideas verbally.
5. Always give students the feeling that you are interested in what they are attempting to say.
6. Work from the concrete to the abstract.
7. Capitalize on the student's strengths.
8. Utilize manipulative objects initially in working with a student who has limited speech.
9. Use words natural to each student's own environment.
10. Keep careful records of students' progress.

READING DISABILITIES

Reading is considered very important in school, so that important that reading difficulties cause considerable alarm. Reading permeates all aspects of education and daily life. Despite our best efforts, including attempts at utilizing "international" symbols for words and ideas, a 1974 University of Texas Research Study found that 23 million Americans were functionally illiterate. A variety of terms have been used in the literature to describe individuals with reading disabilities. Such words as "dyslexic," "word blind," "minimal brain disorder," and even "retarded" have been labels for students exhibiting specific reading difficulties.

There are various types of reading disabilities. As mentioned before, visual and auditory discrimination affect a student's ability to read orally and silently. For example, visual perception may affect the ability of the reader to differentiate between letters such as b, p, q, g, d, e, c, o, m, n, u, and v. Visual perception difficulties cause the student to see a different letter and possibly a different word than what is printed. Further confusion occurs when capital letters E, F, C, G, O, P, T, W, V, and U are introduced, as well as the cursive letters q, g, p, d, e, c, o, m, and n. Students just learning capital letters and the cursive form of writing may view them as an entirely different alphabet from what they already know to exist. Teachers can clear up this confusion through specific remedial activities that point out positioning of letters, give clues to letter identification, and help with configuration recognition.

The role of auditory discrimination is important in differentiating the spoken word and sound blending in oral reading. Students experiencing auditory discrimination difficulties would be unable to differentiate between the words beg-bug, pit-pet, and pin-pen. These same students, if exhibiting visual perception problems would consider written words beg-bag, pit-pet, and pin-pen the same. Auditory cues and attention skills are included in remedial programs for these learners. Another type of disability that follows closely is sound blending, the ability to bring individual sounds together to form a complete word. An example would be the sounds of s, a, and t to form the total word *sat*. Again, the ramifications of the previous disabilities, visual perception and auditory discrimination, are apparent in the ability to blend sounds. Many remedial reading approaches suggest sound blending and sound separation activities to strengthen students' weak areas. A caution to be stressed here is that some children have separated speech sounds so distinctly that it is especially difficult for them to coordinate the sounds into complete and meaningful words.

Letter and word reversals have served as key indicators for additional diagnosing, testing, assessing, and referring of students suspected to have specific learning disabilities. Backward formation of letters and rotated or inverted letters also indicate possible learning disability. At a very young age, preschool through early first grade, reversals do not necessarily indicate a specific learning disability. However, it is important to observe and rate the frequency of reversals, as well as any other patterns of inversions or rotations. If they persist, they will require special attention. Letters most often reversed, inverted, or rotated include b, d, p, q, m, u, n, w, m, and n. Words most often reversed are:

was	saw	rat	tar	cop	poc
tub	but	pin	nip	pets	step
star	rats	pan	nap	lap	pal

Comprehension difficulties also present problems. Comprehension skills are paramount in reading. Disability in comprehension means the inability to understand what is read in printed form. This inability may lie in both literal and interpretive comprehension. Even when students have a flow to their reading, comprehension is not assured. Nila Banton-Smith provides a good example of how one student comprehended the Gettysburg Address:

> Fourscore (a score is what we have after a baseball game is played) and seven years ago our forefathers (this must mean our own and our stepfathers) brought forth on this continent (that's North America—we had that in social studies) a new nation (that's America or the United States, I think), conceived (I wonder what that means?) in liberty (that's what a sailor gets), and dedicated (that's what they did to the building on

the corner) to the proposition (that's what they voted on to give the teachers more money) that all men (what about the women?) are created (we had something about that at Sunday School) equal (we use that in arithmetic problems). [The remainder of the Address was equally garbled in this student's mind.]

This boy could pronounce the words; he could memorize this address and recite it with his classmates; but because of his limited understanding of meanings the entire selection was to him more or less just a confused jumble of words. Its deep significance was lost.

Comprehension is related to both understanding and memory. Difficulty in recalling learned information will affect most aspects of school work. The frustration of teachers will be expressed in statements such as, "He knew it yesterday." "We worked on it this morning, and this afternoon it's just as if we never went through it."

Educational implications

Poor reading and poor self-concept go hand in hand; therefore it is important to pay great attention to self-concept enhancement when working with reading-disabled students. Student success should be maximized in reading skills attainment. It should be coupled with positive reinforcement. Reading based on life experiences is rewarding to students. They read about experiences that they have actually been involved in. The teacher copies the experiences dictated by the student. That copy becomes the book the student uses for instruction.

Commercially produced reading materials are also available in a wide variety of interest areas and reading levels.

Behavioral implications

The process of reading has various social and emotional aspects associated with it. Everyone is supposed to be able to read. The emotions are magnified when the student has to read out loud. Risks are high for showing oneself inferior. Reading out loud subjects one to open scrutiny. No eraser can hide or correct errors that are made.

Students who are experiencing specific reading disabilities will not want to exhibit them in class. The will not volunteer to read. They will withdraw or exhibit avoidance behaviors when they are expected to read. Withdrawal may take the form of maintaining a low profile, not asking questions, or even slumping down at the desk. Avoidance may be similar to withdrawal, yet students avoiding reading may maintain a high profile and bombard the teacher with visions of how "busy" they are. They may ask many questions on a variety of topics. They may attempt to manipulate other students in hopes of getting out of reading.

ARITHMETIC DISABILITIES

Disabilities in the area of mathematics have not been as thoroughly studied and researched as have other areas of learning disability. This neglect results in part from the belief among teachers and parents that arithmetic is not as important to academic or social success as are reading and language. Yet teachers recognize the relationship of specific arithmetic disabilities to other areas of classroom learning. Disabilities in the areas of memory, written language, spatial relations, directionality, and left-right orientation all seem to be involved in the difficulties a student experiences in mathematical learning. As a case in point, Elizabeth Freidus, director of Gateway School, utilized the formation of numerals to facilitate reading readiness in young children and as a remedial approach with older children exhibiting learning disabilities.

Various types of arithmetic disabilities have been noted. Malian and Doyle (1977), in a presentation to the International Association of Children with Learning Disabilities, discussed a diagnostic and remedial approach to arithmetic disabilities. First, diagnosis is used to provide a profile of disabilities for individual students. Through the pinpointing of areas of weakness and strength, specific remedial activities can be applied. Arithmetic remediation uses as its vehicle the specific areas of strength demonstrated by the student. If, for example, a student's best learning modality is visual, then the remedial activities will be couched in the visual domain.

Second, the remediation activities are kept consistent with the procedures used in diagnosis. This format facilitates monitoring, follow-up, and individualized curriculum development.

Educational implications

Instruction for students with arithmetic disabilities encompasses ten concept-skill clusters. The ten clusters are: classification; comparison; ordinal concepts; one-to-one correspondence; amount recognition; counting and language; visual memory; auditory memory; spatial relations; and directionality.

Classification is sorting according to any given criterion. Within this cluster the ability to match, and to classify by size, shape, amount, and color should be present. Difficulties within this area may also result from visual perceptional disabilities.

Comparison is also a basic intellectual function that involves amount, size, and shape. Comparisons allow learners to perceive relations in quantity and degree. Inability to compare accurately hinders the learning of basic mathematical concepts.

Ordinal concepts involves putting items in numerical order. The relation of first, second, third, etc., is important to mathematical concepts.

Amount recognition and *counting and language* involve the ability to recognize quantities presented to a student, to ascertain quickly if amounts vary, and to put numerical concepts into spoken language.

One-to-one correspondence involves the pairings of items, regardless of their physical locations. It is essential for basic number operations of addition, subtraction, multiplication, and division.

Visual memory and *auditory memory* are abilities required for all mathematical functions. They must be strengthened in the student who has learning problems in math.

Additional abilities related to specific arithmetic disabilities are *spatial orientation* and *directional orientation*. The process of teaching multiplication of two-digit number exemplifies the difficulties within this area. In teaching this function the student must first multiply right column bottom to top, the diagonally bottom right with top left, following the place holder "zero" being placed in an additional column on the calculations. The multiplication process then proceeds from bottom left to top right and bottom left to top left. Then the rules of addition from right to left prevail.

$$
\begin{array}{r}
54 \\
\times\ 78\ \uparrow \\
\hline
432 \\
3780 \leftarrow \\
\hline
4212 \\
\hline
\end{array}
$$

Students with perceptual difficulties and problems with space and direction (right-left/ up-down/ sideways) will experience much frustration in this function. In addition, organizational difficulties and coordination problems (fine motor, gross motor) will compound the problem.

Behavioral implications

Frustration manifests itself in behavioral problems among students having difficulty in math. However, as more teachers become interested in the process of learning as well as its end-product, specific problems within mathematical functions are being isolated and remediated. Learning difficulties with facts and operations are being specified, and effective teaching strategies are being developed for dealing with them.

WRITTEN LANGUAGE DISABILITIES

For centuries, the mark of a "literate" person has been the ability to read and write, at least write one's name. This emphasis on writing has never diminished. That has been amply shown in media reports about "Why Johnny can't read," and "Why Suzy can't write."

Everyone agrees on the importance of writing, but experts disagree on the age at which a child should be introduced to formal written language. Early education proponents feel writing should begin in kindergarten. They would build on skills existing in the child, stressing coloring, drawing, and scribbling. Within these behaviors the strokes required for forming letters and numerals are present. The up-down, left-right, and circular movements required in writing numerals lend itself easily to cursive writing.

The maturation proponents, on the other hand, feel that specific fine motor, visual motor, and perceptual motor skills must exist before formal instruction is beneficial. If a child has not developed such skills, they believe it would be counterproductive to introduce controlled writing, which almost certainly would bring frustration.

Additional controversies exist as to whether children should be taught manuscript writing first, following by cursive writing, or taught only cursive writing from the beginning. Both sides can list pros and cons. Since definite answers do not exist for students with writing disabilities, teachers are well advised to look for whatever works with a given student.

Educational implications

Prewriting skills should be assessed for any student suspected of having written language disabilities. Attention should be given to coordination, grasp, and visual perception. Concepts of up, down, top, bottom, and across should be checked. They can be taught through copying and modeling. Copying is an important skill in learning to write. Visual perception, eye-hand coordination, visual memory, and visual association problems can be detected through copying. These specific types of learning disabilities, needless to say, further frustrate the student who is eager to write but unable to do so.

Following remediation of deficits in basic skills, students should practice applying their writing skills to communicate ideas and thoughts. Here organization and sequencing become most important. If these subskills are impaired, they must be remediated before written communication will be effective.

Behavioral implications

The frustration of students who have written language difficulties can be observed in diversionary tactics such as concentrating on a single project and not wanting to change to handwriting. Some students will write anything, scribble, or draw when confronted with a word that they cannot write; they may present papers that are very messy. Sometimes they will write a word, and in anticipation of the teacher's criticism may write over the word, erase it with the finger, or destroy the paper.

Remedial implications

Skills involved in written language should be clearly identified and sequenced. This provides a structure in which a learning-disabled student can function, step by step. Remedial activities can also be organized to avoid certain problems. For example, if a student has developed writing skills but still has residual fine motor problems that make for "messy" work, that student can be taught to use a typewriter. The resulting social and emotional benefits to the student will be great. If a child has strength in the auditory area, he can use a tape recorder for expression while writing skills are being developed.

SUMMARY

Specific learning disabilities involve disorders in the ability to receive, process, or produce language. They are intellectual, not physical, in nature. They are manifested in impaired ability to listen, speak, think, read, write, spell, and do mathematical calculations. To be identified as learning disabled, a student must be academically deficient in reading, math, or written expression *and* must be diagnosed as having a sensory, perceptual, behavioral, or intellectual dysfunction associated with the academic deficit.

This chapter discussed the nature, manifestations, and implications of learning disabilities related to perception, visual and auditory discrimination, spoken and expressive language, reading, mathematics, and written language. Specific strategies were mentioned for teaching learning-disabled students. Throughout, emphasis was placed on the sequencing of requisite skills, teaching to student strengths while remediating weaknesses, and providing the success and progress necessary for adequate self-concept.

The special educator helps the regular classroom teacher. The teacher makes observations that form the basis for referral, screening, diagnosis, programming, and placement of students with academic difficulties.

SUGGESTED ACTIVITIES

1. Interview or invite to class a teacher of the learning disabled. Ask that person to describe diagnostic procedures and specific remedial instruction.
2. Examine diagnostic tests used for the learning disabled. Identify the specific disabilities toward which they are aimed.
3. List several things you could do to raise the self-concept of students who are very poor in reading. Discuss your ideas in class.
4. Obtain a diagnostic prescriptive arithmetic program used for slow learners. Describe the type and sequence of skills that are included.

SUGGESTED READINGS

Anderson, L.: Classroom activities for helping perceptually handicapped children, New York, 1974, The Center for Applied Research in Education.

Banton-Smith, N.: Reading instruction for today's children, Englewood Cliffs, NJ, 1963, Prentice-Hall, Inc.

Barsch, R. H.: Achieving perceptual motor

efficiency; a space-oriented approach to learning, Seattle, 1967, Special Child Publications.

Barsch, R. H.: Perspectives in learning, San Rafael, CA, 1967, Academic Therapy Publications.

Bateman, B.: An educator's view of a diagnostic approach to learning disorders. In Learning disorders, vol. 1, Seattle, 1965, Special Child Publications.

Bateman, B.: Three approaches to diagnosis and educational planning for children with learning disabilities, Academic Ther. Quart. 2:215-222, 1967.

Bryan, T. H.: Learning disabilities; a report on the art, Teachers' College Record 75:395-404, 1974.

Bryan, T. H., and Bryan, J.: Understanding learning disabilities, New York, 1975, Alfred Publishing Co., Inc.

Carter, D. B.: Interdisciplinary approaches to learning disorders, Philadelphia, 1970, Chilton Book Co.

Chaney, C. M., and Miles, N. R.: Remediating learning problems; a developmental curriculum, Columbus, OH, 1974, Charles E. Merrill Publishing Co.

Consila, S. M.: U.S.A. in the 70's—a look at the learning disabled child, Acad. Ther. 9:17-25, 1974.

Cowgill, M., Friedland, S., and Shapiro, R.: Predicting learning disabilities from kindergarten reports, J. Learning Disabil. 6:577-582, 1973.

Cratly, B. J.: Remedial motor activity for children, Philadelphia, 1975, Lea & Febiger.

Crinella, F. M.: Identification of brain dysfunction syndromes in children through profile analysis; patterns associated with so-called minimal brain dysfunction, J. Abnorm. Psychol. 82:33-45, 1973.

Cruickshank, W. M., editor: The teacher of brain injured children; a discussion of the bases of competency, Syracuse, NY, 1966, Syracuse University Press.

Cruickshank, W. M., editor: Psychology of exceptional children and youth, Englewood Cliffs, NJ, 1971, Prentice-Hall, Inc.

Cruickshank, W. M., and Hallahan, D. P., editors: Perceptual and learning disabilities in children: volume I: psychoeducational practices, Syracuse, NY, 1975, Syracuse University Press.

Cruickshank, W. M., and Hallahan, D. P., editors: Perceptual and learning disabilities in children: volume II: research and theory, Syracuse, NY, 1975, Syracuse University Press.

Cruickshank, W., Bentzen, F., Ratzebury, F., and Tannhauser, M.: A method for brain injured hyperactive children, Syracuse, NY, 1961, Syracuse University Press.

Denoff, E.: The measurement of psychoneurological factor contributing to learning efficiency, J. Learning Disabil. 2:636-644, 1968.

Dunn, L. M., editor: Exceptional children in the schools, New York, 1973, Holt, Rinehart & Winston.

Francis-Williams, J.: Children with specific learning difficulties, Elmsford, NY, 1970, Pergamon Press, Inc.

Frostig, M.: Movement education: theory and practice, Chicago, 1970, Follett Corp.

Frostig, M., and Maslow, P.: Learning problems in the classroom; prevention and remediation, New York, 1973, Grune & Stratton, Inc.

Gaddes, W. H.: A neuropsychological approach to learning disorders, J. Learning Disabil. 1:523-524, 1968.

Gardner, W. I.: Children with learning and behavior problems: a behavior management approach, ed. 2, Boston, 1978, Allyn & Bacon, Inc.

Gearheart, B. R.: Learning disabilities; educational strategies, ed. 2, St. Louis, 1977, The C. V. Mosby Co.

Gearheart, B. R., and Weishahn, M. W.: The handicapped child in the regular classroom, St. Louis, 1976, The C. V. Mosby Co.

Goldstein, E. H.: A multidisciplinary evaluation of children with learning disabilities, Child Psychiat. Human Devel. 5:95-106, 1974.

Grzynkowicz, W.: Meeting the needs of learning disabled children in the regular classroom, Springfield, IL, 1974, Charles C Thomas, Publisher.

Hallahan, D. P.: Learning disabilities; a historical and psychological perspective, Ann Arbor, 1971, University of Michigan (Doctoral dissertation).

Hallahan, D. P., and Cruickshank, W. M.: Psychoeducational foundations of learning disabilities, Englewood Cliffs, NJ, 1973, Prentice-Hall, Inc.

Hallahan, E., and Kauffman, J.: Introduction to learning disabilities: a psycho-behavioral approach, Englewood Cliffs, NJ, 1976, Prentice-Hall, Inc.

Hammill, D. D., and Bartel, N. R.: Teaching children with learning and behavior problems, Boston, 1975, Allyn & Bacon, Inc.

Hellmuth, J., editor: Learning disorders, Seattle, 1965, Special Child Publications.

Hewett, F. M.: Hierarchy of educational tasks for children with learning disorders, Exceptional Child. 31:207-214, 1964.

Hoffman, M. S.: A learning disability is a symptom, not a disease, Acad. Therapy 10:28-39, 1975.

Johnson, D., and Myklebust, H. R.: Learning disabilities; educational principles and practices, New York, 1967, Grune & Stratton, Inc.

Kelly, L. J., and Vergason, G. A.: Dictionary of special education and rehabilitation, Denver, 1978, Love Publishing Company.

Keogh, B. K.: Early identification of children with potential learning problems, J. Spec. Educ. (Monograph), May, 1969.

Keogh, B. K., and Becker, L.: Early detection of learning problems: questions, cautions, and guidelines, Exceptional Child. 40:5-11, 1973.

Kephart, N. C.: The slow learner in the classroom, ed. 2, Columbus, OH, 1971, Charles E. Merrill Publishing Co.

Kirk, S.: Educating exceptional children, Boston, 1974, Houghton Mifflin Co.

Kirk, S., and McCarthy, J. M.: Learning disabilities; selected ACLD papers, Boston, 1975, Houghton Mifflin Co.

Kirk, S., and Kirk, W.: Psycholinguistic learning disabilities: diagnosis and remediation, Urbana, IL, 1971, University of Illinois Press.

Koppitz, E. M.: Children with learning disabilities; a five-year follow-up study, New York, 1971, Grune & Stratton, Inc.

Kunzelman, H.: Precision teaching, Seattle, 1970, Special Child Publications.

Learner, J. W.: Children with learning disabilities. Theories, diagnosis, and teaching strategies, ed. 2, Boston, 1976, Houghton Mifflin Co.

McCarthy, J. J., and McCarthy, J. F.: Learning disabilities, Boston, 1969, Allyn & Bacon, Inc.

McIntosh, D. K., and Dunn, L. M.: Children with major specific learning disabilities. In Dunn, L. M., editor: Exceptional children in the schools, New York, 1973, Holt, Rinehart & Winston.

Malian, I. M.: Regular classroom teachers and administrators and children with exceptional needs, Sacramento, 1979, California State Department of Education.

Malian, I. M., and Doyle, B. A.: Is he ready for math?: diagnostic and readiness approach to mastering math, paper presented at the International Association for Children With Learning Disabilities, 1977, Washington, D.C.

Marsh, G. E., Gearheart, C. K., and Gearheart, B. R.: The learning disabled adolescent: program alternatives in the secondary school, St. Louis, 1978, The C. V. Mosby Co.

Meier, J. H.: Developmental and learning disabilities: evaluation, management and prevention in children, Baltimore, 1976, University Park Press.

Mercer, C. D.: Children and adolescents with learning disabilities, Columbus, OH, 1979, Charles E. Merrill Publishing Co.

Myers, P., and Hammill, D.: Methods for learning disorders, New York, 1969, John Wiley & Sons, Inc.

Myklebust, H. R.: Learning disorders: psychoneurological disturbances in childhood, Rehab. Lit. 25:354-360, 1964.

Myklebust, H. R.: Progress in learning disabilities, New York, 1971, Grune & Stratton, Inc.

Rappaport, S., and McNary, S.: Teacher effectiveness for children with learning disorders, J. Learning Disabil. 3:75-83, 1970.

Silver, L. B.: Acceptable and controversial approaches to treating learning disabilities, Pediatrics 36:406-415, 1975.

Simpson, D. M.: Learning to learn, Columbus, OH, 1968, Charles E. Merrill Publishing Co.

Stephens, T. M.: Teaching skills to children with learning and behavior disorders, Columbus, OH, 1977, Charles E. Merrill Publishing Co.

Strauss, A., and Kephart, N.: Psychopathology and education of the brain-injured child: volume II: progress in theory and clinic, New York, 1955, Grune & Stratton, Inc.

Tarnopol, L., editor: Learning disorders in children; psychological diagnosis and remediation, Boston, 1971, Little, Brown & Co.

Valett, R.: The remediation of learning disabilities, Belmont, CA, 1974, Fearon Publishers, Inc.

Wallace, G., and McLoughlin, J. A.: Learning disabilities: concepts and characteristics, ed. 2, Columbus, OH, 1979, Charles E. Merrill Publishing Co.

Weber, R. E., editor: Handbook on learning disabilities: a prognosis for the child, the adolescent, the adult, Englewood Cliffs, NJ, 1975, Prentice-Hall, Inc.

Wood, N.: Verbal learning, Belmont, CA, 1969, Fearon Publishers, Inc.

CHAPTER 9

Teaching mentally retarded students

Myths about the handicapped are widespread throughout our society, in various professions, and within individuals. And of all the handicapped, none is so afflicted with myth as the mentally retarded. These myths have resulted in mislabeling, prejudice, discrimination, and poor delivery of educational services.

What are some of these labels? According to Wolfensberger (1972) they include (1) sick person, (2) subhuman, (3) menace, (4) object of pity, (5) burden of charity, and (6) "holy innocent" or "child of God." Those who work with the mentally handicapped realize that these characterizations are fallacious. They would be laughable if they weren't so damaging.

One thing is not a myth, however: the range of functioning within the categories of mental retardation is varied. Hutt and Gibby (1976) point out that:

> Children vary tremendously in the intellectual effectiveness with which they function, ranging from extremely inferior to extremely superior levels. If we measure their intellectual capacity by means of an intelligence test, we find that a large percentage cluster around the middle portion of the range. By definition, we call these children average. A small percentage rank at such a low level that we term them mentally retarded, and an equally small percentage rank at such a high level that we term them genius. Between the highest and the lowest levels there is a very large range—a continuum—that comprises all the intervening levels of intellectual capacity.
>
> Children range all along this continuum, differing from each other in both the amount of intelligence they possess (quantity) and the kinds of intelligence they display (quality). There is no sharp break along the continuum. For convenience, however, we may term those who rank below an arbitrarily selected point, *mentally retarded*, just as we may term those who rank above an arbitrarily selected point very superior. Those who fall within the lowest portion of the scale differ significantly among themselves. They range from mildly retarded to severely and profoundly retarded.

These varying levels of retardation have been defined and redefined throughout the history of special education. Controversy continues over tests and procedures for determining mental retardation. They are forever being revived and revised. For educators the terms most frequently used are "educable mentally retarded" (EMR) or mild retardation; "trainable mentally retarded" (TMR) or moderately retarded; and "severely/profoundly mentally retarded" (S/PMR). These levels have evolved from medical terminology, and are now used to refer to people who have educational and training needs at specific levels.

The American Association on Mental Deficiency has provided guidelines to the levels of mental retardation (Table 1) in *The Manual on Terminology and Classification in Mental Retardation* (1973). The classification system is arranged according to functioning ability—intellectually (IQ) and behaviorally.

In a report to Congress on the implementation of Public Law 94-142, the

Table 1. AAMD levels of mental retardation*

Degree of mental retardation	Obtained Stanford-Binet (s.d.—16)	Intelligence quotient Weschsler scales (s.d.—15)	Common educational terms
Mild	67-52	Educable	Educable
Moderate	51-36	54-40	Trainable
Severe	35-20	39-25 (extrapolated)	Trainable
Profound	19 and below	24 and below (extrapolated)	Severe/ profound

*From Meier, J. H.: Developmental and learning disabilities: evaluation, management and prevention in children, Baltimore, 1976, University Park Press. Adapted from *Manual on Terminology and Classification in Mental Retardation* (Rev. ed.). Grossman, H. J., et al., American Association on Mental Deficiency, Washington, D.C., 1973, p. 18.

Bureau of Education for the Handicapped cited distributions of handicapped children served in the school year 1977-1978. The mentally retarded population comprised approximately 25% of the total. In the same report the Bureau looked at the various environments in which school-aged mentally retarded children were being served. They reported:

> Over the past 25 years, mentally retarded children have been served primarily in separate classes if their condition was mild or moderate, and in separate facilities if their disability was severe. While figures show that separate classes continue to be the predominant placement for mentally retarded children, it is impressive from a historical perspective that the proportion whose primary placement is the regular classroom is now 39 percent.

Speaking of ramifications for the public schools and regular classroom teachers the report goes on to state:

> Given that trend, and more particularly the provisions of P.L. 94-142, the percentage of school-aged handicapped children served in less restrictive placements will increase. For example, the public schools may serve an increasing proportion of blind children, and serve growing numbers of moderately mentally retarded children in regular classrooms. Data from case studies initiated by the Bureau bear out that expectation, indicating a steadily climbing number of resource room placements and in general a rising trend in the incidence of school-aged handicapped children being placed in less restrictive settings.

LEVELS OF RETARDATION

You know that a variety of levels of retardation exist. You know that a trend is occurring to educate mentally retarded individuals in the regular classroom, with supportive special education. The following sections present a developmental,

educational, and behavioral profile of individuals within the three levels of retardation.

EDUCABLE MENTALLY RETARDED (EMR)

The most acceptable definition for mental retardation comes from the American Association of Mental Deficiency. It has three essential components:
1. Subaverage general intellectual functioning, with . . .
2. Deficiency in adaptive behavior, and was . . .
3. Acquired during the developmental period, which . . .
4. Adversely affects education.
(Grossman, 1973).

The term "mental retardation" as used in this definition does not imply a
specific cause. It is merely descriptive of current behavior. Neither does it imply
permanence of the condition. The term "developmental period" includes conception up to age 16. "Subaverage" refers to an individual's score on a standardized
intelligence test, falling at least two standard deviations below the mean (Bruininks & Warfield, 1978).

All of these characteristics must be present for the definition of mental retardation to apply to an individual. Thus, the "6-hour retarded student" who
consistently fails academic tasks at school but functions adequately in social and
work situations cannot be labeled EMR. Moreover, situations still exist where
culturally biased intelligence tests are being administered to minority students,
and many are being labeled EMR even though their adaptive behavior is well
within the normal range.

In noting the influence of cultural differences and socioeconomic status on
measured intelligence, Heber (1970) states:

> There is a clear difference in the mean I.Q.'s for various socioeconomic groups. These
> in turn give rise to substantial differences in the prevalence of I.Q.'s falling within the
> mentally retarded range. These socioeconomic distinctions remain regardless of
> whether the groups are defined in terms of family, income, quality of housing, pa-
> rental education, or parental occupation.

"Adaptive behavior" is included in the definition of mental retardation. It is
defined as

> the effectiveness and degree to which an individual meets standards of self-sufficiency
> and social responsibility for his or her age-related cultural group. It is the composite of
> many aspects of behavior and the function of a wide range of abilities or disabilities
> involved in one's adjustment to his or her environment. Intellectual, physical, motor,
> motivational, social, and sensory factors in various combinations contribute to the
> total adaptive process. Poor adaptive behavior is one characteristic of the mentally
> retarded. (Kelly and Verguson, 1978.)

Fairchild and Parks (1976) discuss adaptive behavior at three age levels:

> In younger children adaptive behavior typically refers to the development of sensory-motor skills, communication skills, self-help skills, and socialization. In adolescents, it refers to the application of basic academics in daily life activities, application of appropriate reasoning and judgment in mastery of the environment, and social skills. In adulthood, adaptive behavior refers to vocational and social responsibility.

The American Association on Mental Deficiency Adaptive Behavior Scale was developed to provide standardized procedures for evaluating social functioning of children and youth along two major dimensions: development and personality. The Adaptive Behavior Scale provides questions to be answered by the teacher or parent pertaining to the functioning of the student. A profile sheet is provided for identifying strengths and weaknesses. Noting these areas can facilitate classroom programming and guide planning for specific remediation.

A Public School Version of the AAMD Adaptive Scale has also been developed. The authors point out that they view

> assessment as the first step in the diagnostic-prescriptive process in planning education programs for all exceptional children. It is the phase during which all educationally relevant data are gathered and made available for subsequent analysis with the eventual development of an individual educational plan. For this purpose, adequate assessment requires an extensive, comprehensive approach. Interdisciplinary staffing is a necessary diagnostic procedure, and the assessment of a child's adaptive behavior is an integral part of this comprehensive effort. (Lambert, Windmiller, Cole, Figueroa, 1975.)

Components of the Public School Version of the AAMD Adaptive Behavior Scale include (Lambert, Windmiller, Cole, Figueroa, 1975):

PART ONE

1.0 Developmental domains:
    1.1 Independent functioning
        1.1.1 Eating
        1.1.2 Toilet use
        1.1.3 Cleanliness
        1.1.4 Appearance
        1.1.5 Care of clothing
        1.1.6 Dressing
        1.1.7 Undressing
        1.1.8 Travel
        1.1.9 General independent functioning
    1.2 Physical development
        1.2.1 Sensory development
        1.2.2 Motor development
    1.3 Economic activity
        1.3.1 Money handling

As is apparent from the Adaptive Behavior Scale, the subcategories of behavior are subjective in their interpretation. Antisocial and rebellious are not clear-cut behaviors, such that commonality of responses can be documented. For some students, exerting autonomy or independence may even be a behavioral goal. This goal may be confused with maladaptive behavior on the rating scale. Grossman (1973) echos this concern by stating:

At the present time, the value of a single score for adaptive behavior level classification is limited largely to certain administrative purposes and has little diagnostic or program planning import for the individual. Assessment of performance in specific domains of behavior, however, can be very useful in identifying deficits and training needs. As with I.Q. scores, individuals who are classified at the same overall level of adaptive behavior may not be clinically equivalent in that they may vary significantly in the various domains of behavior that comprise the overall rating.

The developmental period lasts from conception to age 16. The most frequent causes of retardation are prenatal complications, including (1) disease such as rubella, measles, infection, and virus; (2) stress, from emotional problems occurring in the mother's life; (3) malnutrition; (4) exposure to x-rays; (5) drugs, including prescribed medications, codeine, heroin, and morphine; (6) physical trauma such as automobile accidents; (7) mother's age; and (8) other undetermined causes. The birth process itself can pose threats to later development. Lack of oxygen may occur if the umbilical cord is wrapped around the baby's neck. The mode of presentation (breech), type of delivery (use of forceps or other instrumentation), prematurity, and mother's condition during pregnancy and labor may contribute to difficulties for the neonate or place the neonate at risk for later handicaps. Other frequent causes of retardation include chromosomal abnormalities (Down's syndrome), early malnutrition, and severe lack of sensory stimulation.

Educational implications

Kirk (1972) clarifies what can be expected of the educable mentally retarded student:
1. Academic skills—can obtain minimum educability in school subjects
2. Social skills—can adjust in order to function independently in the community
3. Occupational skills—can attain an adequate level of job skills for partial or total self-support

Payne and Thomas (1978) suggest that EMR students can be effectively educated within the regular elementary classroom, if they receive individualized instruction and the help of resource specialists. In the upper elementary grades and junior high, they propose that prevocational skills be introduced, along with practical academics necessary for independent living. During high school, they advocate vocational training, possibly within work-study programs.

This plan is consistent with Kirk's ideas, which maintain that the ultimate purpose for education of EMR students is to help them become social participants and wage earners. Their educational goals must be couched in topics such as:
1. Attainment of a style of life
2. Adequate responses to social, personal, and occupational situations
3. Civic responsibilities
4. Self-realization

5. Human relationships

6. A repertoire of general information retrievable quickly and appropriately

7. Effective use of a consistent method of problem solving

The recent interest in career education is most relevant to the educational program of EMR students. Many career education models focus on practical goals that assist EMR students in dealing with life situations.

Teachers usually wonder how EMR students go about learning. The following paragraphs report some of their learning characteristics. This information will help the regular classroom teacher to understand the EMR student:

1. *Concept formation and abstractions may present difficulties.* This is evident in areas as math, time, money relationships, and problems requiring prediction. Concrete, specific materials should be provided to make these abstractions understandable.

2. *Short attention span.* Turnbull and Schulz (1979) point out that students can work for relatively short periods only before they need a change of pace.

3. *Poor memory.* This deficit in EMR students heightens the importance of repetition and organization of materials. Research has indicated that many of the EMR students are at a distinct disadvantage in recalling information immediately after they have received it (Ellis, 1970; Belmont and Butterfield, 1969). Turnbull and Schulz (1979) suggest that EMR students do not automatically use active strategies to remember, as most students do who are not cognitively impaired. Therefore, these students forget much important information. Overlearning and much repetition are necessary.

4. *Perseveration.* This is a behavior of persistently repeating an action, word, idea, or sensation, even when not appropriate. It may interfere with learning. The cause of perseveration is unknown.

5. *Conceptualization and generalization.* These are thinking skills that allow what is learned in one situation to be applied to another situation; EMR students have difficulty with them. This ability must be deliberately taught (Fairchild and Parks, 1976). Students who have difficulty conceptualizing may be referred to as "concrete thinkers" (Turnbull and Schulz, 1979).

6. *Speech and language.* According to Baumeister and Kellas (1971), "If one were to poll those working with mental retardates he/she would undoubtedly find that the inability to learn verbal materials is widely regarded as their most obvious and critical area of behavioral deficiency." Semmel, Barrit, Bennett, and Perfetti (1968) determined that older retarded children respond much like very young nonretarded youngsters. A number of researchers have recommended various procedures and concepts for language training. For example, Rosenberg (1970) proposes five considerations in the language training of EMR students.

1. A complete assessment of the child's language disabilities.
2. Full use of behavior modification.
3. Emphasis on learning the meaning of words. Educable mentally retarded students can string words together, but often do not understand the meanings.
4. Recognition that language training is affected by both the child's and the teacher's use of speech.
5. Since normal children appear to acquire language through activity, language training programs should attempt to reproduce this process by having the retarded child actively participate in the lessons.

When an EMR student is integrated into a regular classroom, the teacher should acquire as much information as possible regarding specific strengths, weaknesses, and physical impairments which may (but do not always) accompany the retardation. Support services within the school will be available, such as a special education teacher, resource room, behavioral interventionist, and aides. A primary responsibility of the teacher is to facilitate peer acceptance and to help maintain a positive self-concept. Enhancement of academic skills for the EMR student is accomplished through the following procedures (Smith and Bentley, 1975):

1. Establishing simply stated objectives with small quantities of materials to be learned
2. Providing practical, concrete, relevant, "hands-on" experiences as often as possible
3. Providing flexibility in selecting and sequencing instruction
4. Focusing on specific target behaviors and reducing distractions
5. Following through with the student, step-by-step, on tasks; steps may have to be broken down quite simply
6. Providing frequent feedback to encourage the student; small improvements warrant praise
7. Devising a variety of approaches for teaching the same concept; drills that are tedious should be avoided
8. Emphasizing the student's strongest learning modality (that is, visual, auditory, tactile), while strengthening modalities that are weak
9. Scheduling frequent review and reteaching to help the student maintain previously learned skills

Behavioral implications

The following global view of EMR students should help teachers understand behavior they observe in the classroom.

1. A general delay in development of EMR students manifests itself in corresponding difficulties in learning to read, write, speak, and calculate.
2. Social and emotional development is also delayed. Consequently, "immature" behavior and poor social judgment are likely to appear.
3. The EMR student has a poor self-concept. Social adjustment and peer relations are seldom positive. EMR students are quite aware of the feelings and opinions held by their peers. The negative attitudes can result in hostility and anxiety.
4. Haring (1974) reported a positive correlation between low intelligence and poor social acceptance. This demonstrates the likelihood of an EMR student being socially rejected and having a lower social status than nonhandicapped peers.

Suggestions for teachers

Teachers, of course, must deal with these realities. Their success will be heightened if they do the following:

1. Maintain an accepting, positive attitude toward the EMR student.
2. Encourage the use of peer tutors. This couples academics with positive social interactions. Other good tutors are parents, community volunteers, and older students.
3. Become a member of a team of educators that mutually contribute information, materials, and behavioral management suggestions. This teaming becomes even more important when the student is involved in a variety of educational environments. For example, an EMR student may go to a special education classroom for part of the day, and then be integrated with nonhandicapped peers for physical education, art, music, etc. Or, the student may be educated in the regular classroom and pulled out for remedial assistance in reading and mathematics. Yet another model proposed by Berry (1972) suggests "split sessions," where part of the child's time is spent in a class with about half the normal number of pupils, and the remainder of his/her time may be spent in another setting.
4. Provide clear routines, with solid structure. This provides security, reduces off-task behavior, and assists learning. Where other students in the class may be able to follow directions and sequences of assignments, the EMR student may remember only the first direction given.
5. Break assignments and tasks within assignments down to very small steps. This wards off frustration and permits a sense of accomplishment.
6. Develop the most positive peer interaction within the class. (Refer to Chapter 5 for specific suggestions.)

TRAINABLE MENTALLY RETARDED (TMR)

The moderately mentally retarded individual is diagnosed very early as being delayed in a variety of areas. In terms of intellectual testing, the moderately mentally retarded student will typically fall between the IQ scores of 40 and 54 on the Wechsler, and 36 and 51 on the Stanford-Binet. Conroy and Derr (1971) delineate expected areas of delay as ambulation, gross motor, fine motor, hearing, vision, behavior-emotional disorders, and toilet training.

Ward (1979) sees four major areas of delay in the moderately retarded individual: physical and motor, speech and language, academic and vocational, and social. These areas are discussed in the following sections.

Physical and motor development

The overall physical development of the moderately retarded individual is delayed. This usually includes height, weight, and musculature.

Ward (1979) points out that multiple handicaps such as hearing and vision problems are also prevalent in this population. Generally, moderately retarded children tire easily and are more susceptible to health problems. Down's syndrome shows distinctive physical features such as low-bridged nose, upward-slanting eyes, small ears, and a protruding tongue. Associated with this syndrome are congenital physical problems such as heart and respiratory difficulties (Gellis and Feingold, 1968).

In addition, motor development, particularly in the areas of gross motor-crawling, standing, and walking, are reported by parents as being delayed. Bruininks (1977) demonstrated delay in running speed and agility, balance, bilateral coordination, strength, upper body coordination, response speed, visual-motor control, and dexterity.

Speech and language development

Language development involves both the understanding of spoken language used by others (receptive language) and the spoken language used by the student (expressive language). Speech defects often noted in TMR students include articulation, voice, and fluency disorders.

Academic and vocational development

The moderately retarded individual will benefit from formal education, particularly a strong readiness and basic skills approach. Vocational activities can then be built on top of the basic skills. Vocational skills to be taught revolve around the goal of facilitating the student's entry into a world of work and being able to maintain his independence in the community. Placement in a sheltered workshop, where actual vocational productivity is possible, is the ultimate goal of training for the moderately mentally retarded.

The National Association For Retarded Citizens (NARC) defines a sheltered workshop as "a work-oriented rehabilitation facility with a controlled working environment and individualized vocational goals, which utilizes work experiences and related services to assist the handicapped person's progress toward normal living and productive vocational status" (Fraenkel, 1962).

Social areas

Moderately retarded individuals can acquire simple social skills. Appropriate behaviors for interacting with others, such as greetings, can be learned. However, most behaviors remain dependent on others for judgment and consequence monitoring. Parents and teachers of moderately retarded children typically worry about behaviors such as running into the street after a ball or accepting rides from strangers.

TMR students are identified early in life. Programs exist throughout the United States to screen, diagnose, and provide infant development programs for the moderately retarded. Integrated preschools, where retarded children are educated with nonretarded peers, are becoming more prevelant. Priority skills include socialization, motor development, speech and language acquisition, and self-help training.

Public schools offer some mainstreaming possibilities for these students. The most likely educational environment for moderately retarded elementary school children would be in a specialized class, with integration into a few activities with nonretarded peers.

At the junior and senior high school levels, program planning involves prevocational and vocational skills training. Often this specialized training for the moderately retarded student occurs in a facility separate from the school (Fig. 6).

SEVERELY AND PROFOUNDLY MENTALLY RETARDED

Individuals who are severely and profoundly mentally retarded will rarely have any mainstream experience. They are taught in separate facilities. Curriculum and instruction are directed to self-help and self-care. Special facilities are needed, including ramps and toilets. The profoundly retarded individuals are seldom able to care for and protect themselves. Many are restricted to bed or wheelchair and require constant supervision.

SUMMARY

Mental retardation covers a wide range of abilities, capabilities, behaviors, strengths, and weaknesses within each classification. Educational programming

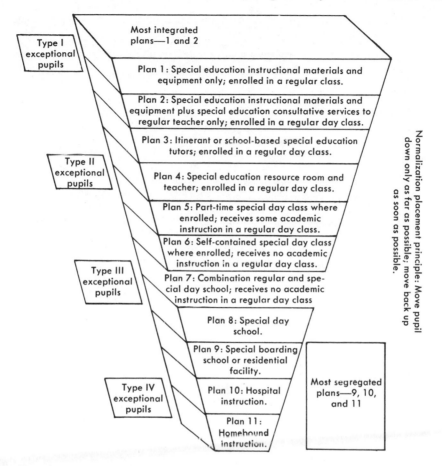

Fig. 6. Dunn's inverted pyramid model of instruction for exceptional pupils. (From Dunn, L. M.: Exceptional children in the schools, ed. 2, New York, 1973, Holt, Rinehart & Winston.)

and planning by the regular classroom teacher are necessary when teaching mildly retarded students (EMR), and to a lesser extent the moderately retarded (TMR). Classroom teachers will seldom be involved in the training of severely and profoundly mentally retarded students.

The classification system in mental retardation is a means of describing ability levels as well as strengths and weaknesses. It is from this system, together with the educational, vocational, social, and emotional needs of the individual, that programming and planning occur.

Mentally retarded students require instruction that has routine and structure. Skill learning should be broken into small steps. Teachers should be warmly accepting. They should use behavior modification liberally and maintain the best peer interactions in the classroom.

The mainstreaming of mentally retarded individuals into the regular classroom will provide a long-term interaction that should dispel many of the myths and stereotypes about them.

SUGGESTED ACTIVITIES

1. Invite a teacher of the mentally retarded to speak to the class about rewards and difficulties of working with mentally retarded students.
2. Arrange a visit to a sheltered workshop where some adult mentally retarded people do productive work to earn a living.
3. The school curriculum for the mentally retarded is arranged into sequential, concrete steps. Obtain a copy of such a curriculum for examination and discussion.
4. Develop a math lesson in adding single-digit numerals. Make it consistent with the learning traits listed for EMR students.

SUGGESTED READINGS

Baumeister, A. A.: Learning abilities of the mentally retarded. In Baumeister, A. A., editor: Mental retardation, Chicago, 1967, Aldine Publishing Company.

Baumeister, A. A., and Kellas, G.: Process variables in the paired-associate learning of retardates. In Ellis, N. R., editor: International review of research in mental retardation, New York, 1971, Academic Press.

Beier, D. C.: Behavioral disturbances in the mentally retarded. In Stevens, H. A., and Heber, R., editors: Mental retardation, Chicago, 1964, University of Chicago Press.

Belmont, J. M., and Butterfield, E. C.: The relations of short-term memory to development and intelligence. In Lipsitt, L. C., and Reese, H. W., editors: Advances in child development and behavior, vol. 4, New York, 1969, Academic Press.

Berry, K. E.: Models for mainstreaming, San Raphael, CA, 1972, Dimensions Publication Co.

Bijou, S. W.: A functional analysis of retarded development. In Ellis, N. R., editor: International review of research in mental retardation, vol. 1, New York, 1966, Academic Press.

Birch, J. W.: Mainstreaming: educable retarded children in regular classes, Reston, VA, 1974, The Council for Exceptional Children.

Blake, K. A.: The mentally retarded: an educational psychology, Englewood Cliffs, NJ, 1976, Prentice-Hall, Inc.

Bruininks, R. H.: Manual for the Bruininks-Osevetsky test of motor proficiency, Circle Pines, MN, 1977, American Guidance Service.

Bruininks, R. H., and Rynders, J. E.: Alternatives to special class placement for educable mentally retarded children, Focus Except. Child. 3(4):1-12, 1971.

Bruininks, R. H., and Warfield, G.: The mentally retarded. In Meyen, E. L., editor: Exceptional children and youth: an introduction, Denver, 1978, Love Publishing Company.

Collins, H. A., Burger, G. K., and Doherty, D.: Self-concept of EMR and non-retarded adolescents, Am. J. Mental Defic. 75:285-289, 1970.

Conroy, J. W., and Derr, K. E.: Survey and analysis of the habilation and rehabilitation status of the mentally retarded with associated handicapped conditions, Washington, D.C., 1971, Department of Health, Education, and Welfare.

Deno, E. N., editor: Instructional alternatives for exceptional children, Reston, VA, 1973, The Council for Exceptional Children.

Ellis, N. R.: Memory processes in retardates and normals. In Ellis, N. R., editor: International review of research in mental retardation, vol. 4, New York, 1970, Academic Press.

Fairchild, T. N., and Parks, A. L.: Mainstreaming the mentally retarded child, Austin, TX, 1976, Learning Concepts.

Fine, M.: Attitudes of regular and special class teachers toward the educable mentally retarded child, Exceptional Child. 33:429-430, 1967.

Fraenkel, W. A.: Fundamentals in organizing a sheltered workshop for the mentally retarded,

New York, 1962, National Association for Retarded Citizens.

Gellis, S. S., and Feingold, M.: Atlas of mental retardation syndromes, Washington, D.C., 1968, U.S. Government Printing Office.

Gohlieb, J.: Public, peer and professional attitudes toward mentally retarded persons. In Begab, M. J., and Richardson, S. A., editors: The mentally retarded and society: a social science perspective, Baltimore, 1975, University Park Press.

Grossman, H. J., editor: Manual on terminology and classification in mental retardation, Rev., Washington, D.C., 1973, American Association on Mental Deficiency.

Guess, P. D., and Horner, R. D.: The severely and profoundly handicapped. In Meyen, E. L., editor: Exceptional children and youth: an introduction, Denver, 1978, Love Publishing Company.

Hallahan, D. P., and Kauffman, J. M.: Exceptional children: introduction to special education, Englewood Cliffs, NJ, 1978, Prentice-Hall, Inc.

Haring, N. G., editor: Behavior of exceptional children, Columbus, OH, 1974, Charles E. Merrill Publishing Co.

Heber, R.: Epidemiology of mental retardation, Springfield, IL, 1970, Charles C Thomas, Publisher.

Hutt, M. L., and Gibby, R. G.: The mentally retarded child: development, education and treatment, Boston, 1976, Allyn & Bacon, Inc.

Johnson, D.: The education of mentally retarded children. In Cruickshank, W. M., and Johnson, O., editors: Education of exceptional children and youth, Englewood Cliffs, NJ, 1975, Prentice-Hall, Inc.

Kelly, L. J., and Vergason, G. A.: Dictionary of special education and rehabilitation, Denver, 1978, Love Publishing Co.

Kirk, S. A.: Educating exceptional children, Boston, 1972, Houghton Mifflin Co.

Knight, O.: The self-concept of educable mentally retarded children in special and regular classes, Dissertation Abstracts International 28:4483, 1968.

Kolstoe, O. P.: Teaching educable mentally retarded children, New York, 1976, Holt, Rinehart & Winston.

Lambert, N., Windmiller, M., Cole, L., and Figueroa, R.: AAMR adaptive behavior scale, public school version—1974, Washington, D.C., 1975, American Association on Mental Deficiency.

MacMillan, D. L.: Mental retardation in school and society, Boston, 1977, Little, Brown & Company.

MacMillan, D. L., Jones, R. L., and Meyers, C. E. Mainstreaming the mildly retarded: some questions, cautions and guidelines, Ment. Retard. 14(1):3-10, 1976.

MacMillan, D. L., and Keogh, B.: Normal and retarded children's expectancy for failure, Dev. Psychol. 4:343-348, 1971.

Malian, I. M.: Regular classroom teachers and administrators and children with exceptional needs, Sacramento, 1979, California State Department of Education.

Malian, I. M.: Modeling techniques and videotape innovation in vocational rehabilitation. In Fink, A., editor: International perspectives on future special education, Reston, VA, 1978, The Council for Exceptional Children.

Malian, I. M.: Mathematics and mental retardation—some research and curricular endeavors, Paper presented to American Association on Mental Deficiency, 1977.

Mercer, C. D., and Snell, M. E. Learning theory research in mental retardation: implications for teaching, Columbus, OH, 1977, Charles E. Merrill Publishing Co.

Mercer, J. R.: Labeling the mentally retarded, Berkeley, CA, 1973, University of California Press.

Meyen, E. L.: Exceptional children and youth: an introduction, Denver, 1978, Love Publishing Company.

Payne, J. S., and Thomas, C.: The mentally retarded. In Haring, N. G., editor: Behavior of exceptional children, Columbus, OH, 1978, Charles E. Merrill Publishing Co.

President's Committee on Mental Retardation: Mental retardation: past and present, Washington, D.C., 1977, Department of Health, Education and Welfare.

Project PREM: Preparing regular educators for mainstreaming, Austin, TX, 1975, State Department of Education.

Robinson, H. B., and Robinson, N. M.: The

168   *Teaching the special students*

mentally retarded child. New York, 1977, McGraw-Hill Book Co.

Robinson, N. M., and Robinson, H. B.: The mentally retarded child: a psychological approach, New York, 1976, McGraw-Hill Book Co.

Rosenberg, S.: Problems of language development in the retarded. In Haywood, H. C., editor: Social-cultural aspects of mental retardation, New York, 1970, Appleton-Century-Crofts.

Semmel, M. I., Barritt, L. S., Bennett, S. W., and Perfetti, C. A.: Grammatical analysis of word association of educable mentally retarded and normal children, Am. J. Ment. Defic. 72:567-576, 1968.

Smith, P. B., and Bentley, G. I.: Participant manual: Mainstreaming, Austin, TX, 1975, Teacher Training Program, Educational Service Center, Region XIII.

Turnbull, A. P., and Schulz, J. B.: Mainstreaming handicapped students: a guide for the classroom teacher, Boston, 1979, Allyn & Bacon, Inc.

United States Department of Health, Education, and Welfare: Progress toward a free appropriate public education: a report to Congress on the implementation of Public Law 94-142: The Education for All Handicapped Children Act, Washington, D.C., 1979, Bureau of Education for the Handicapped.

Wallace, G., and Larsen S. C.: Educational assessment of learning problems: testing and teaching, Boston, 1978, Allyn & Bacon, Inc.

Ward, W. J.: Mentally retarded children and youth: educational, home, and community considerations. In Swanson, B. M., and Willis, D. J., editors: Understanding exceptional children and youth, Chicago, 1979, Rand McNally & Company.

Wolfensberger, W.: Normalization, Toronto, 1972, National Institute on Mental Retardation.

CHAPTER 10

Teaching students with speech impairments

Students with speech impairments comprise the largest single group of people with a handicap. Many of these students receive direct help from speech therapists. Others receive help from the regular teacher. At least half of them, however, receive no help at all. Some of those individuals outgrow their handicap. But large numbers of them retain the impairment their entire lives.

DEFINITIONS OF SPEECH IMPAIRED

What do we mean when we say speech impairment or speech problem? Van Riper (1952) says that speech problems are detectable under two circumstances: first, when a person's speech produces negative reactions in those listening; second, when the speaker experiences great distress as a result of difficulty in communicating. This definition shows that speech disorders can depend on the view of either the speaker or the listener. Public Law 94-142 defines the speech impaired in this way: " 'Speech impaired' means a communication disorder, such as stuttering, impaired articulation, a language impairment, or a voice impairment, which adversely affects a child's educational performance."

Both Van Riper's and the PL 94-142 definitions emphasize speech impairment. Specialists make further distinctions as to speech impairment, language impairment, and communication impairment. They use the term "speech impairment" in a generic sense to refer to disorders of articulation (speech sound production), voice, and fluency (rhythm). Each of these components relates to the mechanics of producing speech. They use the term "language impairment" to refer to disorders in comprehending or verbally expressing the symbols and grammatical rules of language. "Communication impairment" refers in the broadest sense to any speech or language handicap singly or in combination (Bankson, 1978).

CAUSES OF SPEECH IMPAIRMENTS

Bankson tells us that

Some speech problems are related to organic factors such as hearing loss, cleft palate, abnormal dentition, lesions of the vocal folds, or neurological disorders. Other problems may result from faulty learning, such as improper models in the family or environment, or lack of reinforcement from parents and others for adequate speech patterns. Some disorders may result from inadequate environmental stimulation or inappropriate psychological development.

Regardless of whether a given speech impairment results from a neurological disorder or from an inappropriate modeling pattern, the professionals involved in the education and speech therapy of the student have the same task. They must determine whether a genuine speech problem exists, to a degree that it, impairs the student's ability to learn and interact effectively; they must determine the exact nature of the problem; and finally, they must apply the correct therapy for correcting the problem.

EDUCATIONAL IMPLICATIONS

The most serious speech impairments, consistent with definitions in PL 94-142, are stuttering, articulation, language impairments, and voice impairments. These conditions and the means of correcting them are discussed in the following sections.

Stuttering

Weiss (1979) discusses prevelant theories on stuttering. Basically, they can be placed in three categories: (1) physical or constitutional, (2) psychological or neurotic, and (3) learned.

The *physical theory* on causes of stuttering runs the gamut from abnormal tongue to hereditary factors to a recent theory that stuttering is a disorder of timing, which results from disturbed auditory feedback and disrupts the motoric sequencing of speech (Van Riper, 1971).

The *psychological* position considers stuttering an emotional disorder which is a reaction to stress, unconscious needs, hostility, anxiety, or other emotional problems. But many theorists argue that if emotional problems are present in stutters, they are the result, rather than the cause, of the stuttering.

The *learning* view holds that much stuttering behavior is learned. A vicious cycle can be created as a student attempts to speak or relate verbally. He/she may exhibit disfluencies. The listener (parent or teacher) may react or intervene. This in turn causes the student concern and alerts him/her to attend more carefully so as to avoid those utterances. As the student then attempts to avoid stuttering, the expended energy and anxiety to please the listener may in fact cause more stuttering and hence more concern and attention on the part of the listener.

Professionals in the area of speech disorders have classified two types of stuttering. *Primary stuttering* consists of repetitious speech sounds. *Secondary stuttering* consists of nonspeech behaviors such as loss of eye contact; tremors of the lips, eyelids, and jaw; jerks of the head, jaw, and arm; facial grimaces; tongue protrusion; increased body tension; breathing irregularities; and nasal snorts (Weiss, 1979).

Because stuttering calls a great amount of attention to the student attempting to speak, and also results in discomfort for the listener, referrals to speech pathologists are usually made. As with any disturbance, it becomes important to note frequency. Is it occurring every time the student speaks? Or when he/speaks to the teacher? When he/she speaks to the class? Does it occur once or twice a day?

Duration of the stuttering is also important. Does the student stutter the entire time while talking? Or is the stuttering exhibited only in the initial phases of conversation? Identifying the circumstances in which the student stutters may point out stressful situations. For example, does the student stutter during math when he/she must read a problem? Is the stuttering predominantly during English and reading when the student must commit him/herself orally, and take a risk at stuttering in front of peers and teachers?

Turnbull and Schulz (1979) provide general suggestions for the classroom teacher when working with a student who stutters.

1. Avoid calling attention to the stuttering. Let the student finish what he/she is trying to say and maintain good listening habits, such as eye contact and positive facial expressions.
2. Make a special note of the classroom circumstances (discussions, oral presentations, free play) and the times when a student's stuttering seems to be the most severe. On the basis of each student's particular pattern, minimize the troublesome situations and maximize the situations in which the student is most fluent.
3. Cooperatively discuss ways in which the students in the class react positively to stuttering episodes. Classroom peers may tease and mimic if they have not been guided toward reacting positively.
4. As much as possible, reduce anxiety over speaking situations. If the student is particularly fearful of being called on to answer a question orally in class, let him know that he would not be called on unless he raised his hand. This strategy can prevent students with stuttering problems from sweating out every discussion period.

Poor articulation

The most common speech disorder seen within the schools is articulational. Articulation refers to the production of language sounds. An articulatory disorder is present if listeners perceive speech sounds to be omitted, substituted, added, or distorted (Perkins, 1971).

Omission errors involve the dropping of sounds from the full pronunciation of words. They may involve the consistent dropping of a sound—"The ome work was ard"—or an occasional single sound—"When is unch?"

Substitutions occur when one sound is replaced by another sound. Frequently substituted sounds are w for l, as in wove for love; w for r, as in wed for red; b for v, as in bery for very; t for k, as in tite for kite; th for s, as in yeth for yes. Some students will be very consistent in the words or sounds that they substitute. Others may interchange positions of sounds within words.

Additions are the inclusion of extra sounds in words. Examples would be datar for data; sawr for saw; or asslignment for assignment.

Distortions are sounds that are not made correctly. Speakers may come close, but slightly miss the sound. For example a w sound when distorted may be produced as an r sound. Or an l sound may be distorted in production to an r sound.

In classroom situations articulation errors might interfere with student performance in the following ways:

1. Expressive language might be difficult to understand.
2. Phonics training could be held back, affecting spelling and reading skills.
3. The student's social interactions could be damaged.

The teacher needs to be alert to these possibilities and work cooperatively with the student and speech therapist to reduce their effects.

Voice disorder

Classroom teachers will quickly detect voice impairment in students. Voice disorders occur much less frequently than articulation disorders, but they are still of concern because they interfere with interpersonal communications, cause embarrassment, and present adjustment problems (Weiss, 1979). Voice disorders fall into a variety of categories, the most common of which are the following.

Pitch, which refers to the highness or lowness of the student's voice. Proper pitch is related to what is age- and sex-appropriate. Problems occur when the pitch of the voice is inconsistent with age and sex. A male high school senior with a high-pitched voice, or an elementary school female with a low, bellowing voice would be considered voice handicapped. Furthermore, Hallahan and Kauffman (1978) point out that "during normal speech there are smooth transitions of pitch to higher and lower tones. These pitch transitions or intonation help to provide emphasis and make speech more interesting to listen to. It can be extremely distracting to listen to a person who never changes pitch (that is, someone who speaks in a monotone.), speaks with stereotyped inflections (for example uses a "singsong" voice or constant dogmatic emphasis), or uses a voice that constantly cracks or breaks into falsetto."

Intensity refers to loudness or softness of a student's voice. Students, in their oral communication, need to learn to regulate volume. One who constantly speaks too low will cause others to strain in order to hear. This may lead to other students talking above the low-speaking student, or even to ignoring him. By the same token, students who constantly speak too loud disrupt others' work, or exceed the level of comfort in which speech is tolerated. Variances in intensity may indicate a hearing problem in the student. As a precaution, the student should be referred for a routine hearing test.

Quality consists of those characteristics of the voice that make it unique and distinctive. An individual noted to have an unusual voice quality would be referred to as being hoarse, breathy, nasal, harsh, or husky. Some of these traits may indicate that speech is causing strain on the vocal cords. Very often poor voice quality is a result of excessive use of the voice, such as screaming or shouting for long periods of time. There are occasions where benign or malignant growths occur on the vocal cords. A referral is in order if the quality of voice remains poor over a period of time.

Language impairments

Language impairments refer to problems in comprehending, expressing, or otherwise making functional use of spoken language. These impairments involve disorders in auditory reception and expressive language. Auditory receptive skills include ability to receive meaning from spoken language. Expressive skills refer to the ability to produce verbal language. These conditions may operate so that a student comprehends what a speaker says, but is unable to express thoughts in return. Aphasia is one such disorder. It is caused by disease or injury to brain centers, resulting in loss or impairment of the ability to comprehend or produce language (Kelly and Vergason, 1978). Aphasic students may struggle to put together bits and pieces of language to make a response to what is heard.

Additional language impairments may include defects in semantic systems, syntactic systems, morphological systems, phonological systems, and higher level language use (Weiss, 1979). Let us see what these impairments entail.

Semantic system deficits are problems related to word meaning. They involve difficulties both in understanding words and in establishing word relationships. These difficulties are apparent in similarities and differences of words, opposites, synonyms, and antonyms. Inabilities to deal with these relationships prevent the student from comprehending meaning from spoken and written communication.

Syntactic system deficits stem from the inability to employ the conventions of sequencing words and sentences. These conventions include subject-verb agreement, negation, proper form for questions, and other important rules of grammar.

Morphology refers to the study of word formations. *Morphological system deficits* cause difficulties in such things as making a word plural or expressing past, present, and future tenses in a way consistent with the context of what is being communicated.

Phonological system deficits consist of inability to form the sound families that are embedded in the sound system of oral language. Weiss (1979) suggests that, rather than having learned all of the forty-three sounds (phonemes) of English, the child may have mastered only two or three vowels and a scattering of consonants. In other instances, the child with a phonological deficit has all the sounds of English but uses them in ways that are inappropriate to the language.

Higher level language usage includes the ability to classify, compare, develop one-to-one relationships, and integrate these skills into the language system. Students who are deficient in these skills may exhibit difficulties in relating events in stories, following along during oral reading, or sticking to information that pertains to what is being discussed.

Many speech and language impairments occur within the five categories just delineated. Moreover, many of them will be coupled with other speech and language impairments, and will affect work in academic areas. Vellutino (1977) reported that a significant number of children who fail to acquire reading skills also have language problems.

Whether the referral from the classroom teacher results from observed speech and language difficulties, or whether it results from evidence noted within academic and behavioral areas, the regular classroom teacher is key to detecting speech and language impairments. Bankson (1978) reports that children with language disorders commonly comprise up to 60% of a speech pathologist's case load. Again, this shows how frequently these students appear in the regular classroom. The classroom teacher must deal with speech difficulties in accord with the type and severity of the problem. Close contact and communication with the other professionals involved in the student's therapy and education will help the student overcome speech handicaps in the regular classroom. Classroom teachers, then, need to remember the following suggestions when working with the language-impaired child:

1. Refer the child to a professional if problems are suspected in language and speech, particularly if they seem to be a result of hearing difficulties or emotional problems.
2. Accept the student. Focus on developing a positive self-concept by emphasizing strong points.
3. Never pressure a child to respond. An environment should be created to stimulate the student to speak, and to provide opportunities for responses.
4. Establish a goal or objective that the student will be able to accomplish. If a student is receiving services from a speech pathologist, many goals will have already been set. At this point, it is doubly important to develop consistent goals for the student in the regular classroom while following through on the goals established by the speech pathologist.
5. Provide a variety of language experiences through which the student can experience success.
6. Assist the speech pathologist in providing a comprehensive oral language program.
7. Begin with short lessons. At first, a 5-minute period is all that may be profitable. Complete the lesson before the student becomes tired and disinterested.

8. Remember that you are a language and speech model for the students. Speak in simple sentences; speak slowly, clearly, and enthusiastically.

9. Do not expect the student to speak like you. The child should not be expected or be asked to repeat every word that you want him/her to say.

10. Seek information concerning technique that the speech pathologist uses.

11. Begin a remedial program, if the services of a speech clinician are not available. Identify the child's language weaknesses and decide what he needs to learn. If you cannot determine the specific language weaknesses, it is best to use an unstructured approach that provides general language stimulation.

12. Listen attentively and actively to what the student has to say. Do not look away while the student is speaking.

13. Position yourself at the student's eye level when you speak.

14. Reward student efforts to use a word meaningfully. The student should be made to feel extremely proud of his/her words. Do not expect or demand perfection. Talk with the student, giving a chance to add his/her "two cents' worth," even if it is difficult to understand. Try to convince the student that talking is a good way to communicate.

15. When the student says a word incorrectly, don't correct or criticize. Simply say the word, pronouncing it correctly. In this way, an appropriate model is provided. Don't penalize the student by asking him/her to repeat it.

16. Engage in "self-talk" whenever it is appropriate. Talk out loud about what you are doing. Let the student be aware that there are words to describe all sorts of activities. For example, verbalize that the board is being erased, or that desks are being moved, or that lunchtime is approaching.

17. Engage in parallel-talk, that is, verbalize what is happening to the student. For example, as a student is participating in free time activities, verbalize to him/her what he/she is doing. Utilize words to describe his/her activities. This provides words for the student to think with.

18. Encourage group participation, even if at times it means allowing the student to fill a nonspeaking role.

19. Provide a model of acceptance that other students in the class will follow. Demonstrate by actions that speech impairment makes no difference with respect to friendship, academic status, or any other relationship in school.

BEHAVIORAL IMPLICATIONS; SIGNS OF IMPAIRMENTS

The Bureau of the Education for the Handicapped compiled statistics that showed the distribution of children with handicapping conditions being served during the school year 1977-1978. The largest group of handicapped students receiving services were the speech impaired, at about 32%. Their numbers are so large that classroom teachers must be ever watchful in order to identify them. The signs they should look for were listed by DeWeese and Lillywhite (1973). Any one of the following conditions indict that a student's speech warrants a referral to the speech clinician:

1. Failure to speak by age of 2 (this can be ascertained from student's records or parent conferences)
2. Unintelligible speech
3. Delay of more than a year in producing sounds, given the developmental sequence in which most children produce sounds
4. Continual omission of initial consonants (such as *b* in "book," so that the student may say "I read the ook")
5. Substitutions on sounds
6. Excessive use of vowels
7. Inability to produce sentences
8. Continually drops word endings
9. Sentences remain agrammatical (or lacking in proper grammar)
10. Embarrassment about own speech at any age
11. Noticable disfluency
12. Continual distortion, omission, or substitution of any sounds
13. Monotone voice, very loud, very soft, or with a strange quality
14. Inappropriate pitch for age or sex
15. Noticeable hypernasality or lack of nasal resonance
16. Unusual confusion or reversals in connected speech
17. Abnormal rhythm, rate, and inflection
18. Failure to respond well to questions or verbal commands
19. Echoing questions or other verbal materials
20. Unduly rapid speech
21. Indications of pain when speaking
22. Inappropriate speech patterns for age
23. Stuttering

These behavioral indicators may occur singly or in combinations. Each may indicate a different problem, and require its own remedial approach.

SUMMARY

In a report to Congress submitted by The Bureau of Education For The Handicapped, it was established that speech-impaired school-age children were the greatest percentage (32%) of handicapped children being served in 1977-1978.

Furthermore, the predominant educational environment in which these students were being served was the regular classroom.

Speech impairments are many in type and degree of seriousness. They include stuttering, articulation impairments, language impairments, and voice impairments, each of which affects educational performance. Regular classroom teachers should be aware of types and indicators of speech and language impairments. They should know how to contribute to the correction of those impairments. They should assume a team-member role with the speech pathologist, who will likely provide therapy to speech-impaired students on a pull-out basis. They will be instrumental in implementing the remedial activities organized by the speech pathologist. In addition, they will have to develop activities to meet specific needs of speech-impaired students in academic and social areas of the curriculum.

SUGGESTED ACTIVITIES

1. Arrange a visit to a speech therapy center. Observe the clinicians at work with their clients.
2. Obtain a manual that illustrates and describes the placement of tongue and lips for producing the various speech sounds. Practice forming those placements. Instruct a classmate (as you would a child) on producing the sounds correctly.
3. Invite a speech pathologist or clinician to speak with the class about diagnosis and remediation of various speech problems.

SUGGESTED READINGS

American Speech and Hearing Association: Speech and language disorders and the speech and language pathologist, Washington, D.C., 1976, The Association.

Bankson, N. W.: The speech and language impaired. In Meyen, E. L., editor: Exceptional children and youth: an introduction, Denver, 1978, Love Publishing Co.

Barry, H.: The young aphasic child, Washington, D.C., 1961, Alexander Graham Bell Association for the Deaf.

Berry, M.: Language disorders of children: the bases and diagnoses, New York, 1969, Appleton-Century-Crofts.

Bush, W., and Giles, M.: Aids to psycholinguistic teaching, Columbus, OH, 1969, Charles E. Merrill Publishing Co.

Carrell, J. A.: Disorders of articulation, Englewood Cliffs, NJ, 1968, Prentice-Hall, Inc.

DeWeese, D. D., and Lillywhite, H.: Speech disorders in children. In DeWeese, D. D., and Saunders, W. H., editors: Textbook of otolaryngology, St. Louis, 1973, The C. V. Mosby Co.

Egland, G.: Speech and language problems: a guide for the classroom teacher, Englewood Cliffs, NJ, 1970, Prentice-Hall, Inc.

Hallahan, D. P., and Kauffman, J. M.: Exceptional children: an introduction to special education, Englewood Cliffs, NJ, 1978, Prentice-Hall, Inc.

Hansen, S.: Getting a headstart on speech and language problems, Omaha, 1975, University of Nebraska Medical Center.

John, V., and Goldstein, L.: The social context of language acquisition. In The disadvantaged child, vol. 1, Seattle, 1967, Special Child Publications.

Johnson, W., Brown, S., Curtis, J., Edney, C., and Keaster, J.: Speech handicapped school children, ed. 3, New York, 1967, Harper & Row, Publishers, Inc.

Kelly, L. J., and Vergason, G. A.: Dictionary of special education and rehabilitation, Denver, 1978, Love Publishing Co.

Kirk, S., and Kirk, W.: Psycholinguistic learning disabilities: diagnosis and remediation, Urbana, IL, 1971, University of Illinois Press.

Menyuk, P.: The acquisition and development of language, Englewood Cliffs, NJ, 1971, Prentice-Hall, Inc.

Perkins, W. H.: Speech pathology: an applied

behavioral science, St. Louis, 1971, The C. V. Mosby Co.

Project PREM: Preparing regular educators for mainstreaming, Austin, TX, 1975, State Department of Education.

Speech Pathology Department: You, your child and language, Omaha, 1974, University of Nebraska Medical Center.

Turnbull, A. P., and Schulz, J. B.: Mainstreaming handicapped students: a guide for the classroom teacher, Boston, 1979, Allyn & Bacon, Inc.

United States Department of Health, Education, and Welfare: Progress toward a free appropriate public education: a report to Congress on the implementation of Public Law 94-142: The Education For All Handicapped Children Act, Washington, D.C., January 1979, The Bureau of Education for the Handicapped.

Van Hattum, R.: Services of the speech clinician in schools: progress and prospects, J. Am. Speech Hearing Assoc. 18:59-63, 1976.

Van Riper, C.: The nature of stuttering, Englewood Cliffs, NJ, 1971, Prentice-Hall, Inc.

Van Riper, C.: Speech correction: principles and methods, Englewood Cliffs, NJ, 1952, Prentice-Hall, Inc.

Vellutino, F. R.: Alternative conceptualizations of dyslexia: evidence in support of verbal-deficit hypothesis, Howard Educ. Rev. 47:334-354, 1977.

Weiss, M. A.: Speech and language disabled children and youth. In Swanson, B. M., and Willis, D. J., editors: Understanding exceptional children and youth: an introduction to special education, Chicago, 1979, Rand McNally & Co.

Wiig, E., and Semel, E.: Language disabilities in children and adolescents, Columbus, OH, 1976, Charles E. Merrill Publishing Co.

Wood, N.: Delayed speech and language development, Englewood Cliffs, NJ, 1964, Prentice-Hall, Inc.

CHAPTER 11

Teaching gifted students

Leif Fearn, *San Diego State University*

This chapter deals with gifted students. It may seem out of place in this book, since giftedness is clearly not a handicap, at least not in the usual sense of the word. Neither is it mentioned in Public Law 94-142, which has given form to the other chapters contained herein.

Still, two facts point to the need for this material. (1) Most teachers already have gifted students in their classrooms, because many schools do not provide special programs for the gifted. (2) Authorities are beginning to question the wisdom of segregating the gifted. The benefits that accrue to handicapped students when mainstreamed are paralleled by benefits that can accrue to the gifted. They, too, require a balanced view of humanity, and they must prepare to work and live in the greater society. This preparation can best be accomplished within the regular classroom. This does not imply that curriculum, materials, and instruction for the gifted should be the same as for the nongifted. What it does imply is that the gifted, like everyone else, should be considered individuals, with unique needs and abilities. Their education should attend specifically to those needs and abilities.

WHO ARE THE GIFTED?

Gifted children and youth are people who show promise of making superior progress in school. They do not necessarily make this progress, but they do show the promise, and more often than not they fulfill it. Their giftedness usually has to do with achievement in basic school subjects. Sometimes, however, it will show itself in exceptional ability in music, creativity, or artistic performances.

Occasionally, students are identified as gifted through observation of their special talents. But since the main criterion for giftedness is present or potential success in school, identification is usually confirmed through the use of tests. These tests focus on achievement and IQ: the former shows present school success, the latter shows uncommon potential for future school success.

In point of fact, however, gifted students show superior traits in other areas as well. Beyond achievement in school subjects, they often possess potential for superiority as shown in traits such as the following:

1. Sensitivity to the needs of others, often operationalized as an altruistic attitude
2. A need for independence, often apparent in a demand for the right to do and think for themselves
3. A proclivity for creative expression, often apparent in original ideas, fluency of thought, and immense capacity for inquiry
4. A capacity for social leadership that is often shown in the ability to influence peers and manipulate teachers

5. Broad interests that extend in numerous directions; at times, however, the students engross themselves in a single interest for days or weeks on end
6. Seemingly natural talents in such areas as the arts, music, creative expression, or general productivity
7. Noticeable behaviors not typically seen in normal students, such as intensity, persistence, self-assured introversion, and the appearance of detachment from mundane topics

It is important to note that gifted students rarely display all of these characteristics. Most often they show a few of them, but sometimes no more than one or two.

Drews (1963) discussed these trait variations in her study of gifted adolescents. She found that they seemed to fall mainly into one of four clusters, with some overlapping:

Academic achiever	Social effectiveness
Creative performer	Rebellious

In considering Drews' scheme, it is important to keep a significant fact in mind: due largely to the very nature of giftedness, individual differences that exist within any group of gifted students will be greater than the average differences between a gifted group and a nongifted group. That means you can expect great differences among gifted students. These differences are so great that they make it difficult to form generalizations about the gifted.

We have noted some of the traits of gifted students. But what should teachers look for in students which might lead to their being identified as gifted?

The key referral characteristic is marked superiority in one or more areas of productive endeavor. To say that one is markedly superior is to say that the person is very different from the average, at least in some way. Let us see how the notion of "very different" is described.

Suppose you went out and collected 100 fifth-grade girls. They would range from small to big, physically immature to physically mature. It is quite likely that four or five of those girls would have figures very different from the others, different in the sense that they are large and very mature in appearance. Another four or five would have figures very different in that they are small and very immature. If success in some important endeavor depended entirely on mature appearance, the large girls might be considered gifted. On the other hand, if success depended entirely on very immature appearance, the small girls might be considered gifted.

This illustration might seem farfetched, but there is a world in which size makes a difference—professional football and basketball afford much money and recognition to a few people who happen to count size among their various blessings. In that world, great size is a gift. Wilt Chamberlain, Bill Walton, and "Too-Tall" Jones are certainly gifted.

Obviously you can be gifted—markedly superior—in ways other than size. Take the intellect, for example. John Stuart Mill was a markedly superior person in that world. He read earlier than most, became fluent in many languages, comprehended ideas more efficiently than others, and entered a wider range of intellectual pursuits than most. You might be interested to know he was also a feminist long before that posture was acceptable for women, let alone men. By the criteria of the intellectual world, Mill was an eminently gifted individual. The same can be said for Albert Einstein, Thomas Jefferson, W. E. B. DuBois, and Woodrow Wilson; they were all acknowledged to be gifted, though each in ways different from the others.

In the world of the school, gifted students are those whose skills and abilities allow them to stand above others in what is important in school. Thus it is that, when looking for gifted students for diagnostic referral, we seek those people who are intellectually and artistically different, who stand clearly above the mass of their peers.

HOW SHOULD THE GIFTED BE TAUGHT?

This section describes accommodations that should be made for working most effectively with the gifted. It is presented in two parts, corresponding to the two locales presently used for gifted education: the regular classroom and the gifted education classroom.

The regular classroom

Most teachers occasionally have gifted students in their regular classrooms. As mentioned earlier, the gifted are in those classrooms for two reasons. They are there because most schools still do not make segregated accommodations for the gifted; they are also there because, even in those schools with segregated accommodations, identification procedures fail to identify some gifted students.

Teachers have traditionally devised their own procedures for working with the gifted. Those procedures included ignoring them, holding them in line with the total class, encouraging them to work independently, using them as teacher aides, or providing them with individualized tutoring in advanced studies.

Some of these procedures reflect misconceptions about students in the class-room. One such misconception is that gifted students "will make it on their own." That assumption is not only erroneous, it is detrimental to their education. As the gifted seek to fit in, as all of us do, teachers are lulled into the illusion that they have adjusted. The adjustment is not "making it on their own." It is trading off personal education for social comfort. Many gifted students pursue that course. That is one of the main reasons for setting up special educational programs for them.

Enlightened educators, through the years, have used three major approaches to improve the education of the gifted in regular classrooms. Those approaches are *acceleration, enrichment,* and *individualized instruction.*

Acceleration. Acceleration is the process of moving gifted students into aca-demically demanding situations that better fit their skills and abilities. Typically, acceleration has meant moving a student into a higher grade. That procedure is now rare. It has been found that moving a younger student into an older group can damage social development. Still, acceleration sometimes works to the advantage of gifted students. It certainly seemed to do so in the case of Mike Grost (1970), whose abilities so far outdistanced those of his age mates that he entered uni-versity classes as an early teenager. In his case, the dramatic social differences between him and his older classmates caused no difficulty of consequence.

Another way of accelerating students is to keep them in the same grade and class, but provide them content and materials for a higher grade level.

Enrichment. Enrichment, the second major approach to working with gifted students, means a broader, more intense involvement in the study of content designed for that grade level. Enrichment has usually leaned toward research and report writing, both of which allow learners to delve more deeply than normal into selected fields of study.

Individualized instruction. The third major approach to teaching the gifted within the regular classroom is individualized instruction, in which instruction is tailored to the needs, interests, abilities, and working speed of the student. This approach is sound, but most teachers have difficulty implementing it. First, there are too many other students to attend to. Second, teachers usually lack adequate skills and materials for individualizing instruction. When they attempt to do so, the result is often mechanical, relying on packaged materials or programmed instruction.

The main problem with programmed instruction is that it reduces interaction among students, a process generally considered to be very important in education. Desirable alternatives to programmed instruction are available for individualizing instruction. They include diagnostic-prescriptive teaching, the project method, commercial kits and programs, and open experience. Learning centers can also be used effectively in individualized programs for the gifted. (Some of these approaches, together with management strategies, were presented in Chapter 4. Additional approaches are discussed in more detail in *Individualizing Instruction* (Charles, 1980).)

These three procedures for attending to gifted students—acceleration, enrichment, and variations on individualized instruction—have enjoyed only limited success. The preponderance of authoritative opinion is that those three approaches have not adequately met the needs of gifted students; special classes for gifted learners have therefore been formed in many schools. It is important to note that, for the most part, these special classes have not been strongly advocated by teachers. They have come instead from public demands, most especially from the parents of gifted children and youth.

The gifted classroom

If you visit gifted classrooms, you won't see much that is greatly different from what you see in regular classrooms, except that the students are motivated, very capable, and more self-directing than average students. Typically they are engaged in "enriched curricula," which means, more often than not, variations on the general education curriculum that lead learners into greater depth, scope, and complexity. They will probably be working at levels of achievement well beyond those normal for their age.

Two different administrative formats are *segregation* and *pull-out*.

Segregation. The segregated format finds gifted students placed all day, every day, in a classroom called "gifted." Perhaps it has some other name, such as MGM or ELP. That classroom is conducted by a teacher of the gifted. In the room one finds an enriched curriculum with basic skill emphasis, individual study, reporting, research, and study areas that are uncharacteristic for the age level, such as anthropology, higher mathematics, archaeology, and physics. The students also show an accelerated rate of achievement in basic school content. Their reading and mathematics achievement test scores range from two to four or five grade levels above normal. Students are typically happy in the gifted room; they usually prefer the gifted room over the regular classroom. They like the latitude, the enrichment, and the association with classmates similar to themselves.

Pull-out. The pull-out format is seen more often than the segregated format. It finds students from a school or cluster of schools going to a central place one or more times each week. There they find a teacher of the gifted and an environment better suited to their needs. In the pull-out room, they conduct research, write reports, have discussions about worldly issues, and learn accelerated and enriched content. The room also contains a variety of special materials. You might expect to see three-dimensional tic-tac-toe, a chess set, the complete printed works of scholars, scientists, and literary figures, microscopes, cameras, videotape equipment, and sets of science materials. Pull-out learners often do special projects that enhance what they are learning in the regular classroom.

SERIOUSNESS IN GIFTED EDUCATION

Today, gifted education is quite "serious" in its operations. Perhaps the most significant indicator of increasing seriousness is the move toward impact research, that is, research on what gifted education does for gifted students that general education does not. Reports of impact research are still few in number, but they have begun to appear in the literature. A good example is Stanley's (1976) investigation into mathematically precocious youth.

Another example of seriousness is the current focus on identification and programming. Children and youth are now being identified for gifted programs more on the basis of their breadth of exceptionality than on their high IQ scores, although the latter remain of sufficient import that some states fund their schools on a certified per pupil basis, "certified" meaning the achievement of a certain score on an individually administered IQ test.

Most indicative of seriousness, however, is the increasing attention to the specific gifts that these students bring to the classroom. Two examples of such attention are explained in the following paragraphs, which have to do with enrichment and qualitative difference. Both have strong implications for regular classroom teachers who will be working with mainstreamed gifted students.

Programs of enrichment

Enrichment has taken on a much more sophisticated flavor than it had in the past. Helped by the work of Renzulli (1976), enrichment has become a legitimate perspective in gifted education. Renzulli's "Enrichment Triad Model" stresses an enriched curricular structure where student learning goes above and beyond that found in the normal classroom. The model is presented in a sequence of three types, each calling upon teachers and students to fulfill certain responsibilities for personal and educational growth.

What Renzulli calls Type I Enrichment is exploratory. Students are brought into contact with directions for study that may be of interest to them. Students are caused to explore with purpose, that is, identify a direction for study in a reasonable period of time. Type I Enrichment causes students to wonder and ponder about phenomena, to inquire into the structure of knowledge and content. It requires that the teacher provide a wide array of resources into which students can plunge their exploratory energies. It also requires that they notice the work patterns that students display, because those patterns suggest directions for Type II Enrichment activities.

Type II Enrichment is designed to provide students with skills necessary to pursue their identified direction of study. It consists of various methods and learning strategies associated with the pursuit of knowledge. Mainly focused on training experiences in intellectual and affective areas, Type II Enrichment develops the ability to work with new problems and problem-solving situations. Type II Enrichment activities are means to ends, ends that are associated with the generation of knowledge, insight, and perhaps products that display new knowledge and insight.

Type III Enrichment places students in the position of investigator. Its purpose is to cause students to identify and clarify problems that can be solved, develop directions for learning that can be followed, and use their resources and skills to solve the problems. Type III Enrichment brings students into contact with the responsibility to follow through on their commitments to learn. The result of Type III Enrichment is student productions that should, if the process is to have credibility for teachers and students, find their way to some outlet or display.

The Enrichment Triad Model is an attempt to give substance to the concept of enrichment, beyond that normally found. Students are responsible for exploring, focusing, developing skills appropriate to solving problems, pursuing solutions, and reporting their progress or product. It is a systematic perspective on enrichment.

Qualitative difference

The other programming perspective has centered around the concept of "qualitative difference." That term is used to describe differences in *kind* of intellect, ability, or talent, as opposed to mere differences in IQ scores.

To understand better the concept of qualitative difference, consider the nature of typical school education. The content of that education is: (1) the basic skills of reading, writing, and computing; (2) essential subject matter knowledge in the arts, sciences, and social sciences; and (3) interactive group processes to enhance human relations skills and group effectiveness. So long as this content is perpetuated in gifted education, albeit in an accelerated fashion, there is no way to provide qualitative differences for the gifted student. The differences are merely quantitative—differences in amount and speed.

A qualitatively different approach would change the content from that found in typical education to something else. The question is, what else?

The answer is something called "intelligence education," which is recognized as curricular designs in which the major focus is placed on the development of intellectual skills. The following paragraphs present two perspectives for intellectual skill development. They were selected because they are operational and because they enjoy a certain amount of credibility. Those two perspectives are "Structure of Intellect" and "Creative Thinking Skills."

PERSPECTIVE 1: STRUCTURE OF INTELLECT

When Mary N. Meeker (1969) suggested educational implications for J. P. Guilford's model of intellect (1956), she presented the profession with a way to diagnose intellectual processes defined by Guilford. By implication, she also showed how to design the curriculum around those intellectual processes, that is, in ways that would help students learn how to think in specific ways. Meeker's work is chronicled in a long list of publications. She is headquartered at the Structure of Intellect Institute in El Segundo, California.

Meeker has designed instructional materials that key to Structure of Intellect abilities. Those abilities have to do with intellectual functions that people perform. Such functions include cognizing, or comprehending. They include remembering and evaluating. They included producing, which is of two sorts: they produce convergently, which is a narrowing in on single correct responses; they also produce divergently, which is exploring outward so as to produce multiple correct responses of different types. In short, we all possess the intellectual functions of cognition, memory, evaluation, convergent production, and divergent production. Each of these functions involves abilities that can be learned and taught.

People use these functions to think with different kinds of material, or input. In the environment there is *figural* material, or material in the form of pictures, objects, and things. There is *symbolic* material, or material in the form of letters, numbers, notes on a staff, and so forth. There is *semantic* material, or material that is in the form of ideas. Finally, there is material in the form of *behavior,* or what people and objects do. Thus, when people think, they do so by performing intellectual functions on material that is in figural, symbolic, semantic, or behavioral form.

When people think, they attempt to arrange ideas and materials in the environment in certain ways. The arrangements they produce include single pieces of material, called *units*. When grouped into categories, the materials comprise *classes*. Relationships between and among units and classes are called *relations*. Thinking arranges some things in sequences. English sentences, for example, are word sequences. These sequences are called *systems*. When thinking causes materials to undergo changes, the results are called *transformations*. Finally, when people predict, they produce *implications*.

There you have in a nutshell the three dimensions of thinking. People intellectually *do* certain things, with certain *kinds* of material, in an effort to produce certain kinds of *arrangements*. These three dimensions describe our thinking skills and provide a handle on teaching those skills to students.

As teachers become familiar with Meeker's terminology of Structure of Intellect, it becomes obvious that classroom thinking can be defined in terms of these intellectual abilities.

Applying Structure of Intellect notions is one way to provide intelligence education. As you can see, this makes a qualitative difference. A teacher might decide, for instance, to stress and teach the skills of evaluation and divergent production. Instruction can easily be directed at those goals. For example, students can generalize about the initial consonant sound in the word "pig" by formulating lists of words that begin like "pig." This is an example of a divergent thinking exercise. Another example would be having students generate alternatives for filling the boxes in the following equations.

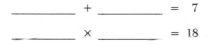

$$\underline{\hspace{2cm}} + \underline{\hspace{2cm}} = 7$$

$$\underline{\hspace{2cm}} \times \underline{\hspace{2cm}} = 18$$

Yet another example would call on students to decide how someone else might have approached the problem differently; this causes the students to evaluate. As teachers understand that students can approach typical problems and tasks in unusual ways, they become able to arrange instruction so that it becomes intelligence education.

Meeker has gone a long step further. She has devised templates (Meeker, 1969) for converting student performance on IQ tests into terms compatible with Structure of Intellect abilities. This allows the IQ tests to be used as diagnostic tests for intellectual functioning. As such they can point out intellectual abilities in which the student is weak, as well as abilities in which the student is strong. Intelligence education would coordinate student work with those areas of strength and weakness. Meeker and her associates have also produced a test that is directed, item by item, to intellectual abilities. Teachers who use the test can send the results to the Institute in El Segundo. For a modest fee, the Institute will return individualized learning materials for each student, based upon the student's performance on the intellectual abilities test.

There are therefore three ways to provide intelligence education within the Structure of Intellect framework: (1) focusing on functions, inputs, and productions; (2) using the templates for diagnostic purposes; and (3) obtaining individualized materials that match diagnosed areas of strength and weakness. Research and development applications are being conducted throughout the

United States. The results of these applications can be obtained from the Institute.

The Structure of Intellect model is surprisingly easy to understand, and the applications are familiar in general teaching practice. It provides a key to intelligence education, where one makes specific application, to specific students, in ways that make a qualitative difference.

PERSPECTIVE 2: CREATIVE THINKING SKILLS

There was an elementary classroom in Southern California in which thirty students and one teacher worked during a recent academic year. The students ranged in age from 8 to 13 years. Seventeen were non-Caucasians, ten spoke a native language other than English, and twenty were categorized as belonging to lower to lower middle socioeconomic levels. Only six qualified as gifted according to the IQ criterion. These students were instructed for a year using an approach called "Creative Thinking Skills." The California Test of Basic Skills was applied in April. Data from that test showed the following. Third-grade students were advanced an average of 2 years in both reading and mathematics. Fifth-graders were advanced by over two grade levels in total reading, and three grade levels in mathematics. Sixth-graders were advanced well over three grade levels in total reading and nearly three grade levels in mathematics.

That classroom was guided by the second perspective on intelligence education, Creative Thinking Skills. The teacher had been trained to help students focus not on creativity per se, but on the skills involved in creative thinking. Those skills and applications, articulated by Fearn (1976), became the format for the educational process in the classroom. All the students participated in creative thinking in all areas of school content, all day long, for the entire school year.

To understand this approach to intelligence education, one must distinguish between what is meant by creativity, and what is meant by creative thinking skills. The term "creativity" has been associated with inventive or creative products. People tend to think of creativity in terms of the masterpieces of such people as Mozart, Einstein, Chagall, and Beckett. Such a view of creativity excludes work done by school students, since they rarely produce masterpieces. Neither does the view correspond with what is learned in school. And if that were not enough, that view of creativity floats in ignorance. No one knows how Mozart did what he did. Many people know about the skills he had, the kinds of things that motivated him, and so forth, but no one has successfully explained, in ways that generalize to either classrooms or studio, the dynamics that produced his compositions.

The term "creative thinking skills" represents something quite different. It refers to operational skills that can be understood, taught, used, and generalized to classroom instruction.

Creative thinking skills fall into three dimensions of attitude and behavior (Fearn, 1977). Thinking does not occur in a vacuum devoid of information and ideas. It always depends on data, knowns, or speculations. Hence, the first dimension of creative thinking skills is *data collection,* learning to become increasingly attuned to collecting the information necessary for thinking. This dimension relies on several discrete skills. One of them is called "awareness," the ability to sense or notice. Awareness is enhanced when learners attempt to visualize mentally a place such as their bedroom and then draw the room or list its contents. Such an exercise causes learners to reconstruct accurately their visual experiences. It causes them to pay attention to details, relationships, and how things work. Other good exercises are drawing bicycles from memory, drawing their thumb without looking, and recalling the appearances of the blouses or shirts they own.

A second skill is "fluency," or putting forth multiple ideas in response to a problem. Fluent thinking is enhanced as learners make lists of things—lists of red things, lists of ways to accomplish seventeen using addition with at least one odd number, lists of ways to measure the height of a building when one cannot get closer than 50 yards.

A third creative thinking skill associated with gathering data is "flexibility," or perceiving problems with different perspectives. Flexibility is enhanced as learners struggle with the problem of cutting a pie into eight pieces of equal size and shape, by making only three cuts. As they solve such a problem, they get a handle on how to approach tasks from multiple perspectives.

The second dimension of creative thinking skills has to do with how people *process data.* Included in this dimension are skills called elaboration and complexity, and an attitude best called persistence. "Elaboration" is the ability to embellish on an idea or problem, to add onto it, to build from a known base. Writing a composition from an outline is elaboration. Making a picture from doodles is elaboration. Building a sentence through the use of modification and increasingly mature clause structure is elaboration.

"Complexity" is the willingness to approach chaotic situations, and find order there. Creative thinking is at least partly a matter of being willing to deal with ambiguity, to work within the context of complex situations. Elaboration and complexity both depend on "persistence." This is the attitude of "stick-to-it-iveness," of never giving up. Instruction in creative thinking skills holds learners responsible for their commitments for working through tasks to completion. Students are taught that they must persist for a reasonable period of time simply to learn the extent to which problems are solvable through sheer effort.

The third dimension to which the creative thinking skill perspective is addressed has to do with the matter of *coming to grips with oneself* in the thinking process. Within this dimension are skills labeled "originality," "curiosity," and "imagination." Originality has to do with new ideas; curiosity has to do with exploring and wondering; imagination has to do with speculations about relationships and their causes and effects.

The creative thinking skills approach structures all teaching and learning sequences around the skills just mentioned. The mathematics format has students solving real-life problems through mathematics. It is helpful for them to translate situations into word problems, written so they can be understood easily.

Students should spend a lot of time making lists of things. They can make lists of things of various colors, of various shapes and sizes, of things that fit combinations of attributes (things that are green, smooth, smaller than a toaster, and organic). They can make wonderful wall posters that contain lists of things that they wonder about, things they have pondered or thought about during the past several months, things that they both did and did not understand. They can read great quantities of material from journals like *The Futurist*, a publication that works almost exclusively within the context of pondering, wondering, and speculation.

Students should also write daily. Their writing should be done in response to tasks like: "Write a sentence that contains the following ideas: old man, tractor, rain, and feelings," and "Write a fifteen-word sentence in which a form of the word 'move' is in the seventh position."

How does a teacher conduct a creative thinking skills classroom? One approach, described by Fearn (1977), is the "full creative thinking skills classroom." It reorganizes all curricular content into creative thinking skills terminology and operations. It provides creative thinking materials throughout the classroom. It holds learners responsible for becoming increasingly aware, persistent, and courageous. It is not a noisy classroom; but neither does it appear very neat and ordered. Most characteristic of the full creative thinking skills classroom is the teacher's willingness to suffer the pain of learner frustration that comes inevitably from the teacher's refusal to release learners from their responsibilities.

The instructional format finds one or more areas of basic content being presented and learned as creative thinking skills. It is not easy to find materials that fit that format, although some such materials are available. One example of curricular material written specifically for creative thinking skill development is the writing program called *The Writing Kabyn* (Fearn and Foster, 1979). This material permits the teacher to conduct a developmental writing program, plus much of the total language arts program, in the form of creative thinking skills development. Other such materials include the Unified Science and Mathematics for Elementary Schools (USMES), and Critical Thinking (Harnadek, 1976).

Finally, teachers might want to bring their students into contact with learning materials designed for creative thinking development. There are several publishers involved in the development and dissemination of such materials, among them, Dissemination of Knowledge (Buffalo, New York), Kabyn Books (San Diego, California), and Midwest Publications (Troy, Michigan).

To summarize, intelligence education is a way of providing qualitative difference that is coming into its own in education of the gifted. It shows considerable promise for being useful to teachers who have gifted students in their regular classrooms. It requires a certain amount of preparation, but does not entail the outlay of impressive amounts of effort or money. One good thing about intelligence education is that it does not exclude the participation of regular students in the classroom. They benefit from it, too. For that reason, intelligence education is a most appropriate way to accommodate gifted students who are mainstreamed into the regular classroom.

QUESTIONS AND ANSWERS ABOUT MAINSTREAMING THE GIFTED

To close this chapter, we will consider some questions commonly asked by regular classroom teachers.

Question: What should I expect of gifted students? How will they behave, and how will they treat me?

Answer: Gifted students will be very well informed in specific topics; they will also be broadly informed. They demand a great deal of attention. They are delightful in their insatiable appetite for knowing. In certain topics older students will know much more than the teacher. But they are not wiser than the teacher. They need teacher guidance, support, and feedback.

Question: What should I do if I have only one or two gifted students in my classroom?

Answer: First, don't make them over into teacher aides. Second, don't forget your own value to them. You must be their teacher, demanding performance, responding to inquiries, providing resources necessary for growth, and insisting on responsibility for educational achievement. Gifted children and youth are more characteristically children and youth than they are gifted. You must work with them on that basis. Third, gifted students, like all others, deserve the opportunity to be learners in an active sense, rather than pupils in the passive sense. Their teacher is responsible for creating an environment that engages them actively in learning. This implies decreasing the amounts of time given to formal instruction, and increasing the amounts of time where students assume responsibility for learning. It means posing problems for students to solve that require persistent application of basic skills and intellectual abilities.

Question: What resources do I need for teaching gifted students?

Answer: The teacher's professional ability to be a teacher is the most powerful resource available. Well-trained teachers are sensitive to the traditional resources found in learning centers, media centers, professional and curriculum libraries, and the larger community. Teachers of the gifted have learned how to use field trips, for instance, as a relatively formal research experiences. They use "mentors," local people with whom they associate learners in "apprentice" relationships. The key is finding resources that provide intellectual and creative stimulation, not just harder work.

Question: What do I do with a student who only wants to read, or work in mathematics, or study anthropology, but wants nothing to do with the other work?

Answer: Gifted students are quite likely to do that, and it is usually troubling for their teachers. Interestingly, gifted students tend to achieve a surprising measure of something akin to a broad educational base, even as they seem to stick to a single topic or area. A student who devotes a month to a single topic in history likely delves into other areas as well. Reading will be involved. Perhaps writing and art will, too. The interest will bring up other questions that the student will want to answer. Eventually the pursuit of those questions broadens the educational base. However, we must remember that school is a place where teachers and learners are responsible for certain areas of knowledge and skill. When students say they don't need to learn how to write because they don't intend to write when they become mathematicians, the teacher must draw the students into writing anyway. Writing is a skill we all use, and teachers and students, as participants in school, are responsible for it.

Question: In a nutshell, what is the key to working effectively with the gifted?

Answer: The key is to allow the gifted to be persons in their own right, to hold them to those things for which they are legitimately responsible as students, and to encourage the fulfillment of their special gifts. That key, as you can see, is not any different from the key to working effectively with all types of students.

SUMMARY

Giftedness is not a handicapping condition and is therefore not included in the provisions of PL 94-142. Still, classroom teachers have gifted students in their classrooms. They need information about how best to teach those students.

Giftedness is defined as the potential for significantly greater than normal school success. Students have been identified as gifted on the basis of IQ scores; increasingly, their breadth of talent is receiving more attention.

Gifted students have been accommodated into the regular classroom in three ways: acceleration, enrichment, and individualized instruction. They have been taught in special classes through two organizational patterns: segregation in gifted classes full-time, and pull-out from regular to gifted classes on a part-time basis.

Heretofore, gifted education has been little more than intensified regular education. The current trend is to seek "qualitatively different" education for the gifted. Two such attempts at qualitative difference are seen in the Structure of Intellect approach and the Creative Thinking Skills approach.

SUGGESTED ACTIVITIES

1. Peruse Mary Meeker's book *Structure of the Intellect*. Discuss her ideas and procedures for strengthening the mind.
2. Invite a teacher of the gifted to speak to the class. Ask about advantages, disadvantages, problems, and joys of working with the gifted. Ask the teacher how a single gifted student might be taught within a regular class.
3. Practice in class some of the thinking skills advocated by Fearn in his Creative Thinking Skills approach.
4. Compose a humane strategy for guiding a student who insists on focusing on his science project all day, to the exclusion of other class activities.
5. Discuss the advantages and disadvantages of special classes, pull-out programs, and mainstreaming as ways to educate the gifted. Overall, which do you consider best?

SUGGESTED READINGS

Charles, C. M.: Individualizing Instruction, ed. 2, St. Louis, 1980, The C. V. Mosby Co.

Drews, E.: The four faces of able adolescents—four types of giftedness, Saturday Review, January, 1963.

Durr, W. K.: The gifted student, New York, 1964, Oxford University Press.

Fearn, L.: Individual development: A process model in creativity. J. Creative Behavior **10**: 55-64, 1976.

Fearn, L.: Teaching for thinking: 311 ways to cause creative behavior, San Diego, 1977, Kabyn Books.

Fearn, L., and Foster, K. M.: The writing Kabyn: sentences and paragraphs, San Diego, 1979, Kabyn Books.

Goldberg, M., Passow, H., Justman, J., and Hage, G.: The effects of ability grouping, New York, 1965, Columbia University Press.

Grost, A.: Genius in residence, Englewood Cliffs, NJ, 1970, Prentice-Hall, Inc.

Guilford, J. P.: The structure of intellect, Psychological Bulletin **52**:267-293, 1956.

Harnadek, A.: Critical thinking, Troy, MI, 1976, Midwest Publications.

Meeker, M. N., Mestyanek, L., Shadduck, R., and Meeker, R.: SOI learning abilities test, El Segundo, CA, 1975, Structure of Intellect Institute.

Meeker, M. N.: The structure of intellect: its interpretation and uses, Columbus, OH, 1969, Charles E. Merrill Publishing Co.

Renzulli, J. S.: The enrichment triad model: a guide for developing defensible programs for the gifted and talented, Gifted Child Quarterly **20**:303-326, 1976.

Stanley, J. C.: The student gifted in mathematics and science, National Association of Secondary School Principals Bulletin **60**:28-37, 1976.

USMES, Education Development Center, Newton, Massachusetts, 1974.

CHAPTER 12

Teaching the visually handicapped and the hearing impaired

This chapter gives attention to two separate areas of handicap—the visually handicapped and the hearing impaired. They are combined in one chapter because they are "low-incidence" handicaps, that is, the number of individuals in each category is small. Regular teachers will find very few students with these two kinds of handicap mainstreamed into their classes.

For that reason, the two groups do not receive as much attention in this book as do "high-incidence" categories, like the speech handicapped, learning disabled, and mentally retarded. Their traits, however, together with a brief review of behavioral and educational implications, are presented so that teachers will have basic information about them. This basic information can serve as a starting place for teachers who wish to explore the categories further. The suggested readings at the end of the chapter include excellent sources for further study.

The visually handicapped

According to the Bureau of Education for the Handicapped the visually handicapped comprise about 1% of all handicapped students being served in school. That is less than 0.1% of all school-age students, or fewer than one out of every thousand. However, of that group of visually handicapped, approximately 60% were being served in regular classes. For that reason, it seems desirable that regular classroom teachers develop an awareness of the educational needs of these students, together with an understanding of how the needs are met.

Public Law 94-142 defines the visually handicapped as those with "a visual impairment which, even with correction, adversely affects a child's educational performance. The term includes both partially seeing and blind children." The National Society for The Prevention of Blindness defines the following additional terms used to describe visual handicaps:

Blindness is generally defined as visual acuity for distance vision of 20/200 or less in the better eye, with best correction; or visual acuity of more than 20/200 if the widest diameter of the field of vision subtends an angle no greater than 20 degrees or, in some states, 30 degrees. A measure of 20/200 visual acuity means that the individual can see at a distance of 20 feet after visual correction only what an individual with normal vision can see at 200 feet. "Blind" people are not necessarily sightless.

The partially seeing are defined as persons with a visual acuity greater than 20/200 but not greater than 20/70 in the better eye after correction. This means that the partially sighted are able to see at no more than 20 feet that which normal people can see at 70 feet.

Barraga (1971) provides an additional definition that fits into the level. It is *low vision*, which describes children "who have limitations in distance vision but are able to see objects and materials when they are within a few inches or at a maximum of a few feet away."

Visually limited people are those "who in some way are limited in their use of vision under average circumstances. They may have difficulty seeing learning materials without special lighting, or they may be unable to see distant objects unless the objects are moving, or they may need to wear prescriptive lenses or use optical and special materials to function visually."

From these descriptions, an operational definition can be composed for use in identifying visually handicapped students. These are students "who differ from the average to such a degree that special personnel, curriculum adaptation, and/or additional instructional materials are needed to assist them in achieving at a level commensurate with their abilities" (Harley, 1973).

Traditionally, the visually handicapped have been identified on the basis of medical definitions, and the label "legally blind" entitled the schools to special teachers, books, and equipment. With the mandate of PL 94-142 and the integration of these students into regular classes, Scholl (1975) proposes a definition for use in educational programming. She describes three groups:

1. Those with no useful vision who are educated through other sensory modalities
2. Those with useful vision but whose major avenue of learning may still be through senses other than vision
3. Those who can learn through visual media even though their vision is severely impaired

Each of these definitions points to the emphasis on using residual vision to the maximum in order to increase visual efficiency. This does not imply that vision will be improved. Barraga (1964) has shown that planned visual experiences do not improve the vision, per se. They can, however, improve the ability to use what vision exists and hence increase visual efficiency.

CAUSES OF VISUAL IMPAIRMENT

Nolan (1978) describes the most common sources of visual handicap:

Causes may include prenatal development deficits, disease, injury, or poisoning. Onset of impairment may be before or at birth. Visual impairments occur because of problems with the surrounding protective structures of the eye, problems with light-focusing parts, problems with muscles which move the eyes, and problems with the eye's neural components.

Nolan goes on to describe the manifestations of:

Trachoma—a severe infection of the eyelid and the outer covering of the eye

Myopia (nearsightedness)—occurs when the eye is too long from front to back, causing light to focus in front of the retina, leaving a blurred image

Astigmatism—a condition in which the light-focusing elements of the eye are not smoothly formed; the result is a distorted visual image.

Cataract—a growth that clouds the lens and restricts the transmission of light

Strabismus—cross eyes or squint caused by defective muscle function; often results in suppression of the weaker eye

Retrolental fibroplasia—a deterioration of the retina caused by too much oxygen supplied to premature infants during incubation

Retinal detachment—a condition, usually occurring in later years, in which the retina falls away from the rear of the eye

EDUCATIONAL IMPLICATIONS

Within the regular classroom various curricular, instructional, and environmental modifications are needed to integrate the visually handicapped student. These are easily made.

Visually handicapped students are very different in many educational ways. Their instruction must take into account their needs, interests, and goals. Furthermore, some students may have disabilities in addition to vision which further complicate the educational programming and demand a more flexible school program.

Regarding curricular modifications, Scholl (1975) suggests that the objective of education should include correcting the handicapping effects to the extent possible. In addition, provision should be made for appropriate materials to be used in meaningful and concrete experiences. These experiences can emphasize the use of other sensory modalities.

Bryan and Bryan (1979) delineate considerations that should receive attention in educating visually handicapped students. Their observations are presented here in slightly modified form.

Learning by touching and hearing. When organizing instruction for the visually handicapped, one should remember that touch and hearing are their main substitutes for vision. Both should be stressed. Fortunately, most curricular topics can be presented adequately through touch and hearing. There are disadvantages to a tactile and auditory curriculum, however. Difficulties occur with spatial relations, and it is impossible to differentiate some important traits of objects and graphic materials.

Mobility training. One of the major tasks to be accomplished by the blind is learning to move about independently. The success that an individual has with the orientation and mobility process is highly dependent upon his perception of the environment. A visually impaired youngster must learn how to use his remaining senses. Specialized trainers, called orientation and mobility instructors, teach techniques for moving safely, for interpreting and being aware of all clues in the surroundings. The youngster can learn to make use of sounds, recognize tactile clues and landmarks, such as the smell of a bakery, the sound of an idling car, and the feel of declining sidewalks near the curbs.

Bryan and Bryan suggest that a mobility training program should contain the following components: attention to physical fitness, motor coordination, posture, freedom of movement, and training to use other available senses.

Developing the intellect. One should always remember academic skills when working with the visually impaired. Academics should always be given priority along with mobility, orientation, body image, motor coordination, and other sensory modalities. Intellectual and affective skills should not take a secondary role.

Braille. Braille is a system of writing that uses raised-dot patterns to stand for letters and words. There are sixty-three characters in braille. They are made up of combinations of one to six dots, arranged in six equally spaced positions, three high by two wide. These six positions make up what is called the braille cell.

Standard English braille consists of 263 meanings assigned to the sixty-three characters. These elements include the letters in the alphabet, letter sequences, words, numbers, and punctuation signs. Various methods exist for writing in braille. One method is the "Perkins Brailler," typewriter of sorts by which embossed dot patterns are produced on paper by depressing keys in varying combinations. Another method to write braille is with the braille slate and stylus. The slate is a hinged frame into which paper is clamped. The front of the slate has rows of openings shaped in outline like the braille cell. Under each opening, the back of the slate contains six depressions arranged like the dots in a braille cell. Using an awl-like device called the stylus, the writer presses the paper down into the depressions, forming the desired combinations of dots.

Large print. Willis, Groves, and Fuhrmann (1979) assert that visually impaired students should learn to read by means of the methods used for the sighted. But they need special materials to accomplish the tasks. Classroom teachers can order enlarger systems that enlarge print so that visually handicapped students can work from the same text as their peers. The American Printing House For the Blind provides educational materials for distribution to legally blind children in the United States. These materials include books in large print, braille, and recorded form. The Printing House provides instructional aids and devices not otherwise available. It also maintains the Instructional Materials Reference Center for the Visually Handicapped, which provides reference services and resource materials for teachers. Other special materials that can be used in the regular classroom include talking books, audio and sensory aids, time compressed recordings, thermoform maps, and raised clock faces.

In-class teaching reminders

During instruction, teachers should remember to do the following:

1. Use the name of the visually impaired student in class discussions when a question is directed to that student.
2. Alternate teaching strategies.
3. Begin instruction at a concrete level, using manipulatives combined with verbal descriptions.
4. Use tape recorders to tape lectures, instructions, tests, and reading assignments.
5. Physically accompany the student through physical education activities or gross motor exercises introduced in class.
6. Emphasize tactile functions such as molding clay, painting with the fingers, weaving, developing collages, and paper sculpting.
7. Provide short breaks in the activities. Vary the classroom activities in order to prevent fatigue. For example, an activity can begin with listening, then proceed to close visual reading, and then move to motor and tactile activities.
8. Use physical contact such as a pat or touch on the arm to indicate praise or approval.
9. Help students to use residual vision as much as possible.
10. Use a buddy system for supportive independence. This also provides a good mutual learning experience.
11. Communicate frequently with resource persons in the school building or district. Familiarization with orientation and mobility skills as well as the ways to properly guide students will be helpful.
12. Include visually handicapped students in physical activities such as running, jumping, wrestling, swinging, rolling, gymnastics, dancing, and swimming. These activities will allow them to interact physically with others in the classroom, which in turn facilitates the development of positive relationships.
13. Do not seat visually handicapped students facing windows. Be sure glare and shadow do not interfere.
14. Keep the classroom noise level down, so the student can hear better.
15. Consult with and make use of the services provided by organizations for the visually handicapped.

BEHAVIORAL IMPLICATIONS

Adjustment to problems. How a student adjusts to visual handicap depends on many things. Scholl (1975) describes some of the variables that may have an effect on the student's vision-related behavior.

1. *Type of onset.* A gradual loss of sight produces different emotional reactions than a sudden loss of sight. Age of onset is also important. This can influence how a person perceives the world and can influence confident functioning within it.

2. *Type and degree of residual vision.* Some limited vision may cause frustration of wanting to see *more* and causing more physical and emotional strain. Additionally, residual vision may cause confusion in the educational process because of vague and imperfect sight. Emotional frustration can occur when teachers and parents expect more of the student because they know that he/she can see more.

3. *Effects.* Some visually handicapped individuals experience pain, as in glaucoma and too much light. Some may be concerned about possible inheritance problems associated with pending marriages. Impairment resulting from venereal disease may affect the parent-child relationship because of feelings of guilt. The visually handicapped student's awareness that vision is getting worse or that, indeed, blindness is imminent, presents social and emotional problems which may be manifested in a variety of ways. Withdrawal, complacence, aggression, and anger may be behaviors resulting from this knowledge.

Indicators of visual difficulty. Not only should classroom teachers be cognizant of social and emotional factors associated with visual handicap, but they should also be aware of behavioral indicators of possible vision problems. The National Society For the Prevention of Blindness lists the following as possible indicators of visual difficulty, which deserve further attention.

1. Rubs eyes excessively.
2. Shuts or covers one eye; tilts head or thrusts head forward.
3. Is sensitive to light.
4. Has difficulty with reading or other work requiring close use of the eyes.
5. Squints, blinks, frowns, or has facial distortions while reading or doing other close work.
6. Holds reading material too close or too far and frequently changes the distance from near to far or from far to near.
7. Complains of pain or aches in the eyes, headaches, dizziness, or nausea following close eye work.
8. Complains of itching, burning, or scratchiness in the eyes.
9. Complains of blurred or double vision.
10. Has a tendency to reverse letters, syllables, or words.
11. Has a tendency to confuse letters of similar shape (o and a, c and e, n and m, h and n, f and t).
12. Has a tendency to lose the place in a sentence or page.
13. Uses poor spacing in writing; has difficulty "staying on the line."
14. Has a tendency to stumble into things or trip over objects.

In addition to these behavioral indicators, classroom teachers need to observe physical appearances of students. Specific appearances indicating vision problems include:

1. Red eyelids
2. Crusts on lids among the lashes
3. Recurring sties, sores, or swollen lids
4. Watery eyes, discharges, or cloudiness
5. Reddened or inflamed eyes
6. Crossed eyes or eyes that do not appear to be straight
7. Pupils of uneven size
8. Eyes that move excessively or unevenly
9. Drooping eyelids
10. Frequent colds and allergies

Students not yet identified as being visually handicapped and who show these signs should be referred for visual screening tests.

TECHNOLOGY FOR THE VISUALLY HANDICAPPED

Modern technological aids specifically designed for the visually handicapped have been readily available for only the past few years. However, their importance in the educational, vocational, and living skills of the visually handicapped has increased to the point that money and large programs have been made available to disseminate these aids. The application of advanced technology to the needs of handicapped people is growing by leaps and bounds. Two examples of the amazing technological products are the Optacon and the Speech Plus Talking Calculator.

Optacon Print Reading Aid. The Optacon Print Reading Aid is a device whose name is an acronym for *Op*tical-to-*Ta*ctile *Con*verter. Through the use of latest developments in integrated circuitry, the Optacon converts print directly to a tactile form that is readable by the blind. It includes a small, hand-held scanner, a kind of camera. The character read by the scanner is felt by the index finger of the opposite hand.

The Optacon is small enough to be completely portable and inexpensive enough to be individually owned. As a direct translation aid, the Optacon is useful for reading a wide range of alphabets, languages, type styles, numbers, graphic symbols, and diagrams.

Speech Plus Talking Calculators. The Speech Plus Talking Calculator is an electronic calculator for use in mathematics that presents results visually on a display, and at the same time auditorily through synthetic speech. It is a great help in mathematics, which has been a source of major frustration for blind children and their teachers. Studies have confirmed that blind students' mathematical competency is well below the norms for sighted students (Nolan, 1964). The lowest achievement levels measured were in the areas where the complexity of operations increased, such as adding or subtracting numbers with three or more digits, dividing or multiplying numbers with two or more digits decimal operations, and negative numbers. The Speech Plus Talking Calculator appears able to prevent the occurrence of these deficits in math learning. Additional commercially produced and inexpensive children's talking calculators have been developed which provide the same kind of auditory feedback.

SUMMARY: VISUALLY HANDICAPPED

The category of visual handicap includes the "blind" and the "partially seeing." Generally, blindness is defined as no better than 20/200 vision after correction. Partially seeing is defined as no better than 20/70 after correction. Both conditions interfere with normal school learning.

There are several different causes of visual impairment, but knowledge of those causes does not help teachers. Of assistance to teachers are knowledge of behavioral traits of the visually handicapped and knowledge of teaching techniques known to be effective in teaching the visually impaired.

The visually handicapped should receive instruction that emphasizes learning through touching and hearing, physical mobility, braille reading and writing, and large print materials and magnifying devices. They should also be provided instruments such as Optacons and Speech Plus Talking Calculators.

Several instructional reminders were presented, as were signs that might indicate to teachers that a student is having difficulties with vision.

The hearing impaired

Public Law 94-142 provides the following descriptions and differentiations for the deaf and hard-of-hearing.

With regard to the *deaf*, the law stipulates that deafness is "A hearing impairment which is so severe that the child is impaired in processing linguistic information through hearing with or without amplification, which adversely affects educational performance." The law defines hard-of-hearing to mean "A hearing impairment whether permanent or fluctuating, which adversely affects a child's educational performance but which is not included under the definition of deaf."

Definitions now existing in medicine can be used to diagnose degrees of hearing loss. This diagnosis is made through audiometric testing, which reveals the degree of severity and the nature of the loss.

A functional educational definition, however, is still lacking. One needs to be agreed upon, which will indicate ranges of hearing ability that can be tied to educational strategies.

Definitions do exist which describe several levels of hearing impairment. These levels are based on degree of loss of hearing acuity, measured by a pure tone audiometer. Again, however, in terms of functionality, the knowledge that a student has a particular level of decibel loss is not directly applicable to classroom programming and management.

Hearing losses are typically classified as conductive or sensorineural. A *conductive* hearing loss is caused by an obstruction in the auditory canal (outer and middle ear) which totally or partially prevents sound waves from reaching the inner ear. If discovered in early stages, conductive hearing loss can often be arrested or circumvented by medical treatment or by means of a hearing aid. The function of the hearing aid is to collect, conduct, and amplify sound waves to assist existing hearing capacity. A *sensorineural* hearing loss is a condition involving impairment of the nerves in the inner ear or in the central nervous system.

CAUSES OF HEARING IMPAIRMENTS

Causes of hearing impairments can be categorized as genetic (endogenous), or externally caused (exogenous)

Larson and Miller (1978) point out that genetic factors have been the leading cause of deafness, except during certain epidemic periods of rubella (German measles). Approximately 50 to 60% of all deafness is attributed to genetic factors. Lowenbraun and Scraggs (1978) report that deafness may be inherited as a dominant trait (14%), recessive trait (84%), or sex-linked disorder (2%). At the present time more than fifty genetic syndromes have been identified in which hearing loss may occur.

External conditions causing hearing impairments include the following:
1. *Disease*, such as maternal rubella
2. *Drugs*, such as kanamycin, neomycin, and gentamycin, taken by the mother during pregnancy; these drugs pass easily across the placental barrier
3. *Trauma*, such as a blow to the head, concussion, or fractured skull; these injuries can result in middle ear bleeding, with resultant injury to the ear
4. *Infection*, viruses (mumps, chickenpox), and meningitis, which is an inflammation of the protective covering of the brain and spinal cord; meningitis deafens an estimated 3 to 5% of the children who contract it and ranks first among postnatal causes (Larson and Miller, 1978)

Knowledge of the *cause* of impairment will not alter the educational or social environment created for the hearing handicapped child. Teachers deal only with the outward manifestations of the handicap. These manifestations include not only hearing impairment but also intellectual development, social adjustment, and the inability to develop speech and language through the sense of hearing.

SPEECH AND LANGUAGE CHARACTERISTICS

Bryan and Bryan (1979) discuss speech and language characteristics of students who are deaf or hard-of-hearing.

1. The hard-of-hearing child is likely to develop speech but will have difficulty with sounds such as s, sh, z, the, t, k, ch, and f.
2. Sounds that present difficulty will either be omitted or will be substituted for by other sounds.
3. The child's speech may have a strange quality, perhaps too nasal, too loud, or too soft.
4. The child's speech may be inapproriate in voice inflection, pitch, and rate.
5. The child will often have difficulty in understanding directions, will misunderstand others, and have difficulty conversing with more than one person.

Bryan and Bryan go on to comment:

The speech and language development of deaf children is even more disrupted than that of hard-of-hearing children. Deaf children, by definition do not spontaneously develop speech. The child must be taught both how to "hear" and how to "speak", that is, the child must be educated in both receptive and expressive communication.

The gap between hearing-impaired children and their normal peers widens with age. This is evidenced in vocabulary and in the ability to express or understand colloquial expressions and verbal mances. These lacks often cause deaf and hard-of-hearing students to exhibit specific learning disabilities in academic areas, particularly in spelling, written expression, and oral reading.

EDUCATIONAL IMPLICATIONS

The greatest concern among the hearing impaired is their inability to communicate effectively. For that reason, educational programs stress the development of communication skills. Controversy exists among educators as to the most effective and efficient method of teaching these communication skills. Three educational approaches, all widely used, have emerged from these controversies: (1) oral communication, (2) manual communication, and (3) total communication. These approaches are discussed in the following sections.

Oral communication. The oral method emphasizes the existing oral environment, given access through the use of a combination of residual hearing, hearing aid, and speechreading (watching others' lips and faces). Many educators of the deaf who align themselves with this oral approach accept Miller's (1970) statement as to the purpose of oral communication:

> We believe that each hearing impaired child should be given every opportunity to learn to communicate through speech, speech reading, hearing if possible, reading, and writing; that he or she be given every opportunity to develop this ability with the help of home, school, and community so that he/she may take his/her rightful place in the world of today.

This approach attempts to enable hearing impaired students to learn intelligible speech, and to learn lipreading. When successful, this provides them a natural manner of communication.

Manual communication. The manual method is a system of communication for the hearing impaired in which fingerspelling or sign language or both are used in place of speech. Fingerspelling consists of a series of finger positions to spell out, letter-by-letter, each word, or words that cannot be communicated through sign language.

American Sign Language is a manual form of communication in which, unlike fingerspelling where entire words are spelled out, entire ideas or thoughts are communicated. In the communication of these ideas, both the finger and the entire hands are used. So are the arms and upper portions of the body. If an idea cannot be conveyed by signing, then it is spelled out. This is common when individual's names need to be communicated.

Signing has been effectively used to communicate with children who have been diagnosed as autistic. In regular classrooms, the introduction of sign language to nonhandicapped children has provided interest, challenge, and understanding of others.

Total communication. Proponents of total communication attempt to combine and synthesize the other two proven approaches to communication for the hearing impaired. Garretson's (1976) theory states that:

1. The total communication concept is a philosophy rather than a method.
2. It combines the oral/aural and manual modes according to the communicative needs and the expressive-receptive threshold of the individual.
3. It is the moral right of the hearing impaired, as with normally hearing bilinguals, to receive and give maximum input to reach optimal comprehension or total understanding in a communication situation.

Denton (1970) describes the total communication approach as including the full spectrum of language modes: child-devised gesture, formal sign language, speech, speechreading, fingerspelling, reading, and writing.

Denton further suggests a sequence for teachers to follow in teaching communication skills to students who have only small amounts of residual hearing.

1. Begin with signs. They are the easiest means of getting the young congeni-
   tally deaf child to communicate or express his own ideas.
2. Use the signs to reinforce speechreading and audition. Here the teacher
   signs and talks simultaneously. The child is using a hearing aid.
3. Make maximum use of residual hearing, with amplification, to develop oral
   skills.
4. Use fingerspelling to facilitate reading and writing.

Statistics from the United States Department of Health, Education and Welfare (1979) revealed that even prior to full compliance with PL 94-142, 50% of
hard-of-hearing students were mainstreamed full-time into the regular classroom.
About 30% were being educated in separate classes within the public schools, with
15% in separate school facilities. A small percentage were involved in other educational environments.

The majority of deaf students were also being served in regular classes (13%)
and in separate classes (40%) within the public schools. These statistics show that
the current educational trends are to place students with hearing impairments into
the regular classroom. Resource teachers provide supportive assistance. The assistance is often given on a "pull-out" basis, where students are instructed in a
resource room setting. The supportive service trains students in the use of hearing
aids and provides auditory training, speechreading, and speech correction.

The teacher's role

The regular classroom teacher fills the role as primary educator in the teach-
ing-learning process for hearing-impaired students. Elements of that role have
been specified within the work of Project PREM (Preparing Regular Educators for
Mainstreaming) (1975). These elements provide reminders for teachers who have
students mainstreamed in their classes.

1. Be aware and possess some knowledge relative to hearing aids and other
   other amplification devices. For instance, teachers should make sure that
   hearing aids fit properly, have fresh batteries, and are used when necessary. The hearing aid cannot completely normalize hearing. Some distortion is inevitable, and all sounds are amplified.
2. Arrange student seating to best advantage. The hearing impaired student
   should sit facing the teacher. He/she should be encouraged to watch the
   teacher's face. The better ear should be toward the teacher and class.
3. As much as possible, the teacher should face hearing-impaired students.
   The use of an overhead projector rather than the chalkboard helps make
   this possible.

4. Speak slowly and distinctly, but not more loudly than normal.
5. Provide feedback to students about their handicaps. For example, the student may need to be told to speak more softly.
6. Fatigue should not be interpreted as lack of interest. Hearing-impaired students must often expend considerable energy to hear others.
7. Rephrase and restate oral information. Students may need to have a word or phrase repeated.
8. Make maximum use of residual hearing. Only a small proportion of hearing-impaired children have total loss.
9. Evaluate the performance of students with hearing impairments according to standards employed with the rest of the class.
10. Use a "listener helper" or "buddy" or provide special help when it is needed.
11. Encourage and facilitate speechreading and desirable speech habits.
12. Frequently evaluate the student's growth in speechreading, auditory discrimination, and auditory comprehension.
13. Be sure to get the attention of the hard-of-hearing student before giving instructions.
14. Write assignments on the board so that students can copy them in a notebook.
15. Work to help the student develop the other senses.

In attempting to implement and follow through on many of these practical suggestions, the teacher should keep in mind all members of the class. Modifications that should be made for the hearing impaired should not interfere with regular class instruction. This can be accomplished by using supplemental materials and the assistance of the special education resource specialist.

BEHAVIORAL IMPLICATIONS

Coping behavior. Children with hearing difficulties often show inappropriate behavior in the classroom. These behaviors can have the appearance of defiance, laziness, manipulation, or withdrawal. They represent coping styles that the student has adopted for operating in the school environment.

Indicators of hearing loss. The regular classroom teacher is in a key position to observe and note students who appear to be experiencing hearing difficulty. Gearheart and Weishahn (1976) describe the following characteristics that may indicate a hearing loss, if repeatedly shown by a student:

1. Tilts head at an angle to obtain a better positioning to hear sound
2. Shows frequent lack of attention
3. Fails to respond when questioned

4. Shows defects in speech, especially when phonetics are important
5. Has difficulty in following directions
6. Has peculiar voice qualities, often high-pitched
7. Is stubborn, shy, withdrawn; misbehaves
8. Is reluctant to participate in oral activities
9. Avoids people
10. Tends to rush words together
11. Is dependent on classmates for instructions
12. Has poor oral reading ability
13. Does best in small groups
14. Usually talks louder than is necessary
15. Shows disparity between expected and actual achievement
16. Watches the faces (especially the mouth and lips) of speakers
17. Has frequent earache, cold, sore throat, and/or fluid running from ears

When a student exhibits one or more of these behaviors, frequently over a period of time, and when they seem to be interferring with learning, the teacher should refer the student for a hearing test.

SUMMARY: HEARING IMPAIRED

Two levels of hearing impairments exist: "deaf," which means severe hearing loss, and "hard-of-hearing," which means moderate hearing loss. Both levels are specified in PL 94-142, and both are diagnosed through hearing tests with audiometers.

The cause of the hearing impairment is not the primary concern of teachers. Their duty is to make effective accommodations in their educational programs. They should know about hearing aids, braille, signing, speechreading, and the total language approach to instruction. They should work cooperatively with resource specialists. They should be sure that hearing-impaired students understand directions and know what is going on in the classroom. Several reminders were presented to help teachers do these things.

Deaf and very hard-of-hearing students are identified early in life. Teachers should be attentive for signs of moderate hearing loss in other students which might have gone previously unnoticed.

SUGGESTED ACTIVITIES

1. Obtain and examine in class devices and materials such as braille print and rulers, braille writers, magnifying devices, hearing aids, and Optacons.
2. Arrange a visit to a clinic where deaf or blind people are taught.
3. Invite a blind person to speak to the class about special problems and successes encountered in school.
4. Learn a few of the basic expressions in American Sign Language.
5. Invite a speech therapist to talk to the class about procedures for teaching hearing-impaired students to speak better.

SUGGESTED READINGS
Visually handicapped

American Foundation for the Blind: A step-by-step guide to personal management for blind persons, New York, 1974, American Foundation for the Blind.

Barraga, N. C.: Increased visual behavior in low vision children, New York, 1964, American Foundation for the Blind.

Barraga, N. C.: Utilization of sensory-perceptual abilities. In Lowenfeld, B., editor: The visually handicapped child in school, New York, 1973, The John Day Company.

Barraga, N. C.: Visual handicaps and learning: a developmental approach, Belmont, CA, 1976, Wadsworth Publishing Co., Inc.

Barraga, N. C., Donward, B., and Ford, P.: Aids for teaching basic concepts of sensory development, Louisville, KY, 1973, American Printing House for the Blind.

Bateman, B.: Sighted children's perceptions of blind children's abilities, Except. Child. **29:**42-46, 1962.

Bishop, V. E.: Teaching the visually limited child, Springfield, IL, 1977, Charles C Thomas, Publisher.

Bryan, J. H., and Bryan, T. H.: Exceptional children, Sherman Oaks, CA, 1978, Alfred Publishing Co., Inc.

Cratty, B. J.: Movement and spatial awareness in blind children and youth, Springfield, IL, 1971, Charles C Thomas, Publisher.

Deahl, T., and Deahl, M.: Integrating partially sighted children in the classroom, Instructor **83:**142-143, 1973.

Fraiberg, S.: Insights from the blind, New York, 1977, Basic Books, Inc., Publishers.

Gearheart, B. R., and Weishahn, M. W.: The handicapped child in the regular classroom, St. Louis, 1976, The C. V. Mosby Company.

Halliday, C., and Kurzhals, I. W.: Stimulating environments for children who are visually impaired, Springfield, IL, 1976, Charles C Thomas, Publisher.

Harley, R. K.: Children with visual disabilities. In Exceptional children in the schools, New York, 1973, Holt, Rinehart & Winston.

Illinois Office of Education: A curriculum guide for: the development of body and sensory awareness for the visually impaired, Springfield, IL, 1974.

Leahy, A.: New opportunities for visually handicapped people through applying today's technology, Paper proposal for First World Congress on Future Special Education, 1977, Stirling, Scotland.

Lowenfeld, B., editor: The visually handicapped child in school, New York, 1973, The John Day Company.

Martin, G. J., and Hoben, N.: Supporting visually impaired students in the mainstream, Reston, VA, 1972, The Council for Exceptional Children.

Meighan, T.: An investigation of the self-concept of blind and visually handicapped adolescents, New York, 1971, American Foundation for the Blind.

National Society for Prevention of Blindness: Estimated statistics on blindness and vision problems, New York, 1966, National Society for Prevention of Blindness.

National Society for Prevention of Blindness: Visual screening in schools, Publication No. 257, New York, 1969, National Society For Prevention of Blindness.

National Society for Prevention of Blindness: Teaching about vision, New York, 1972, National Society for Prevention of Blindness.

Nolan, C. Y.: The visually impaired. In Meyen, E. L., editor: Exceptional children and youth: an introduction, Denver, 1978, Love Publishing Company.

Nolan, C. Y., and Morris, J. E.: The Japanese abacus as a computational aid for blind children, Except. Child. **31:**15-17, 1964.

Project PREM: Preparing regular educators for mainstreaming, Austin, TX, 1975, State Department of Education.

Scholl, G. T.: The education of children with visual impairments. In Cruickshank, W. M., and Johnson, G. O., editors: Education of exceptional children and youth, ed. 3, Englewood Cliffs, NJ, 1975, Prentice-Hall, Inc.

Tait, P.: Play and the intellectual development of blind children, New Outlook Blind **66:**361-369, 1972.

Tuttle, D.: A comparison of three reading media for the blind: braille, normal recording, and compressed speech, Res. Bull. Am. Found. Blind **27:**217-230, 1974.

United States Department of Health, Education, and Welfare: Progress toward a free appropriate public education: a report to Congress on the implementation of Public Law 94-

142: The Education For All Handicapped Children Act, Washington, D.C., January 1979, The Bureau of Education For The Handicapped.

Willis, D. J., Groves, C., and Fuhrmann, W.: Visually disabled children and youth. In Swanson, B. M., and Willis, D. J., editors: Understanding exceptional children and youth, Chicago, 1979, Rand McNally & Co.

Hearing impaired

Bellugi, U., and Klima, E. S.: The roots of language in the sign talk of the deaf, Psychol. Today **6**:661-664, 1972.

Bornstein, H.: A description of some current sign systems designed to represent English, Am. Ann. Deaf **118**:454-463, 1973.

Bothwell, H.: What the classroom teacher can do for the child with impaired hearing, Natl. Educ. Assoc. J. **56**:44-46, 1967.

Bryan, J. H., and Bryan, T. H.: Exceptional children, Sherman Oaks, CA, 1979, Alfred Publishing Co., Inc.

Carhart, R.: Development and conservation of speech. In Davis, H., and Silvermann, S. R., editors: Hearing and deafness, ed. 3, New York, 1970, Holt, Rinehart & Winston.

Charrow, V. R., and Fletcher, J. D.: English as the second language of deaf children, Dev. Psychol. **10**:463-470, 1974.

Davis, H., and Silverman, S. R., editors: Hearing and deafness, ed. 3, New York, 1970, Holt, Rinehart & Winston.

Denton, D. M.: Total communication, Maryland school for the deaf, Maryland, 1970.

Frick, E.: Adjusting to integration: some difficulties hearing impaired children have in public schools, Volta Rev. **75**:36-46, 1973.

Furth, H. G.: Thinking without language: psychological implication of deafness, New York, 1966, The Free Press.

Furth, H. G.: Deafness and learning: a psychosocial approach, Belmont, CA, 1973, Wadsworth Publishing Co., Inc.

Garretson, M. D.: Total communication, Volta Rev. **78**(4):88-95, 1976.

Gearheart, B. R., and Weishahn, M. W.: The handicapped child in the regular classroom, St. Louis, 1976, The C. V. Mosby Co.

Gildston, P.: The hearing impaired child in the classroom: a guide for the classroom teacher. In Northcott, W. H., editor: The hearing impaired child in a regular classroom, Washington, D.C., 1973, Alexander Graham Bell Association for the Deaf.

Hedgecock, D.: Facilitating integration at the junior high level, Volta Rev. **76**:182-188, 1974.

Larson, A. D., and Miller, J. B.: The hearing impaired. In Meyen, E. L., editor: Exceptional children and youth: an introduction, Denver, 1978, Love Publishing Company.

Lowenbraun, S., and Scraggs, C.: The hearing handicapped. In Haring, N. G., editor: Behavior of exceptional children, ed. 2, Columbus, OH, 1978, Charles E. Merrill Publishing Co.

McGee, D. E.: The benefits of educating deaf children with hearing children, Teach. Except. Child. **2**:133-137, 1970.

Malian, I. M.: Regular classroom teachers and administrators and children with exceptional needs, Sacramento, 1979, California State Department of Education.

Meadow, K. P.: Development of deaf children. In Hetherington, E. M., editor: Review of child development research, vol. 5, Chicago, 1975, University of Chicago Press.

Myklebust, H. R.: The psychology of deafness, ed. 2, New York, 1964, Grune & Stratton, Inc.

Miller, J. B.: Oralism, Volta Rev. **70**:211-217, 1970.

Northern, J. L., and Downs, M. P.: Hearing in children, Baltimore, 1974, The Williams & Wilkins Co.

Project PREM: Preparing regular educators for mainstreaming, Austin, TX, 1975, State Department of Education.

Rister, A.: Deaf children in a mainstream education, Volta Rev. **77**:279-290, 1975.

Schlesinger, H. S., and Meadow, K. P.: Sound and sign: childhood deafness and mental health, Berkeley, CA, 1972, University of California Press.

Watson, F. J.: Use of hearing aids by hearing impaired pupils in ordinary schools, Volta Rev. **66**:741-744, 1964.

CHAPTER 13

Teaching the orthopedically impaired and the health impaired

"Orthopedics" refers to diseases and deformities of the muscles, joints, and skeletal system. Familiar orthopedic impairments include cerebral palsy, amputations, and arthritis. "Health impaired" refers to relatively permanent malfunctions of vital organs and body tissues. Familiar health impairments are allergies, asthma, epilepsy, and diabetes.

Public Law 94-142 lists orthopedic and health impairments as separate categories of disability; they are considered here in a single chapter. They, like visual handicap and hearing impairment, are low-incidence handicaps, that is, very few students are afflicted with them to the point that their education is hampered. Gearheart and Weishahn (1976) estimated their combined total number at around 275,000 students of school age. This would comprise no more than 4 to 5% of all students identified as handicapped.

These small numbers in no way reduce the severity of the handicaps. Nor do they suggest that teachers need not take the education of these students seriously. They simply mean that teachers will seldom encounter these students in their regular classrooms.

Bigge and Sirvis (1978) relate the historical development of services to orthopedically and health impaired students:

> Historically, educational programming for the physically disabled population began with those children who were hospitalized with disabilities resulting from diseases such as polio and tuberculosis. Generally, however, children with more severe disabilities such as cerebral palsy began to alter the direction of special education programs. While early programs had been merely supplements to extensive medical treatment in hospitals, a team approach to treatment evolved. It recognized the importance of educational intervention as well as medical services and gave equal status to educational programming.

This perspective indicates that physically handicapped students have been recognized as able to function, with environmental modifications, in the educational world. For example, a cerebral palsied student who has only lower limb involvement, with no intellectual difficulties, need not be "institutionalized" or maintained at home because of the physical condition. This contradicts the myths pertaining to the physically handicapped that if they cannot walk, talk, or function normally, they cannot be very intelligent.

In attempting to define the physically handicapped population, Wald (1971) presents these observations:

> The crippled and other health impaired population appears to be seen in three dimensions: physical definition, functional problems, and programmational modifications. The population is comprised of those children and adults who as a result of permanent, temporary, or intermittent medical disabilities require modifications in curriculum and instructional strategies. Frequent separation from family and lack of adequate parental guidance contribute to secondary emotional problems of the

crippled or other health impaired population. The child's physical limitations are often the basis of functional retardation as well as sensory, perceptual and conceptual deficits. The development of realistic expectation levels requires the identification of additional and unique instructional materials, equipment, and strategies for evaluation.

Public Law 94-142 seemed to delve into the educational aspects of Wald's definition. The Education of All Handicapped Children Act of 1975 defines *orthopedically impaired* to mean "a severe orthopedic impairment which adversely affects a child's educational performance." The term includes impairments caused by congenital abnormality (clubfoot, absence of some member, etc.), impairments caused by disease (poliomyelitis, bone tuberculosis, etc.), and impairments from other causes, (cerebral palsy, amputations, and fractures or burns which cause contractures).

Other health impaired, according to the federal definition, means "limited strength, vitality, or alertness, due to chronic or acute health problems such as heart condition, tuberculosis, rheumatic fever, nephritis, asthma, sickle cell anemia, hemophilia, epilepsy, lead poisoning, leukemia, or diabetes which adversely affects a child's educational performance."

It is important to remember that these orthopedic and health impairments are to be considered handicaps only if they "adversely affect" the student's ability to participate and take advantage of the educational environment.

The Bureau of Education for the Handicapped states that about 40% of all orthopedically and health-impaired students are served in the regular classroom. The same data show that this population has the largest percentage (about 25%) of students being educated in educational environments other than school classrooms.

Orthopedically impaired

Several types of orthopedic impairments affect the education of students. They are all quite serious. Some lead to early death. Most, however, are fairly rare. The most common of these afflictions is cerebral palsy. It receives most of the attention in our consideration of orthopedic impairments.

CEREBRAL PALSY

Cerebral palsy is characterized by varying degrees of disturbance of voluntary movements. "Cerebral" refers to the brain, and "palsy" refers to a weakness or lack of control. It is not a progressive disease, but a complex neuromuscular disability caused by damage to the motor control center of the brain. This damage limits motor coordination. In most cases cerebral palsy is congenital, which means the damage to the brain occurred during pregnancy or at birth. However, infectious diseases (meningitis or encephalitis) or severe head injury can cause cerebral palsy at any time in life.

Types. There are different types of cerebral palsy. Classification specifies the limbs involved and the types of motor disability. Denhoff (1976) lists the various types according to limbs involved, which in turn indicates the location and extent of damage to the motor center of the brain. The percentage of individuals included within each type is given in the following list.

> *Hemiplegia:* One half (right side or left side) of the body is involved (35 to 40%)
> *Diplegia:* Legs are involved to a greater extent than the arms (10 to 20%)
> *Quadriplegia:* All four limbs are involved (15 to 20%)
> *Paraplegia:* Only the legs are involved (10 to 20%)
> *Monoplegia:* Only one limb is involved (rarely occurs)
> *Triplegia:* Three limbs are involved (rarely occurs)
> *Double hemiplegia:* Both halves of the body are involved, but unlike quadriplegia the two sides are affected differently (rarely occurs)

Educational implications

The education of the cerebral-palsied student will occur under the direction of professionals. Each member of that team will contribute to enhancing the regular classroom environment for the student. Along with the various academic and social goals will be the long- and short-term goals of related services such as physical therapy. This therapy is used to train the body to take over needed muscle functions to achieve more controlled mobility. Activities by the physical therapist can be adapted for regular classroom follow-through. Communication between the classroom teacher and the physical therapist is essential.

An occupational therapist can help with activities for daily living, occupational mobility, and fine motor remediations. A speech pathologist can provide therapy for communication skills. Medical intervention may involve surgery to improve motion or to prepare the student for braces. This interdisciplinary team makes a continuum of services available to the cerebral-palsied child in the least restrictive environment.

Cerebral-palsied students who are severely or multiply handicapped may not be able to function in the regular classroom. However, the mildly impaired will require little special accommodation, if any. Each type of cerebral palsy has its own set of needs, and each child should be taught with attention to those needs.

Functions that require specific motor responses present the greatest problems in educating cerebral-palsied students: these include reading, writing, speaking, and other activities that require coordination. Accommodations for meeting these needs include taping paper to the desk, devising means of keeping pencils from rolling, and using small balls of clay on pencils to hold the pencil more securely. In addition, book holders, mechanical page turners, adjustable chalkboards, and adaptive typewriters can be provided. The buddy system, mentioned so often before, may again be employed, whereby the nonhandicapped peer serves as an aide to the cerebral-palsied student.

Physical modifications in the school include ramps for wheelchairs and hand-bars by drinking fountains and restrooms. Rubber mats should be placed over slippery floors, and any other changes that permit greater freedom of movement should be made.

Behavioral implications

The physical behavior of students with cerebral palsy varies with the type of motor disability. The student with *spastic cerebral palsy* has jerky or explosive movements when a voluntary motion is made. About 50% of cerebral-palsied individuals shows spasticity. *Athetoid cerebral palsy* causes purposeless and involuntary movement of some parts of the body such as the legs, arms, hands, or mouth. Thus, there is trouble with guiding the direction of voluntary movement; about 25% of cases of cerebral are classified as athetoid. *Atoxic cerebral palsy* is characterized by poor balance and problems with spatial relationships. The individual is awkward, with poor coordination. About 25% of the cerebral-palsied population is classified as atoxic. *Rigid cerebral palsy*, characterized by continuous muscle tension, and *tremor cerebral palsy*, with rhythmic involuntary movement of certain muscles, are rare forms of the disease.

A large percentage of persons with cerebral palsy also have impairments in either vision, speech, language, hearing, intelligence, or sensorimotor integration.

Additional behavioral characteristics for the classroom teacher to be aware of include accident proneness, mood fluctuations, perseveration, short attention span, hyperactivity, and speech inadequacies that result in withdrawal, shyness, and avoidance of communication. Cerebral-palsied students within the regular classroom may be required to wear braces, use crutches, or be confined to a wheelchair. These obvious reminders that a student is different may cause the cerebral-palsied student to experience feelings of self-consciousness, which may in turn cause behavioral problems.

Instructional suggestions

Metsker (1977) presents instructional suggestions for the cerebral-palsied student in the regular classroom. You may note that, with the exception of wheelchair accessibility, most ideas have been an integral part of the mainstreaming plan for other special students.

1. Promote self-acceptance by using role playing, dramatic, musical, and artistic activities, discussions, and successful academics.
2. Provide warmth, support, and a fulfilling classroom environment by making learning meaningful, accepting differences, and showing how school tasks are worthwhile.
3. Insist that all programs and facilities be made accessible for wheelchairs and crutches. Widen aisles for mobility and provide easels to hold books and papers.
4. Encourage other students to socialize with the student by stressing strengths and abilities of the student.
5. Encourage independence and mobility. Let others help only to prevent frustration and not to promote dependence. For example, if others constantly push the student's wheelchair, that student may become passive and dependent, and will not develop self-confidence nor improve strength, endurance, or grasp.
6. Do not omit cerebral-palsied or other orthopedically handicapped students from field trips.

OTHER TYPES OF ORTHOPEDIC IMPAIRMENT

As mentioned earlier, cerebral palsy is the orthopedic impairment most often seen in the regular classroom. Other conditions with which the classroom teacher needs to be familiar include the following.

Spina bifida. Spina bifida is a congenital malformation of the spine characterized by lack of closure of the vertebral column, which often allows protrusion of the spinal cord into a sac at the base of the spine. The degree of severity may vary, but this condition often causes paralysis of the lower extremities, changes in tactile and thermal sensations, and a lack of bowel and bladder control. Whenever possible, surgery is performed at an early age to reduce the handicapping effects (Kelly and Verguson, 1978).

Poliomyelitis (polio). Poliomyelitis is an acute disease that inflames nerve cells of the spinal cord or brain stem and leaves a residual paralysis. Vaccines now have the potential of eliminating this disease, which was formerly much more widespread.

Multiple sclerosis (MS). Multiple sclerosis is a disease or progressive deterioration in which the protective sheath surrounding the nerves degenerates and causes failure in the body's neurological system. This results in increased motor incoordination and loss of sensory modalities.

Paralysis. Paralysis is an inability to move, which occurs as a result of disease or injury to the spinal cord or brain. The behavioral characteristic involves an inability to move or feel the part of the body that has been afflicted.

Amputation. Amputation is the surgical removal of a limb from the body. This may be necessitated by an accident or by disease or infection. The term "congenital amputee" is used when a limb is missing or mostly missing at birth. Artificial limbs (prostheses) can usually be fitted to the student.

Muscular dystrophy (MD). Muscular dystrophy is a progressive disease in which the body is unable to utilize vitamin E and the muscles are replaced by fatty tissue. Gradually, power is lost in various parts of the body, particularly legs and trunk. In advanced stages, respiratory problems are common. Onset may be in early childhood or early adolescence. The student is usually faced with the prognosis of early death (Project PREM, 1975).

Juvenile rheumatoid arthritis. Juvenile rheumatoid arthritis is a disease, sudden or gradual, temporary or permanent, that produces painfully swollen joints, impaired mobility, and sometimes deformities.

Bone diseases. Bone diseases include cancer, osteogenesis (a rare bone disease resulting in fragile bones), and osteomyelitis (an infection resulting in inflammation of the bone marrow).

Congenital malformation. Congenital malformations include clubfoot, deformed or absent limbs, and skeletal deformities.

Suggestions for teachers

Students with orthopedic impairments such as these may require the use of crutches, braces, wheelchairs, prostheses, catheters, or other types of medical equipment. Project PREM makes these suggestions for the classroom teacher:

1. Become familiar with the function and use of equipment required by orthopedically impaired students.
2. Become aware of signs that indicate a malfunction in devices, such as worn-out or missing parts, braces, and shoes that are too small or are rubbing.
3. Find out from the student, parent, resource teacher, or any other appropriate person the exact nature of the impairment and its effect, if any, on learning.
4. Engage in communication with other professionals involved in the treatment, therapy, and educational planning of the student. Provide specific information with respect to behavior, fatigue, moods, and specific situations when the behavior is observed.
5. Be reinforcing to any therapy the student may receive by knowing the reasons for therapy and activities that should and should *not* be performed by the student.

6. Ask if any mechanical devices such as adaptive typewriters, book holders, page turners, weights, etc., can be obtained to aid in using academic materials.
7. Do not expect less of the student because he/she is impaired. Find alternative ways to cover the same material (tape recorders, readers, records, etc).
8. Be alert to signs of infection that may coincide with the disease.
9. Be supportive, not condescending, and help the student gain and/or maintain a positive self-concept.
10. Discuss the condition with the rest of the class at an appropriate time (the student may even do this) in order to alleviate anxiety or misconceptions.
11. Communicate with resource personnel regarding adaptation of material and additional resources.

Health impaired

Public Law 94-142 lists a variety of health impairments, some of them very serious. This list includes the following.

Heart conditions. Heart conditions include a number of impairments resulting from malformations, mechanical imperfections, or injuries to the heart, its muscles, or vessels leading to and from it.

Rheumatic fever. Rheumatic fever is a disease, contracted following a streptococcal infection, that is characterized by acute inflammation of the joints, fever, skin rash, nosebleeds, and abdominal pains. The disease is considered serious because it often damages the heart by scarring its tissues and valves (Kelly and Vergason, 1978).

Tuberculosis. Tuberculosis is a bacterial infection, typically of the lungs. Can also infect other organs as well as skin, heart, and bones.

Nephritis. Nephritis is an acute or chronic inflammation of the kidneys. The kidneys may deteriorate, causing a great deal of pain. The prognosis is poor and the treatment calls for absolute bed rest.

Sickle cell anemia. Sickle cell anemia is a condition of the blood in which the red blood cells assume a sickle shape and do not function properly in carrying oxygen. The condition is genetic and largely limited to the Negro race. It results in low vitality, pain, and interferences with cerebral nutrition, and when severe enough may cause mental retardation or death (Kelly and Vergason, 1978). In the United States, it is estimated that about 2.5 million black people carry the trait and the 45,000 to 75,000 have the disease (Luckmann and Sorensen, 1974).

Hemophilia. Hemophilia is a condition, usually hereditary, characterized by failure of the blood to clot following an injury. Profuse bleeding, internal as well as external, occurs from even slight injuries. It is found primarily in males.

Lead poisoning. Lead poisoning occurs from large ingestions of lead. This may result from swallowing paint chips or chewing lead toys or other objects. Lead poisoning can result in impairment of different parts of the nervous system. It often leads to muscle deterioration and foot or wrist drop.

Leukemia. Leukemia is a serious disease of the blood-forming organs, marked by an increase in the number of white blood cells and resulting in progressive deterioration of the body.

Challenges to teachers

Many of these health impairments require hospitalization, for specific treatment or tests, assessments, and monitoring of the disease. The challenge to the regular classroom teacher becomes (1) the organization of work to be taken to the student to maintain academic level in the classroom, and (2) the reintegration of the student once he/she returns. Regular classroom teachers should obtain the support of the other members of the class in this process, as they will be instrumental in the social and emotional aspects of the student's return to class.

• • •

Public Law 94-142 also gives attention to health impairments that can affect education but that do not produce effects severe enough to require hospitalization. Students with these impairments can be considered "at-risk." Examples of some of these more common health impairments include asthma, epilepsy, and diabetes. Their manifestations, treatments, and educational accommodations are discussed in the following paragraphs.

ASTHMA

Bronchial asthma is a condition in which the bronchial tubes become constricted and excess mucus is produced in the bronchial tubes or lungs, obstructing breathing and producing spasms in the bronchial musculature. An attack of asthma may be caused by a specific sensitivity to an allergen, too much physical exertion, or by an emotional reaction. Asthma can develop at any age. Persons with allergies may later develop asthma.

Educational implications

The following are a group of suggestions for teachers who have an asthmatic student in their classroom.

1. Help the student avoid contact with known or suspected allergens, such as pollen, molds, fabrics, animal hair, and bird feathers.

2. Protect the student against overexertion in physical education activities.
3. Provide assistance, follow-through, and monitoring of drugs and medications that have been prescribed for the student.
4. Seek information from parents and school nurse on what to do if the child has an asthmatic attack.
5. Provide feedback to parents and professionals involved in the medical management. Take note of events leading up to the attack, any unusual behavioral manifestations during the attack, and behavior following the attack.
6. Help other members of the class to understand the situation. This will deter anxieties and possible ridicule.

Behavioral implications

A student having an attack of asthma may have difficulty in breathing, show a loss of color, wheeze, and perspire excessively. An attack may last for minutes, hours, or days. A student experiencing an asthmatic attack may become frightened because of the hard breathing and associated behaviors. Other behaviors may include high anxiety, lack of self-confidence in physical activities, and being more dependent on adults (Connor, 1975).

EPILEPSY

Epilepsy includes a number of neurological (central nervous system) conditions referred to as convulsive disorders. It involves the impairment of normal brain functioning. The seizure results from an abnormal chemical-electrical discharge from damaged nerve cells in the brain. The seizure sometimes results in muscular convulsions and partial or total loss of consciousness.

Educational implications

As stated before, the students with a health impairment may or may not have a corresponding learning difficulty. If learning problems are evident, epilepsy may be secondary to the learning disabilities. If it is determined that the epilepsy is adversely affecting the student's learning, then educational intervention can call on resource assistance from the special education teacher. More than likely, the student will require medical intervention. The Epilepsy Foundation of America (1973) outlines some suggestions for teachers:

1. Keep calm when a major seizure occurs. You cannot stop a seizure once it has started. Do not restrain the student or try to revive him/her.
2. Clear the area of hard, sharp, or hot objects that could cause injury. Place a pillow or rolled up coat under the student's head.
3. Do not force anything between the student's teeth. If the mouth is open,

you may place a soft object like a handkerchief between the teeth on one side of the mouth.

4. Turn the patient's head to the side, and make sure that breath is not obstructed.

5. Do not be concerned if the student seems to have stopped breathing. Yet, you *should be* concerned if the student seems to pass from one seizure into another without gaining consciousness. (This is rare, and requires a doctor's help.)

6. Carefully observe the student's actions during the seizure for a full medical report later. When the seizure is over, let the student rest.

Behavioral implications

There are three major types of epileptic seizures.

1. *Grand mal.* This type usually involves spasmodic movements of the entire body, followed by a loss of consciousness. After the convulsion has ceased the person may sleep for several hours and later feel weak and confused. The frequency of grand mal seizures can vary widely, from one or more per day to only a few per year.

2. *Petit mal.* This type of seizure is much less dramatic than the grand mal. It is most common in children. It lasts from 5 to 20 seconds. It can occur occasionally or many times an hour. It usually involves little or no loss of consciousness. The person may stop, stare "vacantly" about, and then resume activities. It is seldom obvious to the individual or to others that a seizure has occurred.

3. *Temporal or psychomotor.* This type of seizure is characterized by unusual behavior. The person appears to be very confused, may without interruption still perform a routine task, chew or smack lips, or become dizzy, fearful, or angry. After the seizure is over the person is usually not able to remember what happened.

There is no exact figure of how many people have epilepsy. In 1975 the Epilepsy Foundation of America estimated that at least 2% (or one million) Americans had epilepsy (Hitzing, 1976).

DIABETES

Diabetes is a metabolic disorder. The body is unable to utilize carbohydrates properly because of a failure of the pancreas to secrete adequate insulin. The result is an abnormal concentration of sugar in the blood and urine.

Educational implications

Diabetic students are educated in the regular classroom. The teacher need only be aware of the medical regimen required and reinforce the child in maintaining firm control of diet and regularity of medication. Social and emotional difficulties may arise when a student, particularly an adolescent, must self-inject insulin. The stigma of "shooting-up" drugs and other connotations should be dealt with in frank discussions with other members of the class. Other suggestions for the classroom teacher include:

1. Check with parents concerning the schedule of midmorning snacks and lunch.
2. Provide calm, soothing activities immediately prior to lunch.
3. Keep a supply of candy, raisins, or sugar cubes in the event of insulin reaction.
4. Inform others who work with the student of his/her diabetes and inform them of what to do in case of insulin reaction or diabetic coma.
5. Do not panic; keep calm if the student does have an insulin reaction or diabetic coma.

Behavioral implications

Classroom teachers need to be alert to symptoms of diabetes. They are excessive thirst, excessive urination, weight loss, rapid weight gain, slow healing of cuts and bruises, pain in the joints, drowsiness, visual difficulties, and skin infections. If these symptoms persist over a period of time, the school nurse or the student's parents should be contacted. Treatment includes a strictly regulated diet, or daily injections of insulin together with proper diet, exercise, and rest.

Symptoms. The classroom teacher should also be aware of the symptoms of insulin reaction (too much insulin being produced) and ketoacidosis (not enough insulin or diabetic coma). The teacher should notify medical personnel at the first sign of a problem. Delayed identification of the student's symptoms and improper treatment may result in death. The symptoms of insulin reaction are a *rapid onset* of nausea, vomiting, palpitations, irritability, shallow breathing, cold moist skin that may be pale, hunger, and/or dizziness. In this case the classroom teacher should give the student sugar, candy, juices, soda pop with sugar, or any other sugar with which the insulin will react. The symptoms of ketoacidosis are *gradual onset* of fatigue, drinking large amounts of water, frequent urination, excessive hunger, deep breathing, and/or warm, dry skin. The treatment for ketoacidosis is to give the student insulin. The classroom teacher should keep the student warm, and notify parents and appropriate medical personnel.

SUMMARY

Orthopedic (skeletal and muscle) impairments and health impairments (organic malfunctions) are low-incidence handicaps but are quite serious in many cases.

The most common orthopedic impairments are cerebral palsy and amputations. The classroom teacher must learn to make necessary accommodations for student movements and for use of braces, wheelchairs, artificial limbs, and other devices.

The most common health impairments are allergies, asthma, epilepsy, and diabetes. Teachers should help monitor medication and diet, recognize various symptoms, know what to do in the event of attacks and seizures, and help the student and other class members to understand and accept the handicap, its manifestations, and its requirements.

SUGGESTED ACTIVITIES

1. Practice, in class, the care of a student during a pretended grand mal epileptic seizure.
2. Invite a diabetic person to speak to the class about life habits, medication, and diet in controlling the condition.
3. Arrange a class visit to a hospital unit for the orthopedically handicapped. Note the types of handicap, the corresponding behaviors, and the special equipment needed.

SUGGESTED READINGS

American Diabetes Association: Diabetes mellitus. Diagnosis and Treatment, vol. 2, New York, 1971, American Diabetes Association.

Arthritis Foundation: Arthritis, the basic facts, New York, 1974, Arthritis Foundation.

Bharani, S. N., and Hyde, J. S.: Chronic asthma and the school, J. School Health **46:**24-30, 1976.

Bigge, J. L., and O'Donnell, P. A.: Teaching individuals with physical and multiple disabilities, Columbus, OH, 1977, Charles E. Merrill Publishing Co.

Bigge, J. L., and Sirvis, B.: Children with physical and multiple disabilities. In Haring, N. G., editor: Behavior of exceptional children, ed. 2, Columbus, OH, 1978, Charles E. Merrill Publishing Co.

Bleck, E. E., and Nagel, D. A., editors: Physically handicapped children: a medical atlas for teachers, New York, 1975, Grune & Stratton, Inc.

Bruya, M. A., and Bolin, R. H.: Epilepsy: a controlled disease, Am. J. Nursing **76**(3):388-397, 1976.

Christiansen, R. O.: Diabetes. In Bleck, E. E.,

and Nagel, D. A., editors: Physically handicapped children: a medical atlas for teachers, New York, 1975, Grune & Stratton, Inc.

Chutorian, A. M., and Myers, S. J.: Diseases of the muscle. In Downey, J. A., and Low, N. L., editors: The child with disabling illness: principles of rehabilitation, Philadelphia, 1974, W. B. Saunders Co.

Cobb, R. B.: Medical and psychological aspects of disability, Springfield, IL, 1973, Charles C Thomas, Publisher.

Collier, B. N.: The adolescent with diabetes and the public schools: a misunderstanding, Personnel Guidance J. **47:**753-757, 1969.

Connor, F. P.: The education of children with crippling and chronic medical conditions. In Cruickshank, W. M., and Johnson, G. O., editors: Education of exceptional children and youth, ed. 3, Englewood Cliffs, NJ, 1975, Prentice-Hall, Inc.

Cruickshank, W. M., editor: Cerebral palsy: a developmental disability, ed. 3, Syracuse, NY, 1976, Syracuse University Press.

Denhoff, E.: Medical aspects. In Cruickshank, W. M., editor: Cerebral palsy: a developmental disability, ed. 3, Syracuse, NY, 1976, Syracuse University Press.

Epilepsy Foundation of America: Recognition and first aid for those with epilepsy, Washington, D.C., 1973, Epilepsy Foundation of America.

Friedland, G.: Learning behavior of a preadolescent with diabetes, Am. J. Nursing **76:**39-61, 1976.

Gearheart, B. R., and Weishahn, M. W.: The handicapped child in the regular classroom, St. Louis, 1976, The C. V. Mosby Co.

Ghory, J. H.: Exercise and asthma: overview and clinical impact, Pediatrics **56**(Suppl.):844-846, 1975.

Hitzing, W.: Developmental disabilities, Omaha, 1976, The Center For the Development of Community Alternative Service System.

Holley, L.: The physical therapist: who, what and how, Am. J. Nursing **70**:1521-1524, 1970.

Kelly, L. J., and Vergason, G. A.: Dictionary of special education and rehabilitation, Denver, 1978, Love Publishing Co.

Luckmann, J., and Sorensen, K. C.: Medical-surgical nursing: a psychophysiologic approach, Philadelphia, 1974, W. B. Saunders Co.

McAnarney, E. R., Pless, I. B., Satterwhite, B., and Friedman, S. B.: Psychological problems of children with chronic juvenile arthritis, Pediatrics **53**:523-528, 1974.

McElfresh, A. E.: What is hemophilia? J. Pediatrics **84**(4):623-624, 1974.

Metsker, C. J.: Hints and activities for mainstreaming, Dansville, NY, 1977, The Instructor Publication, Inc.

Mitchell, M. M.: Occupational therapy and special education, Children **18**:183-186, 1971.

Muscular Dystrophy Association: 1976 fact sheet, New York, 1976, Muscular Dystrophy Association.

Project PREM: Preparing regular educators for mainstreaming, Austin, TX, 1975, State Department of Education.

Reed, E. W.: Genetic abnormalities in development. In Horowitz, F. D., editor: Review of child development research, vol. 4, Chicago, 1975, University of Chicago Press.

Sirvis, B.: The physically handicapped. In Meyen, E. L., editor: Exceptional children and youth: an introduction, Denver, 1978, Love Publishing Company.

United States Department of Health, Education, and Welfare: Progress toward a free appropriate public education: a report to Congress on the implementation of Public Law 94-142: The Education For All Handicapped Children Act, Washington, D.C., January 1979, The Bureau of Education For the Handicapped.

Wald, J. R.: Crippled and other health impaired and their education. In Connor, F. P., Wald, J. R., and Cohen, M. J., editors: Professional preparation of education of crippled children, New York, 1971, Teachers College Press.

Wright, B. A.: Physical disability: a psychological approach, New York, 1960, Harper & Row Publishers, Inc.

PART FOUR

A look into the future

CHAPTER 14

Future special education

Since 1975 we have seen a quickening in the movement to provide quality education for handicapped students. More handicapped youth than ever have been identified and are receiving quality instruction. Increased numbers are being mainstreamed, included for part or all of each day in the regular classroom. New diagnostic measures have appeared, together with improved teaching techniques. New media and technology abound. These advances have snowballed so rapidly that one wonders where they lead.

We cannot see into the distant future, but the force of present trends will surely maintain its momentum for another decade. When we project those trends, they show special education in a light rather different from today. Key among the trends are those involving mass education, removing myths about the handicapped, increasing skills of teachers, the urgencies of Public Law 94-142, the use of new technology, and changes in the preparation of prospective teachers. The following sections, each headed by a summarizing statement, explore these thrusts. In so doing, they present a preview of future special education.

Special education will follow the best trends in mass education

Education for the future. In 1974 Alvin Toffler wrote, "All education springs from some image of the future. If the image of the future held by society is grossly inaccurate, its education system will betray its youth." Some people feel that our educational system is already committing this act of betrayal. Parents of handicapped children have tended to think so, though for reasons other than that expressed by Toffler. But the opinion is far more widespread than that. It is voiced in writings about "Why Johnny Can't Read," "Why Suzie Can't Spell," and "Why Tommy Can't Talk." These commentaries could well be subsumed under the general title "Why Students Don't Learn."

Learning how to learn. But if nonlearning is the problem, what is the solution? Psychologist Herbert Gerjuoy of the Human Resources Research Organization suggests a solution in his observation that "Tomorrow's illiterate will not be the man who can't read, he will be the man who has not learned how to learn" (Toffler, 1974). In this view, learning how to learn becomes the prime objective of education in general. As Gerjuoy continues, "The new education must teach the individual how to classify and reclassify information, how to evaluate its veracity, how to change categories when necessary, how to move from concrete into abstract and back, how to look at problems from a new direction—how to teach himself" (Toffler, 1974).

Lifelong learning. If we pay heed to these cogent observations, the implications for exceptional learners are great, indeed. Imagine trying, for the most able learners, to couple the new life-instruction with the present explosion in knowledge. Self-instruction presents far greater challenges yet for handicapped students. The growth of knowledge, moreover, is absolutely staggering. It has been pointed out that:

Half of what a person learns is no longer valid at middle age

One third of the items on supermarket shelves did not exist 10 years ago

One half of the labor force is now earning a living in industry that did not exist when the United States began over 200 years ago

Three fourths of all people employed by industry 12 years from now will be providing goods not yet conceived (Zigler, 1971)

These present-day facts cannot fail to impact the future of education. Individuals with exceptional needs will of necessity be affected as much as anyone else. Educators must struggle with attending adequately to the needs of exceptional students, not only their needs of daily living, but their ability to cope and to continue learning in the future. All individuals will be caught up in a changing view of education that seems to be leading in the following directions.

1. Learning will be viewed as a continuing process, throughout life. Schools will facilitate this process of lifetime learning and take the lead in moving toward a concept of life-span education.
2. Learning will focus ever more closely on the skills that permit people to cope successfully with very rapid change. Our schools are not presently geared for this purpose. Significant reorientation and reorganization will be required.
3. Life-span education will incorporate the notion of relearning. Incredible advances in media, technology, and systems for processing knowledge will permit us continually to update what we know. The situation will be complicated by increased life span, new employment opportunities, and newer ways of imparting information.
4. A fundamental goal of education will be openness to new learning. We must become increasingly able to receive, analyze, evaluate, and incorporate new information. We need to develop within ourselves mental file boxes with a vast number of compartments, managed by a sorting and retrieval system that allows us to store and remember what we have learned.

These directions will be necessary if education is not to betray us. The advances in communication, transportation, and technology require them. Overlying that is a state of educational diffusion, which compels us to share with all learners, young and old, the ideas, values, attitudes, beliefs, and legal challenges that energize the social mix of which all of us are a part.

Myths now prevalent about handicapped individuals will largely disappear

Our personal attitudes, values, and beliefs result partly from our perceptions and partly from folklore passed along by people around us. Both these sources strongly affect our beliefs and attitudes about handicapped people. Some of these beliefs and attitudes are accurate and realistic. Others are so inaccurate and stereotyped as to be considered myths.

There have always been numerous individuals with exceptional needs in our society. We have, in the past, looked at those people, and if they appeared or behaved noticably different from the majority, we considered them flawed, abnormal, and of diminished value. Surrounding that view of diminished value have been erroneous stories of what handicapped people are like, of how they came to be that way, and of how they should be educated. Those erroneous stories are referred to as myths about the handicapped. Most of those myths are harmful. Fortunately, they are being dispelled. Within the next decade they will be supplanted in large measure by accurate facts about the handicapped.

Meanwhile, it serves a valuable function to point out some of the more harmful myths. This clarification makes it possible for all of us to focus on the errors and thus to supplant them with the truth in our own thinking. The following observations about myths of the handicapped are adapted from Wolfensberger (1972), Human Policy Press (1974), and Hallahan and Kauffman (1978).

Myth: Handicapped people are sick, subhuman, and a potential menace.
Fact: In only a few cases are the handicapped sick, in the sense of being infected with disease germs. Sickness, in the sense of mental illness, is not a category of handicap. It afflicts normal and handicapped people alike. The handicapped are human equally with others, and deserve and demand to be treated as such. Not even in the wildest imagination can handicapped people be considered a menace.

Myth: Handicapped people should be looked upon as objects of pity.
Fact: Assigning pity where it is neither deserved nor wanted is grossly dehumanizing. Handicapped people have special needs. They should have those needs attended to. The needs do not include the desire to be pitied. They do include the desire to be treated with dignity.

Myth: Most handicapped people receive special education in school.
Fact: The United States Office of Education has found that only half of the exceptional children in this country receive special education services. Public Law 94-142 will certainly increase this percentage, but it is still presently true that great numbers of handicapped students do not receive services.

Myth: Mentally retarded people do not grow in intellectual ability.
Fact: Improvements in intellectual functioning are possible for almost all people for the majority of their life-spans. Many of us do cease growing, normal and retarded

alike. But that need not be the case. If it were, a primary or preprimary curriculum would suffice for the mentally retarded. It would be static, nonfluid, suitable only for a tiny child.

Myth: The teacher should know whether the child's retardation is the result of brain damage.

Fact: It is not imperative that the teacher know the cause of a particular individual's retardation. Diagnosis of brain damage might be important for the medical people, but it helps teachers not at all when it comes to planning and delivering educational programs. The only thing teachers need to know is the child's needs and levels of functioning. That is the basis upon which sound instructional programs can be built.

Myth: All learning disabled children have disorders of the central nervous system.

Fact: Great numbers of students have learning problems without any evidence of central nervous disorder. It is true that brain damage often results in learning disability. However, the spectrum of disabilities is vast. As professionals have zeroed in on the causes and natures of learning disability, they have progressed through terms such as dyslexia, brain-injured, minimal brain dysfunction, and specific learning disabilities. While these terms have helped educators, they have done nothing to refute the erroneous belief that brain injury and learning disability always go hand in hand.

Myth: Most emotionally disturbed children go unnoticed.

Fact: Emotionally disturbed children are easy to spot, if one but knows the signs to look for. The two main signs are gross aggression and pervasive withdrawal, each of which has several manifestations. These signs do not point out the causes of the disturbances; causes are identified by trained personnel.

Myth: Deaf students cannot speak so as to be understood.

Fact: Most students with hearing loss learn to speak acceptably. Only those profoundly deaf from infancy have great difficulty speaking. Students with light to moderate hearing loss may speak perfectly and go unnoticed for years in the regular classroom. Students who have even limited ability to hear can be helped with hearing aids, speechreading, and special instruction from speech therapists.

Myth: The blind have an extra compensating sense, or have greater acuity than normal in their other senses.

Fact: This is one of the most prevalent myths about the handicapped. The blind *do not* have an extra sense. They are able to develop an "obstacle sense" if they are able to hear. They also learn to make fine discriminations in the sensations they receive through the senses. But these are learned, adaptive behaviors, not traits that occur automatically. They simply represent better use of sensory abilities that all of us have.

Myth: The more severely crippled, the less intelligent people are.

Fact: Physical crippling and mental impairment are usually entirely separate. Cerebral palsy is a good case in point. Some cerebral-palsied individuals are so afflicted that they cannot move about or even sit alone, yet they may be brilliant intellectually.

This myth is very strong. It illustrates the extent to which highly observable handicaps evoke images of reduced mental capacities. It has been found that teachers are influenced by this myth. Studies have shown that they show a decided preference for working with behaviorally handicapped students (who usually look normal) over working with physically handicapped students, whose emotional behavior and mental capacity may be normal.

The mainstreaming of handicapped individuals is bound to chip away at these myths until they have disappeared. The educational setting provides a perfect milieu for dispelling them, for it is in the classroom that individual capabilities, transcending the various forms of handicap, can be demonstrated.

Regular teachers will become increasingly adept at diagnosing and remediating the needs of all students, but special teachers will still be needed

The courts of the land have ruled that handicapped citizens have a right to protection, least restrictive alternatives, educational placement, residential placement, equal opportunity, just payment for work done, and the right not to be deprived of life (McGee and Malian, 1977). Their rights to the best free education possible have been elaborated and codified in Public Law 94-142, the provisions of which have been detailed in earlier chapters.

Effects of PL 94-142. The requirements set forth in PL 94-142 have influenced teaching practice strongly. That influence will continue to grow. Its prime effect has been to require that handicapped students be looked at carefully on an individual basis, that their specific individual needs be assessed, that their abilities and disabilities be diagnosed, that individualized education plans be formulated, and that individualized instruction be made a reality in the classroom.

As teachers move to comply with these requirements, their attitudes change and their skills improve. The attitude change is beginning acceptance of every student on an individual basis, to take them as and where they are, and to attempt to teach them what they need to know. The skill improvement includes increased ability to diagnose, remediate, individualize, and manage the behavior of individuals and groups.

These attitudes and skills have been the hallmark of special education. This is not to say that regular classroom teachers lacked them. Wherever you go in public and private schools, you will find teachers who diagnose, remediate, individualize, and manage behavior beautifully. But this is not the case across the mass of teachers. Teachers who do these things still comprise a small minority. Teachers who do them with consummate skill comprise a tiny percentage, indeed.

Increasingly, then, the prize skills of special education will become diffused throughout the teaching ranks. This process will take some time to complete. Most new teachers must demonstrate these skills before they can be credentialled. Inservice teachers, however, who will comprise the major part of the teaching force for the next two decades, often have little exposure to the requirements of PL 94-142. Most school districts have not been aggressive in providing inservice training for mainstreaming. Mainstreaming requirements thus register on inservice teachers only when they begin to work directly with handicapped students, whose education is guided by IEPs and a team of professionals and parents.

Continued need for special educators. Because the diffusion cf skills and attitudes is occurring slowly, special educators will maintain high-priority positions. They will continue to play key roles in organizing, monitoring, assessing, and assisting in the IEP. They will coordinate the teams of teachers, parents, and students. They will provide services to handicapped students both in the regular classroom and on a pull-out basis to special rooms. They will have major responsibility for providing inservice education. And of course they will provide educational services directly to those students who cannot participate effectively in regular classrooms.

Formalized communication and teamwork between special educators and classroom teachers will become the rule rather than the exception

Equal partnership. Communication and teamwork between special educators and classroom teachers is mandated in PL 94-142. The two groups are directed to work together. Each contributes its expertise, shares its views, expresses its difficulties, suggests its solutions. Both are involved in all phases of diagnosis, placement, instruction, management, and reporting.

Where the two groups are able to establish an equal partner relationship, communication flows and positive progress is facilitated. Trouble occurs when unequal relationships exist. If special educators dominate the team, teachers will be made to feel inferior and incompetent. They will sour on the notion of mainstreaming, and they will not seek help from specialists. If teachers dominate the team, special educators will feel they are on foreign terrain when in the classroom. They will tend to withdraw into their special centers and communicate by memo rather than through direct involvement. Thus, it is essential that these teams establish ground rules that specify duties, functions, procedures, and lines of responsibility.

Mainstreaming, a routine matter. As this positive teamwork develops, the entire process of mainstreaming becomes routine. Fears and mysteries dissolve. Ties between school and parents grow stronger. Students receive the best educational program that the state of the art allows. These are the goals of mainstreaming. Teamwork makes them possible.

All students will at last receive the best education possible

We have focused almost exclusively on the education of handicapped students. That, after all, is the purpose of mainstreaming and, in turn, the reason for this book. PL 94-142 sets forth clear educational requirements regarding identification, assessment, diagnosis, placement, and individualized instruction. These requirements, applied to the regular classroom, imply many details of behavior management, diagnostic-prescriptive teaching, nonprejudicial evaluation, and classroom organization that apply not only to handicapped students but to all students in the classroom.

Thus, mainstreaming requirements force the use of instruction, evaluation, and management techniques consistent with what is believed to be the best in educational practice. The benefits of this instruction accrue to handicapped students. They accrue likewise to nonhandicapped students in the same class. This fact has caused many observers to consider mainstreaming a real boon to education in general.

Handicapped students will receive instruction through new media and technology, and in some cases in new locales

New technology. In 1970 Alvin Toffler made several "future-shockish" predictions, many of which have already come true. One of them had to do with the mode of delivering education in the future. It had strong implications for special education and mainstreaming:

> A good deal of education will take place in the student's own room at home or in a dorm, at hours of his choosing, with vast libraries of data available to him via computerized information retrieval systems, with his own tapes and video units, his own language laboratory, and his own electronically equipped study carrel.

This prediction is already realized in terms of both hardware (the mechanical devices) and software (printed material, auditory tapes, and visual material). Future availability and applications appear limitless. Readily available today are such innovations as computer-assisted instruction, synthetic voice composers, Optacons, which translate print into sound, communication boards for the communicatively handicapped, biofeedback monitors for the behaviorally disordered, and videotaped modeling for the physically and behaviorally impaired. One can foresee these and other innovations coming into widespread use by the end of the next decade.

New organization and requirements. Organization and locales for delivering education will certainly undergo modifications, too. DeLorenzo, in a keynote address to the First World Congress on Future Special Education, held in Scotland in 1978, spoke of future special education in which:

1. Referrals to special environments are rare. Regular teachers, school psychologists, principals, and other school personnel have been trained extensively in helping students with special needs to survive in mainstream settings.
2. Elderly and retired persons substantially supplement the efforts of regular school personnel. They put their experience and career training to work by providing regular part-time instruction.
3. Students stay in school as long as it takes them to learn what they need to know.
4. Any time after they are 15 years old, students may leave school and go to work for themselves or for someone else. But they are still free to take advantage of the educational system whenever they want and for whatever purpose.
5. There is no longer any isolated "special" education. All education is special, and each student may pursue whatever course of learning he or she desires for as long as he or she wants to pursue it.
6. A critical aspect of the educational system is the participation of parents. Parents are teachers at home, and a significant portion of each child's education is dependent upon the guidance the child receives at home.
7. The heart of the educational system is a computer-controlled satellite technology that provides a dissemination and utilization system. This brings coherence and direction to the various aspects of diagnosis, assessment, teaching, evaluation, and guidance.

Teacher training programs will reduce the major boundaries that separate regular from special teachers.

Personnel development. Heretofore, a rather distinct cleavage has existed in most educators' minds between special education and regular education. A similar distinction has existed in their views of the roles of special education personnel and regular classroom teachers.

As indicated earlier, the boundaries that separate these two groups are beginning to fade. PL 94-142 requires several tasks that must be carried out together by specialists and teachers. These requirements thrust teachers into realms that have been the province of specialists, such as diagnosis, remediation, and the management of behavior disorders. In the same way, it has thrust special educators into what has been the province of the teacher, specifically, classroom instruction, total class management, and group evaluation.

This joint collaboration is mandated by law. Law, however, is not sufficient to bring it about alone. Also required are specific skills, attitudes, and understandings. PL 94-142 addresses this need for personnel development. It stipulates that school agencies must:

1. Develop a personnel development plan that provides a structure for personnel planning, focusing on preservice and inservice needs
2. Conduct and report a needs assessment that identifies needed areas of personnel training, together with a prioritized ordering of those needs
3. Identify the target population for personnel development, including general education and special education, instructional and administrative personnel, support personnel, and other personnel such as paraprofessionals, parents, and volunteers

Functions of educational agencies. This mandate directly affects state agencies, local agencies, and institutions of higher education. They are encouraged to collaborate so as to provide the necessary training for knowledge, skills, and competencies in the following areas:

1. The specific requirements of Public Law 94-142
2. The litigation concerning education of the handicapped that preceeded PL 94-142
3. The legal rights of handicapped children, their parents, and their teachers
4. The characteristics of special learners
5. Instructional and curricular modifications needed for special learners
6. Parent-professional relationships
7. Planning and implementing Individualized Education Programs (IEPs)
8. Monitoring and reporting student progress

It has been left to the various states to specify the training programs and specific competencies they will institute in order to meet federal requirements. No state may do less than comply with the stipulations of PL 94-142. States may, if they wish, go beyond those stipulations by adding additional skills and competencies. Chapter 1 presented, as an example, the specific competencies that must be demonstrated by teacher trainees and administrator trainees before they will be granted the credential to work in California.

Parental involvement. The importance of parental involvement in aspects of teaching and teacher training bears repeating. Parents of exceptional children comprise the segment of the lay population that is most interested, most knowledgeable about, and most involved in their children's education. Many are participants in strong parent organizations that keep up to date with, even push for, litigation and new laws. They are highly insistent that their children's rights be observed and that they have the right to due process when they disapprove of what is being done.

Parents of the handicapped are very watchful and insistent, but they are also very supportive. They are eager to communicate, eager to help, eager to push for facilities. Experienced teachers know that parents are their best allies. This observation is doubly true for the parents of the handicapped.

• • •

This concludes our attempt to predict the future of special education during the next decade. In short, the crystal ball says that the emphasis on providing quality education for the handicapped will continue unabated. It will push special education and regular classroom education much closer together, even wiping out some of the lines that separate them. Incredible advances will continue in media and technology, which will find their ways into education for everyone. All teachers, administrators, and other school personnel will become skilled in diagnosis, instruction, evaluation, and guidance of all students, handicapped and nonhandicapped alike. The overall result will be educational programs of higher quality than ever before provided.

SUGGESTED ACTIVITIES

1. View the film "Future Shock." What evidence do you see that its predictions have begun to occur? Which of its separate topics seems to have greatest implications for the education of school students?
2. Invite a long-time college professor or school official in special education to visit the class and describe what has happened during the past 30 years in special education. Ask that person to speculate on what he or she sees in the future for special education.
3. Assess yourself in terms of the specific teaching competencies suggested by PL 94-142 (a list is presented in Chapter 1). How well do you match up to them? How can you remediate your deficiencies? To what extent do you feel the competencies prepare you to work with handicapped students in the regular classroom?
4. Which of the myths about the handicapped did you believe in the past? (Be honest, now.) Are the myths dispelled from your mind, or do vestiges still remain? If they remain, how will you keep them from interfering with your work with handicapped students?

SUGGESTED READINGS

Anon.: Handicapism, Syracuse, NY, 1974, Human Policy Press.

Callahan, W. G.: Futurisms: a question-answer approach for beginners in the field, Stirling, Scotland, 1978, Unpublished paper for The First World Congress on Future Special Education.

DeLorenzo, E. G.: Planning the future of special education. In Fink, A. H., editor: International perspectives on future special education, Reston, VA, 1978, The Council For Exceptional Children.

Hallahan, D. P., and Kaufmann, J. M.: Exceptional children: introduction to special education, Englewood Cliffs, NJ, 1968, Prentice-Hall, Inc.

McGee, J. J., and Malian, I. M.: Belief systems: human and legal rights, San Juan, Puerto Rico, 1977, Paper presented to the American Occupational Therapy Association.

Skinner, B. F.: Beyond freedom and dignity, New York, 1972, Bantam Books, Inc.

Stanovich, K. E.: Technology and mentally handicapped individuals: speculations on the future. In Fink, A., editor: International perspectives on future special education, Reston, VA, 1978, The Council for Exceptional Children.

Toffler, A.: Learning for tomorrow: the role of the future in education, New York, 1974, Vintage Books.

Toffler, A.: Future shock, New York, 1970, Bantam Books, Inc.

Turnbull, H. R., and Turnbull, A.: Free appropriate public education: law and implementation, Denver, 1978, Love Publishing Company.

Wolfensberger, W.: Normalization, Toronto, 1972, National Institute on Mental Retardation.

Zigler, W. L.: Social and technological development, Syracuse, NY, 1971, Educational Policy Research Center, Syracuse University. Cited in Corrigan, D.: Future: implication for preparation of educational personnel, J. Teacher Educ. 25(2):100-107, 1974.

Index